GEORGES RIVER BLUES

SWAMPS, MANGROVES AND
RESIDENT ACTION, 1945–1980

GEORGES RIVER BLUES

SWAMPS, MANGROVES AND RESIDENT ACTION, 1945–1980

HEATHER GOODALL

Australian
National
University

ANU PRESS

WORLD FOREST HISTORY SERIES

Australian
National
University

ANU PRESS

Published by ANU Press
The Australian National University
Acton ACT 2601, Australia
Email: anupress@anu.edu.au

Available to download for free at press.anu.edu.au

ISBN (print): 9781760464622
ISBN (online): 9781760464639

WorldCat (print): 1275422853
WorldCat (online): 1275422837

DOI: 10.22459/GRB.2021

The World Forest History Series aims to produce rigorous histories of forestry that inform
contemporary environmental policy debates and provide enduring scholarly landmarks for future
generations of historians and environmental researchers. The series is affiliated with the Centre for
Environmental History at The Australian National University.

Series Editors: Gregory A. Barton, Professor of History, University of Western Sydney, Affiliate, Centre
for Environmental History, The Australian National University; Brett M. Bennett, Senior Lecturer in
History, University of Western Sydney, Affiliate, Centre for Environmental History, The Australian
National University.

Cover design and layout by ANU Press

Cover: Ruth Staples was a courageous Georges River campaigner who lived all her life around Lime
Kiln Bay at Oatley West. She kept on fighting to regenerate the river until her death, aged 90, in 2020.
Photograph by Mick Staples, Ruth's husband, while on a family holiday at Thredbo, 1966, courtesy
Haworth family collection.

This book is published under the aegis of the Environmental History Editorial Board and the Social
Sciences Editorial Committee of ANU Press.

Contents

Part I: Introducing the Picnic River

Part II: Initial Shock

Part III: Death of the Picnic River

Part IV: The 'Mangrovites' Fight Back

Part V: Conclusions

Usage and Spelling

Terminology: The collective terms 'Aboriginal people' (as a noun, with 'Aboriginal' as an adjective), 'Indigenous' and 'First Nations' are all in use currently. Each term presents problems but I have used 'Aboriginal people/Aboriginal' most often as this has generally been preferred by the Aboriginal people I have interviewed. However, I have used the other listed terms at times and I recognise that usage and preferences change over time and context. Most recently, for example, the term 'First Peoples' has been chosen in Victoria where the First Peoples' Assembly of Victoria is negotiating with the state government on a future treaty. Initially used in British Columbia, Canada, in the First Peoples' Cultural Council, this term has less historical baggage, but has not yet become widely used in Australia.

Spelling: While Aboriginal languages are known to have a number of consonants not familiar to English speakers, there are three consonants that have voiced and unvoiced pronunciations. These pairs – t/d, k/g (hard 'g') and p/b – do not have different meanings in any Aboriginal languages, leaving written users to choose to use either the voiced or the unvoiced option. Early English recorders used various conventions for transliterating what they heard, and so early spellings vary widely. For consistency, this book uses the voiced option of each pair: d, g and b. So Dharawal rather than Tharawal; Bidjigal rather than Pitjikal; Gandangara rather than Kantankara; and Dharug rather than Tharuk.

List of Maps

List of Figures

Abbreviations

ACF	Australian Conservation Foundation
ALP	Australian Labor Party
BLF	Builders Labourers' Federation
CCP	County of Cumberland Plan
CPA	Communist Party of Australia
CRAG	Coalition of Resident Action Groups
CRIL	Cooks River Improvement League
CRVA	Cooks River Valley Association
EIS	Environmental Impact Statement
GROLPA	Georges River Oyster Lease Protest Association
LGA	local government area
LKBPC	Lime Kiln Bay Preservation Committee
MSCEU	Municipal and Shire Council Employees' Union
NCC	Nature Conservation Council
NPWS	National Parks and Wildlife Service
OFF	Oatley Flora and Fauna Society
PPRA	Picnic Point Regatta Association
SPCC	State Pollution Control Commission
SSRS	Society for Social Responsibility in Science
TEC	Total Environment Centre
UNSW	University of New South Wales
WWI	World War I
WWII	World War II

Acknowledgements

Dharawal and Dharug lands on the estuary of the Georges River have seen many histories. This book is about a brief period along that estuary – from 1945 to 1980 – when Aboriginal people continued to live along the estuary but were seldom consulted in its events. Instead, the majority of the population for this brief period were Irish and Anglo settlers, with increasing numbers of even more recent immigrants from Asia and the North Africa/West Asia area (also known as the 'Middle East').

This book is built on memories – the memories of those recent settlers and immigrants, but also those of the Aboriginal people who continued to live on the river. I have been particularly grateful in all my Georges River work to have had the interest and insights of Aboriginal people who had been involved with the river, including those who have passed away: Jacko Campbell, Gubbu Ted Thomas and most recently Ellen James and her granddaughter Tracey Whetnall. I have continued to draw on those who remain today, like Shayne Williams and Denis Foley, while analysts of colonialism Peter Read and the late Tracey Banivanua Mar have been continuing inspirations.

My own memories of growing up on the river, in an Irish-Scots family in the 1950s, drew me back there, but I have now learnt far more from the many non-Indigenous Georges River people who gave their time, their memories, their interest and their support to the project. I want to thank Carol Jacobsen, Dave Koffel, Laurie Derwent and Alexandra Knight who have each been so patient in answering my many questions and in digging around for photographs and papers.

The book arose initially from a project shared with Denis Byrne and Stephen Wearing, begun in 2004, researching the Georges River National Park, on which we worked with inspired and inspiring researchers Jo Kijas, Allison Cadzow, Hesham Abdo, Stephen Gapps, Joy Suliman, Wafa Zaim,

Alison Phan and Huy Pham. We drew on the advice and continued interest of the Muslim Women Association and Hajeh Maha Abdo. From this work, Allison Cadzow and I published *Rivers and Resilience* (2009, UNSW Press), following the continuing histories of Aboriginal people along the Georges River to the present.

Georges River Blues has since drawn further on the ecological insights and the personal experiences on the river of Neil Saintilan and Jeff Kelleway, while those from further afield, like Alan Reid, Peter Fairweather and Philip Sutton, each contributed to the campaigns in the book and to the project itself. I continue to learn from William Gladstone, who not only has an endless knowledge of marine biology and conservation but is also a brilliant photographer.

The field of environmental history and humanities has been nurtured by a community of analysts and activists in Australia, India and Europe. I have learnt from all of them and particularly thank Haripriya Rangan, Emily O'Gorman, Mahesh Rangarajan, Meera Oommen, Libby Robin, Tom Griffiths, Katie Holmes, Andrea Gaynor, Kartik Shanker, Ruth Morgan, Margaret Cook, Gunnel Cederlof and Thom van Dooren.

Local knowledge has been fundamental to *Georges River Blues*. The skills of local studies and heritage librarians at Bankstown, Canterbury, Hurstville and Fairfield libraries have been invaluable. I particularly wish to thank John MacRitchie of the Georges River Council Library and Marilyn Gallo at Fairfield Museum. Inspiring research and creative outcomes have been achieved at the Bankstown Arts Centre by Vandana Ram, its director, while collaborations initiated by Tim Carroll (*Out Loud*) with school students have generated important oral histories. Just as important has been the work of local writers, researchers and archivists like Esme Clisby and Alan Fairley, without whom the stories of local campaigners would be lost forever. Dave Koffel gave me generous access to his valuable archive of the Lime Kiln Bay Preservation Committee, and Alexandra Knight, who has gathered her family's extensive records and unique slides of the environmental and educational work around Oatley Bay, shared her archive with me.

Douglas Coles, my cousin, introduced me to the Milperra history he knew from his father who had struggled to farm a soldier settler block there after returning from World War I. I am grateful to local analyst and historian Andrew Molloy, who has worked tirelessly to record local people's memories and to gather and protect their archives. I have learnt too from the boys with whom I shared my Salt Pan Creek childhood – my brothers Mark and Craig and our friend, Glenn Goodacre – who remembered the river mud and mangroves that I missed out on. Christine, my best friend and Glenn's sister, and their parents, Val and Elliott, could share more about the river from living at Picnic Point. My daughters Emma and Judith, even though they are inner-city girls, have supported this project over many years (especially Judith who deserved a Brownie badge for her fortitude on a really tough Georges River bush walk). My husband Paul Torzillo was on hand to rescue me from the river when I was young – but has unfailingly encouraged me to return to make more sense of it in later years.

Bringing the book into being has needed many hands. Friends and researchers Helen Randerson and Allison Cadzow have brought new insights to still more research and editing. Sharon Harrup has crafted fine maps that tell these stories. Rani Kerin has been an invaluable copyeditor, while ANU Press manager Emily Tinker and the series editor, Brett Bennett, have been supportive and consistently optimistic, even when I wasn't.

My special thanks are to the whole Haworth family. Especially to Ruth, who passed away recently, but whose inspiration and tenacity sustained this book. And to Bob, for his endlessly inquiring curiosity, patient teaching, eloquent maps, esoteric (but always apposite) literary quotations, incisive political analysis, rarely ruffled good humour, great bushwalkers' lunches and amazing memories of a life dedicated to social and environmental justice.

Preface

In 2000 the Georges River seemed very familiar to me. But I had not counted on how much I hated and feared mangroves. I had grown up on the western side of Salt Pan Creek, at Padstow, in the 1950s and 1960s. I thought I knew the river because I had travelled by train to and from school every day for many years, over the rattly bridge across Salt Pan, on my way to Tempe then Kogarah then later into the city before I moved away in 1973. Yet it turned out that I only knew a short stretch of the river – the estuary from Milperra downstream to Salt Pan Creek. I was to find there had been a very different river downstream, from Lime Kiln Bay past the Woronora River to Towra Point. And the past, as they say, is another country, so even my stretch of the Georges River had a different history than I had expected.

I was able to learn something of the past of the river when I worked with Denis Byrne, Stephen Wearing, Allison Cadzow, Jo Kijas and Stephen Gapps on the history and present-day usage of the Georges River National Park, mainly on the northern side of a short stretch of river from East Hills to Salt Pan Creek. Our team of historians, a cultural archaeologist and a leisure sociologist traced the continuing history of Indigenous peoples on the river and the contemporary meanings of the park for Arabic-speaking and Vietnamese local residents. Yet there was one group whose story we did not tell. These were the people I had known best, the residents from the Irish and Anglo world who had lived on the river as settlers and later factory workers until the time I left.

I might have taken this unfinished work no further, but the local government authority where I now live in inner-city Glebe has begun to plant mangroves along the nearby waterfront of Blackwattle Bay to allow environmental regeneration. I was disturbed by the plantings – at first horrified to see what I saw as a threatening and invasive creature, however endemic – and then surprised by my own emotional responses.[1] Where had this come from when I had learnt so much over the years about the important role of mangroves in ecological relationships? I realised I needed to return to the Georges River research to understand my own reactions to this plant and the ideas that swirled around it when I was growing up in the 1960s and 1970s.

I had continued to visit old friends and relations on the river since that early work, so I began exploring their memories of the river. It became clear that not only had river residents been vitally interested in the river in the 1950s, when they had campaigned for their own national park, but also that they had gone on to take part in many campaigns in the 1960s and 1970s to try to restore the river to ecological health as well as to sustain the rich social relationships they valued. I had moved away to become a student in the inner city, learning about other stories and other places – and I had missed some very important episodes in the river's story. Returning to this story, I realised I needed to broaden and deepen the focus if I was to better understand what these stories could teach me about the river I thought I knew.

Heather Goodall
September 2021

---

1   I was not the only Glebe resident who was troubled: see McManus, 'Mangrove Battlelines'.

Part I: Introducing the Picnic River

1

A City River and its Bush

This book aims to explain a series of resident-driven conflicts that took place along the Georges River estuary from 1945 to 1980. In colloquial language shared across Australia, any disputes are known as 'blues'. In order to understand these Georges River blues, we need to engage the social and political history of the estuary with the environmental history of the living, non-human world – the birds, fish and oysters, but particularly the riverine vegetation and the mangroves – in this time of major change. The histories of the people and the living animals, birds and plants there had always been related but they all became caught up in post–World War II Reconstruction. Until 1945, British settler development on the river had been slow, despite leaving lasting impacts. This had generated an illusion of stability that, while welcomed by many human residents who confidently assumed that this would always be the 'picnic river', was deplored by developers and speculators alike.

The war brought sudden change. It led to the push for more factories, more building and subdivision for housing to bring people to work in the factories, and more 'social' housing for the many people 'slum cleared' out of the crowded inner city. The areas along the northern side of the river rapidly became more densely populated and suburban. While the upstream areas of the estuary saw the most industrial development, the downstream reaches, where the river was far wider and the views more impressive, began to see a boom in expensive waterfront developments, although the infrastructure like piped sewerage often lagged far behind the lucrative land sales.

The more-than-human world bore heavy impacts from these changes. Many species of birds that had lived along the river were displaced by the development and reclamations of the 1950s. The mangroves remained, but their behaviour began to change. Mangroves had never been what would today be called a 'charismatic species'. Like me, many people found them inhospitable, full of spiders and snakes, with sticky, sucking mud and spikey vertical roots all around them. For reasons only partially understood at the time, mangroves began to expand in the quiet bays along the Georges River estuary, pushing themselves into the awareness of residents and civil authorities alike, becoming invested with intense but widely different emotions. Oysters had already been transformed from a naturally occurring delicacy to a commercial farm product, winning the support of governments as a luxury export industry, despite the heavy manual labour needed to cultivate, shuck and bottle them. Yet the emergence of more expensive waterfront developments was beginning to put a premium on unimpeded water views. Oysters were being transformed once again, from a premium industry to a polluting eyesore, leading to the stigmatisation not only of the industry but also of the people who farmed them. This meant that, in both human and more-than-human terms, the outcomes from these Georges River blues were very mixed.

***

This book traces the emergence of suburban resident environmental activism in Australia from 1945 to 1980 by focusing on the lower Georges River, the estuary running through southern Sydney, flanked by sandy, swampy banks and sandstone cliffs. This waterway had risen as a freshwater river in the Southern Highlands, flowing first north and then swinging towards the east near what became Liverpool before turning south at Chipping Norton. Finally, it made one more turn, bending towards the east at Voyager Point and then on into Botany Bay. A geological shift, millennia ago, tilted the coastline upwards where Botany Bay met the sea, drowning the lower reaches and allowing the salt water and the tide to penetrate far upstream. So the Georges River flows onwards, but not as freshwater. Instead, it is an estuary – saline and tidal – from Liverpool downstream until it enters Botany Bay at Towra Point (see Map 1.1). Much of the land along the river's banks is low-lying and waterlogged, with water rising on high tides and flowing out across wide areas in floods. Today those areas would be recognised as wetlands, but in the 1970s – even after the *Ramsar Convention on Wetlands of International Importance Especially as Waterfowl Habitat* was declared in 1971 – the term 'wetlands' was unfamiliar in Australia. Instead, these Georges River lowlands were known until at least the 1980s as 'marshes' or 'swamps' – or sometimes just 'bush'. This book follows the language used in the resident-driven environmental campaigns along the Georges River estuary from 1945 to 1980 to explore how these low-lying places were seen and valued – and, hence, why they were fought over so bitterly.

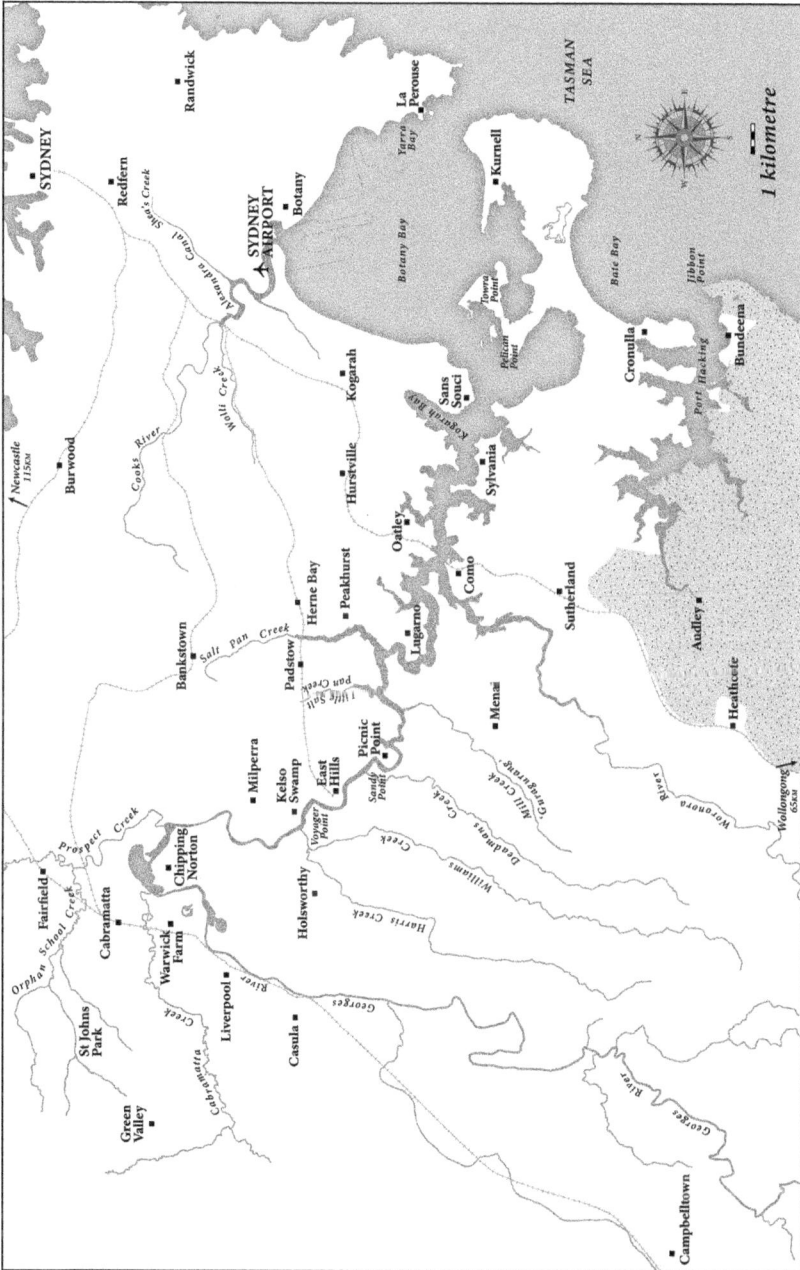

Map 1.1: A city river.

Cartography: Sharon Harrup.

Much of this book is about the living networks of this estuary: the animal, insect and human interactions. This estuary has offered a rich habitat for salt water fish and crustaceans, and for birds, small reptiles and marsupials, with its riverbank vegetation characteristically made up by some mangroves, behind which were low-lying saltmarsh areas, often inundated at high tide, then salt-tolerant species like casuarinas (often called she-oaks but resembling pines because of their thin, grey, needle-shaped foliage[1]) and, finally, as the land rose above the salty watertable, taller shrubs and trees like melaleucas (known as paperbarks).

But rivers are still more than this. The material of the bed of a river – its soil and rock, as well as the interactions of the chemistry of soil, water and living material – contribute to the quality of water and the living networks that it sustains. The water itself is clearly essential in coastal rivers, but its flow rates and salinity have all changed over time, with interactions with surrounding environments, built or otherwise, as well as with the craft that might be employed on it by people. The shifts from canoes to rowboats and then to powerboats, for example, had significant effects not only on water quality but also on turbulence and suspended material, shaping the interactions of both human and more-than-human species. So, at times, despite our focus on living networks, geological and hydrological questions need to be considered as well.

The water and surrounding land areas identified in this book as the tidal, estuarine Georges River – from Liverpool downstream to Towra Point at the river's mouth onto Botany Bay – also relate more to human, land-based administrative divisions than to geographic definitions. Local government councils are prominent in this study because they took active roles in implementing – or resisting – the dredging and 'reclamation' projects that were the focus of most campaigns. Here the term 'upper' estuary refers to the area from Liverpool weir downstream to the Salt Pan Creek. The northern shore of this part of the river is managed by – from the west – the local government areas of Liverpool, Fairfield and Bankstown municipal (and later city) councils, while the southern shore is managed by Liverpool in the west and then the Sutherland Shire. The term 'lower' estuary refers to the section from the eastern shore of Salt Pan Creek downstream to Brighton, managed on the north by Hurstville and Kogarah councils and, on the south, entirely by the Sutherland Shire.

---

1   *Casuarina cunninghamiana* or *Casuarina glauca* (swamp she-oak).

This still does not exhaust the meanings that the Georges River carries. Like any waterway, this river is understood very differently for the people who live along and hail from it. While the following chapters will tell more of their stories, the Georges River has continued to hold many human meanings at the same time. For thousands of years it had been a productive river for the Dharawal, Dharug and Gandangara peoples who lived along its shores, as well as being the source of the many narratives that sustained a rich culture across the region. Despite losing many people to invasion violence and illness, Indigenous owners survived along the river, taking marriage partners from inland and continuing to live in sheltered spaces of their country along the river.[2] The river land soils were not well suited to European agriculture, but there were still avenues for the river to offer productive environments for the settlers too, with small commercial ventures arising from fishing, timber and lime, along with the cultivation that could be sustained on sandy soils, like poultry, vineyards, orchards and, later, on the waters themselves, oyster farming. Such productive uses supported only a sparse settler population in the nineteenth century, although there was some increase in numbers before World War II (WWII). So the Georges River remained a 'picnic' river – a place known for its bush, fishing, duck shooting and boating; a place to go for a day trip away from the crowded city.

With WWII, however, this changed dramatically – as later chapters will trace. Noel Butlin has argued that the major impact of postwar industrialisation and migration was to fall most heavily on the Georges River estuary, leading to this 'picnic' river becoming subdivided and developed, crisscrossed with rail lines and roads, a drain for large volumes of human and industrial waste. Its landscape became recognised by all its residents as 'suburban' while its waterway became more polluted. It was here, along this damaged, suburban river, that so many battles broke out to try to save its bush and waters – and, downstream, its lucrative views. These were the Georges River blues. They had mixed social, political and environmental outcomes, and they have been ignored in conservation histories. Yet they were at least partially successful in retaining something of the meaning of the Georges River as a rich, productive and 'bush' river.

---

2   Goodall and Cadzow, *Rivers and Resilience*.

Recognising this complex history and demography, I realised I needed to extend the frame we had used in earlier research in a number of ways if I wanted to understand what had motivated these Georges River blues – the many conflicts that took place in the postwar decades to try to save a damaged river and its bush.

A Longer Time Frame

First, I needed to take a longer view chronologically. Although it concentrates on the post-WWII period, this book first sketches out the period from colonisation up to the Depression. Next it explores the period from the end of WWII, through the 1950s campaign for the Georges River National Park and its aftermath in expanding official and bureaucratic controls. It continues by considering the pressures escalating on the river and finally investigates the burst of environmental activism in the later 1960s through to 1980.

History, Colonisation, Migrancy and Culture

Second, taking a longer time frame meant I needed to consider how these actors saw themselves in relation to invasion, colonisation and continuing interaction with Indigenous peoples. My previous work about people on the Georges River has concentrated on specific cultural groups, although each group has been heterogeneous with many complex internal differences. I have worked with and written about Indigenous peoples in *Rivers and Resilience*, Vietnamese Australians in *Waterborne* and Arabic-speaking communities in *Waters of Belonging*, all on the Georges River.[3] While this book focuses on environmental campaigns conducted largely by residents with Anglo-Celtic settler or immigrant backgrounds, this demands inquiry into how those Anglo-Celtic residents saw themselves in relation to other communities and their relationships to the river.

---

3   Goodall and Cadzow, *Rivers and Resilience*; Cadzow, Goodall and Byrne, 'Waterborne: Vietnamese Australians'; Goodall, Byrne and Cadzow, *Waters of Belonging*.

A Wider Geography

Third, I needed to take a wider geographic focus. This book looks beyond the early national park to consider the lands and waters of the estuary, with a focal area from Milperra downstream to Towra Point at the mouth of the Georges River as it enters Botany Bay. This immediately showed the significance of two places that had a powerful influence on the residents of the Georges River estuary.

One was the nearby national park, just to the south of the Georges River, which was set aside in 1879 to be the first reserved land called 'national' in Australia. It was managed by one of the same local government councils (the Sutherland Shire) that would become involved later in the Georges River National Park. The first national park was renamed the Royal National Park to honour Queen Elizabeth's visit in 1954, and it will be referred to as 'the Royal' throughout this book.

The second key place was the Cooks River to the north, which, like the Georges River, flows into Botany Bay. A small drowned valley estuary, the Cooks River lies much closer to the city of Sydney, so it suffered a heavy impact from the city's early industries. Rising near Greenacre, it flows eastwards, with important tributaries Shea's Creek, from its north, and Wolli and Muddy creeks, from the south.

Although both the Royal National Park and the Cooks River were important to Georges River residents, they carried opposite meanings. The Royal was a vision to which Georges River people strived, hoping to have the bushland along their own river acknowledged as being as important as the bushland in the national park to the south. The Cooks River was, on the other hand, a grim warning about what a river could become. While the soils along the Cooks River were far more suitable for European farming than those of the Georges, supporting early arcadian visions and attracting affluent and powerful landowners, it was also the site of the early settlement's most noxious industries. Organic waste from slaughterhouses, wool scours and tanneries polluted its waters along with the human waste that flowed from the major population expansion from the 1860s to the 1880s, as well as inner-city sewage, into Shea's Creek. The CSR sugar refinery at Canterbury, from 1842 to 1855, and other early heavy industries in the east of the catchment, added to the damage to the river's waters. However, because it was segmented early in its colonial history by dams at Tempe in 1832 and a weir built in 1842 near what became Canterbury Road, the impacts were varied along the river's short length. There could still be illusions of arcadian river pastimes even while other segments of the river were being 'improved' by concrete and canalisation – as was Shea's Creek between 1886 and 1900, becoming Alexandra Canal. This book will consider the Cooks River, not in detail as Tyrrell has done, but as it was seen by Georges River residents: 'a river despoiled' – a lesson about what could befall the Georges River if it were not defended.[4]

The damage to the Cooks River took place throughout the whole two centuries of colonisation while, as the following chapters show, the Georges River saw much slower damage across the nineteenth century, leading to the illusion of stability that was shattered by the rapid changes of the mid-twentieth century. This book focuses on responses to that sudden change along the Georges River from 1945 to 1980. It does not consider the major conflicts over Botany Bay, beginning in the 1970s but coming into full view in the 1980s as the emerging organised environmental justice movement battled with huge transnational companies against industrial and environmental damage. The blues on the Georges River had different protagonists. On one side were local people, including those living and working on land as well as those who lived along the river but worked on its waters, fishing or farming oysters. At the outset of the campaigns, these different groups of local people seldom worked together – in fact, they were often barely on speaking terms. Yet they were all confronting their own municipal authorities over directions for urban planning and sanitation in very local conditions. The battles in the Georges River estuary were not so dramatic as those later in Botany Bay but they were just as bitter and the resident groups just as tenacious. Oral histories conducted over the last 20 years and the many archival sources from the period from local organisations, newspapers and government inquiries allow an opportunity to look closely at how these widespread resident environmental action campaigns developed.

---

4   W. B. Malcolm, NSW Fisheries Branch, on plans for extensive bacteriological testing of the Cooks and Georges rivers and Botany Bay in 'Exhaustive Pollution Tests Soon', *Bankstown Torch*, 20 August 1969, 1, 3.

What is 'Suburban' Environmentalism?

Fourth, if I wanted to understand this activism I was hearing about in the oral histories, and reading about in the archives – as well as to explore the relationship with the Indigenous and multicultural histories I knew on the Georges River – then I needed to take a closer look at the writing on 'suburban environmentalism'. This led me to consider the way histories of cities and their environments have been addressed as well as how the histories of the Australian environmental movement have been written.

The word 'suburban' simply refers to a residential land area related to, but at some distance from, an urban area, yet it has developed denigratory meanings. While there has been a general equation of 'suburban' with middle class, the Georges River was a complex area in class terms. Certainly, all suburbs are not the same – just as not all environmentalists are the same. I needed to explore suburban environmentalism on this river by recognising its substantial working-class populations as well as the continuing presence of Indigenous peoples, the gentrifying new Anglo residents, and the incoming migrant and often non-Anglo communities. The book traces seven resident environmental campaigns on this estuarine stretch of the Georges River: one in the 1950s, one in the 1960s, then five occurring virtually simultaneously across the decade between 1967 and 1977, with one of them stretching to 1980. All of these campaigns had a vision of the river at their core. Each exhibited distinctive features that set it apart from the others, yet there were many shared concerns and all of them were in communication with the others, whether in friendship or conflict.

The twentieth century saw the expansion of suburbs around cities in the UK, the US and Australia. Much literature has been dismissive of suburbs, depicting their residents as embodying a conservative social order that emerged in the later nineteenth century, and focusing on private ownership of land and the privacy of spaces within fence lines. This social order – thought to be expressed in suburban architecture – assumed the dominance of men over women but also expected the control of humans over their private land-based gardens, in which natural processes were to be tamed and reordered, however they might be artfully arranged as 'wilderness'. Both literature and theatre have denigrated suburbs as barren wastelands of cultural mediocrity and environmental erasure.[5] In Australia there has been scathing and sustained criticism of suburbanism for its alleged isolating individualism, pressure for conformity, anti-intellectualism and repression of women.[6] Contributing to this narrative were the chemical and technological advances arising from WWII that were seen as conquering nature: herbicides, pesticides and the green revolution were all said to be fulfilling 'modern' human mastery over nature.

While many of these criticisms had elements of truth in them, each must be qualified to understand postwar environmental activism on the Georges River. Head and Muir[7] and, most recently, Andrea Gaynor have challenged the narrative that suburban land-based gardening confirmed human dominance over the more-than-human world. Gaynor points out that attempts to garden either for food or ornamentation in suburban conditions nurtured among gardeners an embodied and everyday interaction with the natural world that often contradicted the view that human dominance was growing over nature through technological and chemical industries. Their experiences were often far more ambivalent, with many of them forced to grapple with the refusal of the natural world to bow to such controls.[8] In fact, many species of animals, insects and plants demonstrated a tenacious resilience in the changing chemical environments with which they were faced, adapting and evolving in ways that led to a reassertion of their numbers and impact, much to the frustration of gardeners and the medical world.

Christopher Sellers has argued for the importance of seeing suburbs in the US as broader geographic areas rather than focusing only on privatised individual houseblocks. Sellers identifies the emergence of mid-twentieth-century environmentalism in the interactions that suburbs allowed for residents who continued to engage with rural hinterlands as well as the interstices of the suburbs themselves, created by rivers and creeks, marshes or parks. He argues that suburban environments were valued by residents not because they set up privatised and individualised spaces that excluded

---

5   Sellers, *Crabgrass Crucible*. For denigratory approaches in Australia, see the work of Robin Boyd in architecture (e.g. *The Great Australian Ugliness*, 1960), Patrick White in fiction (e.g. *Riders in the Chariot*) and Barry Humphries (as Edna Everage) in theatre.
6   Gilbert, 'The Roots of Anti-Suburbanism in Australia'.
7   Head and Muir, *Backyard*. Further authors on Australian suburban environmentalism have been Benson and Howell, *Taken for Granted*; Davison, 'Australian Suburban Imaginaries of Nature'; Davison, 'Stuck in a Cul-De-Sac?'; Davison, 'The Trouble with Nature'; Hogan, '"Nature Strip"'.
8   Gaynor, *Harvest of the Suburbs*; Gaynor, 'Grappling with "Nature"'.

nature, but because they allowed residents to be more actively involved in the environments outside their own fence lines – in the broader regions beyond but still close to their suburbs. Sellers proposes that the personal, embodied interactions with the natural world that suburbs made possible stimulated the environmental activism of the 1960s and 1970s. He points out that it was the collective and shared experiences of nature that generated this activism. Instead of suburbs creating isolated individuals craving solitary experiences in pristine nature, Sellers argues that suburbs fostered a sense of collective and socially responsible environment interactions that generated – in the climate of the 1960s and 1970s – a grassroots environmental movement, fuelled by direct experiences and local collective action.[9] I go a step further in this book to argue that it was the slow building of alliances between groups that initially had divergent interests that eventually offered the most effective resistance to the environmental damage of reclamation.

Writing about suburban environmentalism, including that of Sellers, has seldom considered urban rivers where significant industrial working-class populations existed, even when change was occurring. A number of important analyses have addressed the histories of Australian urban rivers, including Ian Tyrrell's valuable study of the Cooks River, discussed earlier, and those of Margaret Cook, Grace Karskens, Paul Boon and others. In all of these, however, there has more often been a focus on middle-class residents than on industrial workers or low-income groups who may have lived on these rivers.[10] Recognising the mixed and changing demographics of the Georges River estuary, this book traces the form and the strategies of environmental activism on the estuary in and between both working-class and gentrifying resident groups.

The Nation and the Bush

Another area of important reflection about environmentalism in Australia is related to urban areas in a different way. This is the concept of 'the nation', with places so often identified as symbolic of – and indeed,

---

9   Sellers, *Crabgrass Crucible*.
10   Tyrrell, *River Dreams*; Cook, *A River with a City Problem*; McLoughlin, *The Middle Lane Cove River*; McLoughlin, 'Mangroves and Grass Swamps'; McLoughlin, *The Natural Environment of Bankstown*; Rosen, *Losing Ground*; Rosen, *Bankstown*; Boon, *The Hawkesbury River*; Otto, *Yarra*; Karskens, *People of the River*.

contributing to – national identity. One way in which places have been identified as emblematic of 'the nation' has been by the enshrining of an area – initially an area of land – as a 'national park'. The current meanings of the term 'national park' have been shaped by the body of ideas about conservation that developed late in the twentieth century, arising partly from the emerging science of ecology and partly from the anachronistic application of US history to Australia.

The existence and uses of the Royal National Park shaped all the Georges River environmental campaigns from the 1940s onwards. Indeed, the first campaign considered in this study aimed to create a new 'national park' on the Georges River itself. This campaign succeeded with the declaration in 1961 of a national park on some sections of the northern and southern foreshores of the Georges River from west of East Hills to east of Salt Pan Creek. The expectations of the campaigners for this Georges River national park was that it would include 'natural bush', which had become firmly established in the early twentieth century as being vegetation native to Australia, symbolising its unique qualities and its independence (at least in popular imaginations) from British colonial founders.[11] Although this national park was short-lived – being demoted in 1967 to a 'State Recreation Park' – the brief existence of the park as 'national' had done two important things. First, it had brought three councils into close collaboration on environmental matters: Sutherland, Hurstville and Bankstown. Second, it left lasting memories among the residents all along the river about the types of protections to which they could aspire as well as the types of betrayals against which they had to guard.

The concept of 'the bush' was central to this vision. The Royal National Park was deliberately a reservation not over cultivated gardens but over 'native bush', the land and waterscapes being regarded, even in 1879, as offering not only healthy recreation but also immersion in unique and valuable environments. The early British disparagement of Australian landscapes had been inverted among Australians by the late nineteenth century, when the 'bush' was coming to symbolise not only Australia's unique environments but also its difference from its coloniser, Britain. At the same time, the term 'the bush' was used to refer to harsher areas remote from the coastal cities where unemployed workers during the 1890s depression travelled in search of work. More positive meanings re-emerged – in popular imagination if not in legal fact – as the colonies

---

11   See Chapter 4, this volume, for a discussion of the campaign.

became a 'nation' with Federation in 1901. Floral emblems were imbued too with the emotional impact of World War I, which led to so many Australian deaths and created new myths about the unique character of Australian soldiers, said to have been created in encounters with 'the bush'. At the same time, the endearing depictions of native Australian vegetation in the children's books of May Gibbs – particularly the gumnut babies, Snugglepot and Cuddlepie, with their friends and enemies – created generations of affectionate commitments to the, by now many-layered, idea of 'the bush'.[12] It was this concept of 'the bush' on which residents of the Georges River were basing their campaign for a park that was 'national'.

Melissa Harper has demonstrated that recreation – rather than biological conservation – was the intended use of the early Australian national parks. Recreation was certainly a concern of the lead campaigners for the Georges River National Park, but they were insisting that this should be in a landscape that included 'bush'.[13] The early US 'national parks' at Yellowstone (1872) and Yosemite (1890) were very different from the national park set aside in the Sutherland area by the New South Wales Government in 1879, renamed the 'Royal National Park' after Queen Elizabeth's visit in 1954.[14] The US national parks were protected with the future in mind because their landscapes were considered awe-inspiring and their living species were considered pristine. Conversely, the Royal National Park was set aside in 1879 to provide recreation within an environment of distinctly 'native bush' for the nearby inhabitants of Sydney whose urban life was believed to need supplementing with fresh air and opportunities for healthy recreation within what was regarded as a 'natural' environment. It was these living, neighbouring people who were considered to be 'the nation' rather than either the 'future' or the moneyed elite who were the only group who could afford to travel to the remote US parks. The Georges River campaigners were insisting that it was working-class and local communities that were 'the nation' for whom the national park – land *and* water – was to offer recreation, rather than to those from further away, and certainly not for elites.[15]

---

12   Although she did no service to banksias, on which, to this day, I look with completely undeserved mistrust.

13   Harper, 'The Battle for the Bush'; Harper, *The Ways of the Bushwalker*.

14   Harper and White, 'How National Were the First National Parks'. This park will be termed the Royal National Park throughout this piece to distinguish it from the Georges River National Park (1961–67).

15   Goodall and Cadzow, 'The People's National Park'.

Much of Harper's work is consistent with Seller's recognition of the important role of informal social interactions in the activities that were important in the natural environment. Her 2017 review of the literature on what she calls 'bush-based recreation' identifies the sociality of picnics as a core element in the goals for national park uses in the nineteenth and early twentieth centuries. Cadzow has traced the gendered dimensions of bush-based exploration within landscapes regarded as uniquely Australian, identifying the entanglements of gender both in attitudes to environments and in the social and power relationships of these explorations – entanglements that continue to emerge in the informal social interactions of picnics and river-based events.[16] Gender was an important issue in the postwar decades on the Georges River, when expectations of gendered roles – from boys' recreation to activist public life – shaped all uses of river and river lands, and it emerges in the following pages in motivations to activism as well as in the forms that such activism took.

Sociality or Solitude?

I have used the term *sociality* throughout this book to indicate human social interactions that are desired, expected and valued. Such gregarious interactions may occur in everyday living or working contexts and often in recreational settings like picnics in parks or fishing on riverbanks. While not necessarily formally planned, such interactions are not competitive; nor are they unwelcome or intrusive. They are instead an expected and encouraged experience.[17]

Analyses of Australian conservation, however, invariably shift the focus away from informal and locally organised sociality when they consider the campaigns for parklands in Australia in the mid-twentieth century, concentrating instead on the campaigns for remote and wilderness conservation allowing solitude and contemplation, or on the emergence of scientific conservation advocates.[18] In these studies, and in archival

16   Cadzow, 'Waltzing Matildas'.
17   A widely used term for informal social interactions in the disciplines of sociology and anthropology. See for example Strang, 'Substantial Connections'; Clark, 'Social Actions, Social Commitments'; Enfield and Levinson, *The Roots of Human Sociality*.
18   Harper 'The Battle for the Bush'; Harper, *The Ways of the Bushwalker*; Harper and White, 'How National Were the First National Parks'; Hutton and Connors, *A History of the Australian Environment Movement*; Mulligan and Hill, *Ecological Pioneers*; Robin, *The Flight of the Emu*; James, *Cosmopolitan Conservationists*; Griffiths, 'Environmental History, Australian Style'.

collections such as the Dunphy Papers, the campaigns of the Georges River and their wider motivations disappear from view entirely, despite Myles Dunphy's family residence in the heart of the Georges River and only 10 metres from the Oatley Park fence at Oatley West. Yet the campaign for the first Georges River National Park (1950–61) was quite explicit in its goals for recreational access for local working-class people to the foreshores and waters of the river, on lands that included picnic areas as well as playing fields but that retained what they called 'bush' or 'native' environments.[19]

Tyrrell has noted the interest in informal social activities on the Cooks River through this period, alongside the interest in engineering 'improvements' that were characteristic of the Cooks River Improvement League (CRIL, from 1908 to the 1930s) and the early Cooks River Valley Association (CRVA, from the 1950s). Such an interest in informal social activity was often fostered, Tyrrell points out, by women, despite their usually subordinate roles in the campaigns of CRIL and CRVA.[20] The emphasis of the CRVA turned, however, more towards 'modern environmentalism', which Tyrrell identifies with contemplation and solitude, after 1976.[21]

On the Georges River, this interest in picnics and informal opportunities for sociality in bushland did not disappear with the demise of the national park in 1967, when it was judged 'too small' and 'not wilderness' enough to qualify as a national park under the newly established state government National Parks and Wildlife Service.[22] As will become clear in later chapters, the desire to take part in picnics and informal outdoor social events in native bushland became even more strongly expressed during the campaigns of the 1960s and 1970s than it had been in the 1950s. There may have been more women in active roles in the Georges River campaigns, particularly at Lime Kiln Bay and Poulton Park as the following chapters suggest, but they were still in a minority. Nevertheless, the men who took part in the Georges River campaigns from 1950 onwards also argued that the informal sociality of picnics could be retained alongside more formal opportunities for recreation like playing fields for competitive sports,

---

19   Goodall and Cadzow, 'The People's National Park'. Closer attention is paid to suburban interest in environments in Dorothy Kass's valuable study of the introduction of nature study, particularly of education about birds, in the New South Wales primary schools curriculum in 1905. See Kass, *Educational Reform*.
20   Tyrrell, *River Dreams*, 162–64.
21   Ibid., 175–81.
22   Goodall and Cadzow, 'The People's National Park', 30.

which seemed increasingly to be the goal of municipal councils. None of these campaigns advocated the ideal of 'nature' as a place of contemplation and solitude. It was the informal sociality offered by bushland family and community picnics, all gendered and shaped by cultural diversity – the sharing of food and informal social interactions as well as ceremonies like the celebration of birthdays, the naming of children or the performance of prayers – that allows us to see the continuities between the goals of suburban environmentalism on the Georges River and the uses of natural spaces including the river before and since suburbs came into existence.

The central point for the Georges River campaigners about all such informal, outdoor and social activities was that they were taking place in 'the bush' – which is today understood across many communities in Australia as symbolic of 'the nation' but also open to 'the people' – partly because it was so often seen as 'wasteland'. While 'the bush' had many meanings, it also had connotations of 'the wild', the uncontrolled and undisciplined – of the imagined essence of the unique continent that was embraced by its many peoples. The central attraction for those living around the Georges River was not only the water of the river but also the bush of its banks, and the elements of this fragile and intractable vegetation that could be encouraged or coaxed into gardens. The goal of the campaign to save Poulton Creek and its surroundings near Oatley Bay was to 'Keep bushland in our suburbs'.

Environment and the Law

In another departure from earlier work, this book takes a different view of the very substance of the 'environment'. Australia's legal and administrative structures make a clear distinction between dry land and land under water. Crown land and all private property above the high-water mark is dealt with by the Lands Department whereas the underwater land of the estuaries like the lower Georges River are owned by the same body that manages harbours and coastlines: the Maritime Services Board.[23] In the period under discussion here, from the 1940s to 1980, the New South Wales Fisheries Branch had a role in regulating many aspects of the estuary. It managed leases for oysters, the construction of jetties and the conduct of dredging, which might affect fish and all aquatic animal

---

23   New South Wales Coastal Conference, *Estuary Management Manual*, 21.

and vegetation species, although this power was seldom used before the 1960s.[24] Only after 1979 could council zoning affect the ways in which estuary underwater land and foreshores may be used, including in the use of dredging.[25]

Yet many of the people in the human societies along both sides of the river held a different view, in which the river was an integral part of the imagined environment within which they lived. They may fish in the river, swim in it, gather oysters from the shore or from racks in the water, boat on it or simply observe the river's flow. In all these cases, in company or alone, they understood the river as an intimately connected part of their environment. In ecological terms – considering biology, geology and hydrology – the river waters and the river lands were interdependent and interacting, continuously shaping and reshaping each other. While the human perception of the river may have been more limited and fixed than the ecological – in that humans, for example, expected rivers to have fixed 'beds' and so they identified floods as unusual or even unnatural – nevertheless, the human view of their world, in cultural and imaginative terms, was closer to the ecological than it was to the legal.

Seeing the World as More-than-Human

Just like the river itself, the living beings in the more-than-human world all play important and active roles in this history, but history has often been written as if it were separated into human history and 'nature', where 'nature' – or living, non-human species – was little more than a backdrop to human actions.

Tracing out the stories of resident human environmental campaigns raises questions around what non-human species were fought over, what species were seen and what were unseen, what has been remembered and what forgotten. The history of these human resident campaigns on the Georges River estuary brings a number of non-human groups into view, most notably oysters and, because of their absence, the birdlife of the disappearing swamps. But it was mangroves that came to bear the most emotive and contradictory baggage arising from the conflicts between

---

24   Ibid., 20; New South Wales, *The Fisheries and Oyster Farms Act 1935*.
25   New South Wales Coastal Conference, *Estuary Management Manual*, 14, through the *Environmental Planning and Assessment Act 1979*.

humans over environmental change. No species is isolated from others, but the ecology of mangroves – that network of interacting living beings within which mangrove species existed – was lost to view. It was mangroves alone that became the object of such emotional attention.

The possibility of writing *relational* environmental histories, in which the relationships between changes over time in human and non-human species are understood to be in interaction, has been explored by Emily O'Gorman and Andrea Gaynor in their paper 'More-than-Human Histories', drawing on work from across the environmental humanities.[26] *Georges River Blues* does not achieve such a relational history, but it is written with the hope that it takes a step towards that approach. The goals and concerns of the Georges River resident campaigners were always interrelated with the changing behaviour of living mangrove species on the river, as well as the intensifying – and contesting – emotions that were being inscribed onto the plants over the time frame of this study. It is these interrelationships that the book seeks to trace. The human histories cannot be understood without seeing their interaction with the changing behaviours of mangroves as well as the changing *imagined* depictions of mangroves among all the contending parties.

Mangroves: Emerging from the Swamp

The concept of 'the bush' has been undifferentiated so far in this chapter, and for many people it has been a broad term. Yet mangroves have come to occupy a distinct and contested place within that broader concept of 'the bush'. The vegetation of low-lying sheltered bays and river shores is now understood to be complex, including microscopic creatures as well as a large diverse group of plants classified as 'macrophytes', meaning simply plants that are visible to the naked eye and that tolerate a fully or intermittently flooded environment. Some macrophytes are always below the waterline. In estuarine swamplands, they may be seagrasses or similar plants, while other macrophytes tolerate tidal inundation, with the whole plant or its roots fully underwater at high tide and above the water at low tide. In Botany Bay and the Georges River, the visible component of the macrophytes in the low-lying, watery areas was made up of a number

---

26   O'Gorman and Gaynor, 'More-than-Human Histories'; Adam, 'Mangroves and Saltmarsh Communities'.

of small plants and taller reeds in waterlogged soil known collectively as saltmarsh, and between the water and the saltmarsh were small numbers of mangrove trees.

Mangroves were just the largest of the macrophytes in estuarine low-lying watery lands – usually closest to deep water, with much of their root system in silt where little oxygen existed. Some mangrove species draw in oxygen from buttress roots above the silt. In the temperate zone like Sydney, the dominant variety, *Avicennia marina*, is characterised by thin pneumatophores that rise vertically up through the silt from horizontal, submerged roots, making the mud around them look spikey and forbidding.[27] The other variety is *Aegiceras corniculatum*, otherwise known as the river mangrove, able to thrive in less saline waters and generally smaller and with more rounded leaves than *Avicennia m.*[28]

Figure 1.1: Within a Georges River mangrove stand, low tide.
This photograph suggests the eerie wildness inside a Georges River mangrove stand.
Photographer: John Dowling, Illawong. 'The Tide is Out'. Courtesy of Inmagine Group.

---

27   Adam, 'Australian Saltmarshes in Global Context'. Adam draws on comparative data from temperate saltmarsh areas in South Africa, south-west and south-eastern Australia, New Zealand and temperate South America.
28   Ibid.

Figure 1.2: Mangrove pneumatophores, the upright roots allow the plant to bring in oxygen.

Mangroves grow in deoxygenated mud, so the pneumatophores rise vertically from underground horizontal roots, allowing the plant to access oxygen from the air. Wikipedia, Creative Commons.

Figure 1.3: Georges River saltmarsh at Mill Creek (Guragurang), 2009.

The foreground includes the succulent Sarcocornia quinqueflora (known as samphire) and Juncus kraussii (sea rush). In the middle and rear distance are mangroves (Avicennia marina) in front of taller, salt-tolerant plants such as varieties of Melaleuca and Casuarina. Geographer Dr Robert Haworth can be seen striding across the saltmarsh on the right. This photograph was taken from the middle of the saltmarsh, looking towards the landward side. There were mangroves behind the camera, between the saltmarsh and the river. Photographer: Heather Goodall.

Figure 1.4: Looking downwards, showing inundated roots of saltmarsh.

Another view of saltmarsh at Guragurang (Mill Creek) in 2009, looking down through the rushes or reeds to show the inundated roots of the saltmarsh species, *Sarcocornia quinqueflora*. Photographer: Heather Goodall.

Temperate zone mangroves were known in earlier decades to be a favoured site for oyster spawn attachment and had generally been seen as valuable for aquatic creatures like fish, but there had not been a detailed study of the temperate mangrove stands until the 1970s, perhaps stimulated by the political activity we chart later in this book. The early research about temperate mangroves and saltmarsh had seen them in a biological succession, in which bare shore might be colonised first by saltmarsh plants that would eventually be 'succeeded' by taller salt-tolerant plants like mangroves.[29] Research on saltmarsh began even later, in the 1990s. The archaeology investigating the relationship between mangroves and saltmarsh suggests that, rather than a succession, mangroves and saltmarsh were interacting and often competing species. The border between mangrove stands and saltmarsh was generally distinct, but it was not fixed, instead moving backwards and forwards as conditions changed.[30]

Beneath the saltmarsh, there is, most commonly, waterlogged soil, intensely saline, on which only the salt-tolerant saltmarsh species are viable.

29   Pidgeon, 'The Ecology of the Central Coastal', cited in Adam, 'Australian Saltmarshes in Global Context'. See also Adam, 'Mangroves and Saltmarsh Communities'; Rogers, Saintilan, Davies, Kelleway and Mogensen, *Mangrove and Saltmarsh Threat Analysis*.
30   Adam, 'Australian Saltmarshes in Global Context'; Saintilan, Rogers and Howe, 'Geomorphology and Habitat Dynamics'.

Figure 1.5: Georges River seagrasses: *Zostera capricorni* (foreground) and *Posidonia australis* (at rear).
Photograph taken at Port Stephens, New South Wales. Courtesy of photographer: Professor Tim M. Glasby.

Less well recognised, however, are the macrophytes below the surface of the waters. In the sheltered areas of Georges River estuary, where mangroves could be found along with saltmarsh before the British invasion, the plants below the waterline often included seagrasses, usually *Zostera capricorni* but also the broader leafed *Posidonia australis* (strapweed).[31] Not to be confused with seaweeds (which are algae), seagrasses are land grasses that are adapted to living under the water, flowering in season and, in low nutrient conditions, far better than seaweeds at extracting resources from the waters they inhabit. Seagrasses prefer shallow, slow-moving, clear waters that give them access to sunlight to allow photosynthesis. The tiny creatures that live on seagrass leaves offer excellent food for the immature fish and crustaceans who shelter among the waving stems. The seagrasses are not themselves eaten, but their leaves die and decay, forming detritus that becomes entangled in mangrove roots, which, in its turn, offers

---

31   West et al., *An Estuarine Inventory*; West, *Seagrasses*; Larkum, Kendrick and Ralph, *Seagrasses of Australia*.

nutrition for immature fish and crustaceans who shelter among the mangroves. The larger mangroves also offer shelter for seagrasses, slowing the flow of water and perhaps reducing waves.[32]

To better understand how mangroves came to change their meanings so much from the mid-twentieth century, it is helpful to return to the way they had been seen earlier. Although we know that much of the landscape of Australia was alien and disturbing for the British, it is also true that, from their first landings on the coastal estuaries of Botany Bay and Port Jackson in 1788, these settlers had found some geographies they recognised. The bays and inlets had tidal, low-lying swamps that were similar to those they knew from the coasts of south-east England and the Thames estuary. They even found plants in these estuarine swamps that seemed familiar, like the *Sarcocornia quinqueflora*, which was similar to the plant they knew as samphire (the *Crithmum maritimum* of English coasts). Once they crossed the Blue Mountains, they found inland marshes that looked like the fens of eastern England.

The mangroves seen in Botany Bay by James Cook and Joseph Banks were associated with the western areas of the bay and, while they lined the water's edge, did not appear to extend deeply on the landward side. Neither *Avicennia m.* nor *Aegiceras c.* appear on the definitive Banks and Solander list of species seen on that visit.[33] John Hunter explored along the lower Georges and Cooks rivers while Cook's party was anchored in Botany Bay but, despite charting as far inland as Salt Pan Creek, he did not record extensive mangrove stands.[34] In temperate zones like Sydney, mangroves consisted only of a few species.[35]

Tropical mangroves were different. In British India, from which many settlers came to Australia, as well as in Queensland and Papua New Guinea, there were many more species of mangroves present and they were more expansive, occupying far greater areas. Tropical mangroves were to become disturbingly familiar again to Australians during WWII, when many young men served in Papua New Guinea and other islands of the South Pacific.

---

32 New South Wales Department of Primary Industries, *Seagrasses: Prime Facts*.
33 Australian Botanic Garden, 'Banks and Solander Species List', accessed 11 October 2020, www.australianbotanicgarden.com.au/science/the-botany-of-botany-bay/plants/banks-and-solander-species-list.
34 Hunter, *An Historical Journal*; Adam, 'Mangroves and Saltmarsh Communities'.
35 Adam, 'Australian Saltmarshes in Global Context'.

Swamps and Myths

In temperate zone areas like Sydney, at the beginning of the twentieth century and, indeed, from the beginning of British settlement, mangroves had been unremarkable – just one piece of awkward places known as 'swamps'. Although familiar, swamps carried a heavy burden of fear and prejudice that reached deeply back into the myths the settlers brought with them from Europe. Swamps were places that were seen as unnatural – waterlogged places that were not water but not land either. Such beliefs about swamps were widespread within many European cultures and had persisted through the colonisation of Australia and later waves of migration. Beliefs and fears about swamps had been reinforced by European medical teaching from its Roman origins. Swamps were believed to hold damp, rotting material within them that generated 'miasmas' – mists so fine as to be invisible but often malodorous – that were understood to circulate diseases like cholera or malaria (or fen ague) between humans.[36] By the 1880s, the mosquitoes that were associated with swamps had been identified as the vectors for disease as well as irritants.[37] Yet diseases were only one part of the mythology of swamps. Even more dangerous were the malevolent forces still thought to be associated with these waterlogged places, making them sources of danger and evil whether on inland plains or coastal lowlands.

This inherited burden of myths and fears about the danger of mangroves and swamps had been intensified for Australians by their WWII battle experiences in the inhospitable mangrove forests of South-East Asia. The Australian parliamentarian Henry 'Jo' Gullett remembered the 'jungle' from his WWII experience in Papua New Guinea as 'sunless, dripping, curiously silent, without birds or wild animals, yet somehow alive, watching, malignant, dangerous'. He associated it with 'a nagging insistent consciousness of one's physical weakness'.[38] John Cross, author of *Jungle Warfare: Experiences and Encounters*, praised Gullett's accuracy and added his own conflict memories of the jungle, including mangroves, as being in:

---

36   Halliday, 'Death and Miasma'; Nash, *Inescapable Ecologies*.
37   Cox, 'History of the Discovery'.
38   Gullett, *Not as a Duty Only*, 95.

A state of permanent semi-twilight, gloomy even when sunshine does dapple the jungle floor with shadows, and dark in creeks and narrow valleys at noon. It is a state of permanent dampness, rain or sweat, of stifling, windless heat, of dirty clothes, of smelly bodies, of heavy loads, of loaded and cocked weapons, of tensed reflexes … Such conditions of rain, mud, rottenness, stench, gloom … are sufficient to fray the strongest nerves. But add to them the tension of the constant expectancy of death from behind the impenetrable screen of green.[39]

There did not need to be malevolent spiritual forces lurking among mangroves when there might be enemy soldiers hidden in every dark recess. The long-lasting psychological damage caused by the terrifying conditions of war has been identified recently as post-traumatic stress disorder, but such damage was seldom recognised in the mid-twentieth century. Yet, so many of the South-East Asian battles were fought out in impenetrable jungle conditions that mangroves were inevitably inscribed with the disturbing emotions faced by so many young Australian troops. Returning to Australia and seeing mangroves expanding in the south-eastern estuaries must have offered an ominous warning of impending danger. It is impossible to investigate systematically how many people associated the expanding mangroves they saw in the Georges River with their residual wartime fears. Some hints, however, were given by advocates of mangrove removal, like the editor of the *St George and Sutherland Leader* who explained his distaste of mangroves (a plant he had described as an 'eyesore') after 'witnessing first-hand what damage mangroves can do in Papua New Guinea and Queensland'.[40]

* * *

---

39   Cross, *Jungle Warfare*, 18–20.
40   'Editorial: Why Keep an Eyesore?', *Leader*, 7 August 1974, 2. The editor's comment about 'witnessing harm' was in response to a letter to the editor entitled, 'Swamp Must be Preserved', *Leader*, 21 August 1974, 21. Chapters 7 and 11 will discuss the wartime experience of Hurstville Municipal Engineer A. H. Brewer in relation to mangroves as expressed in Hurstville Council Minutes, 6 March 1969, item 274, Local Studies Archive, Hurstville Library, Georges River Council Libraries.

There seems to have been only very slow mangrove regrowth after some early settler use on the Georges River. It was apparently only after the 1930s that mangrove expansion began to be noticed by the people who lived along the river. Instead of simply being one part of a bigger entity – the swamp – the term 'mangrove swamp' became more common from mid-century, as will be seen in the following chapters. There was a growing implication that the mangroves *caused* the swamp.

Yet, even in the early days, mangroves had shared with swamps the quality of being ambiguous. They lived between land and water, obscuring the water's edge, smudging any clear distinction between dry land and river or sea. And they can live in brackish water, undrinkable and saline although sometimes mixed with fresh, but always lost irretrievably to humans to drink. They seemed twisted, misshapen and unruly. Yet, for those same reasons, they offered sanctuary and protection for humans and animals. Mangrove roots are confronting, either winding through the air or spiking up in pneumatophores, seeking oxygen above the waterlogged soil, allowing the plant to thrive. Not only do these roots bring oxygen into the plant, they also catch and hold detritus from the passing water, offering food to both the plant and the small creatures sheltering among those roots. Hydrogen sulphide (or rotten egg gas) is one of the chemical by-products of rotting vegetation in anaerobic conditions. Yet all the odours are invariably blamed on the mangroves; the harder they work, the more rotting plant material they gather, the more garbage and filth they save from travelling downstream, the worse they stink. The less likely they are, therefore, to be embraced as a 'flagship' or 'charismatic' species.

As they expanded, the intractability of mangroves made them easier to hate but their visibility forced humans to notice them. This unavoidable presence made mangroves easier to defend than what lay around them, often unnoticed – the broader wetland. As this book will show, for those who desired to transform the bays into golf courses and playing fields, the highly visible and expanding presence of mangroves 'proved' that the bays were 'stinking, mosquito-infested swamps' – that is, 'wastelands'. For the defenders of the bays in the 1960s and 1970s, however, the presence of mangroves 'proved' that the waters could become clean and healthy again. Mangroves offered essential sources of nurture, food and protection for young fish, crabs and other species: they gave hope for the future. So, whether they were hated or defended, mangroves became the metonym – the symbol – for the whole imagined environment.

The increasing episodes of environmental activism along the Georges River from 1945 to 1985 did not emerge coincidentally. Nor was the expansion of the mangrove stands accidental over the same years. While mangroves on temperate rivers like the Georges were never so extensive as in tropical lands, they carried the mythologies of forests in many cultures, embodying beliefs and fears, surprises, mysteries and horrors, so that their expansion troubled emotions as much as evoking rational responses. Activism and mangroves both grew in specific conditions, shaped by history, shifting environments and changing attitudes. The entanglements between them, and what is beneath the surface of each, are explored in the following pages.

2

The Picnic River: Pleasure Grounds and Waste Lands

The Georges River estuary was no rich farming site. On the contrary, along its tidal, saline length, from Liverpool to its junction with Botany Bay, the Georges River banks were mostly sandy soils, low-lying swamps with some mangroves on the water's edge or, in the downstream reaches, sandstone escarpments.[1] Yet residents along the estuary frequently interacted with the broader riverine environments in ways that were highly socialised, rather than solitary. This became most evident in the 1940–70s environmental resident action campaigns, but the earlier history of the river had shaped its later developments. This river became known as a 'picnic river' – far enough away from the city to have escaped some of its worst pollution in the nineteenth century but close enough to visit – particularly once the railway lines went through. On the way to the Royal National Park, by the later years of the century, Georges River had become a destination in its own right, to which people could escape from the everyday city to picnics or pleasure grounds.

***

Over generations, Aboriginal people on both the northern and southern sides had found the river lands and its waters highly productive, shown by the many cooking hearths, middens and art sites along its shores. There was sustained community knowledge of the river's foods and crafts such as woven goods from its reeds, which were still being talked about to John

1   For discussion of the 'Banks and Solander Species List', see Benson and Eldershaw, 'Backdrop to Encounter'; Hunter, *An Historical Journal*.

Lennis during his childhood at Herne Bay on Salt Pan Creek in the 1940s. An Indigenous horticulturalist later working with Gandangara Land Council, Lennis remembered that, for him and his family, 'the Georges River was the playground'.[2]

The soils, however, were not suited to European agriculture. There were some patches of rich volcanic soils, such as Lugarno, but little intensive farming could be done on the rest of the riverbank. Instead, land use in some areas included low intensity uses like orchards or poultry farming, which meant that much of it was still considered to be underutilised and, therefore, 'wasted'. The main European clearing and intensive farming was done away from the river, on the richer, shale-derived soils where townships like Bankstown developed. Areas closer to the river were cropped for timber, contributing to erosion, while on the riverbanks themselves, there was, as discussed earlier, some use of the estuarine vegetation in the early years of British settlement, when either saltmarsh or mangroves or both were harvested and burnt for alkaline ash to make soap. The types of vegetation used and the amounts harvested were not enumerated and this early industry had declined by 1840.

Dharawal and Dharug people along the river had posed sustained resistance to early colonisers, but they had been badly impacted by the violence of the invasion and then by the illnesses brought by the settlers. Nevertheless, people remained – like Biddy, born perhaps in the 1840s on northern Dharawal land on the southern shore of the Georges River, living and raising children on southern Dharwal land around Wollongong, but returning to the Georges River by the 1860s, marrying an Englishman, Billy Giles, and living on Mill Creek (Guragurang). Biddy became a guide for many white settlers in their fishing and hunting excursions as they travelled between the townships of Sydney and Wollongong. Their memoirs of these trips often include Biddy's teaching about her country, as well as her visits along the way to the many small Dharawal families living along the river.[3]

Even after the numbers of Aboriginal people on the river had been reduced, European population remained sparse. There was little interest in buying or trying to farm the marginal river lands. Yet those 'wastelands' were used vigorously, along with the river itself for fishing and swimming. Before World War I (WWI), there were three uses to which the river lands were put. There were minimally developed 'pleasure grounds' for private or

2   Lennis, interview.
3   Goodall and Cadzow, *Rivers and Resilience*, Ch. 4.

commercial picnics; military training grounds and barracks; and sheltered, informal living spaces, where residents lived in huts, camps or tents. The most active commercial enterprise had developed on the river waters themselves: the cultivation of oysters. Even the 'wasteland' spaces were used productively. Rabbits and small game were hunted by settlers as well as by the Aboriginal people who still lived there, and on the swamps, ducks were hunted and birds' eggs gathered. Yet these informal uses, on which people often depended for daily food and even a small income, were not seen as 'real' farming. Even less recognised, however, were the simultaneous environmental changes that were to have a powerful impact on the political campaigns of the later twentieth century. Each of these human uses, discussed below, caused changes to the riverine bed, waters or shores.

Picnics and Pleasure Grounds

A few of these river lands were already identified as 'parks' in the later nineteenth century. The largest in the area was, of course, the national park at Audley, declared in 1879. This huge park was well known and frequented by people from the growing city of Sydney on the Harbour to the north but also by those from the large towns like Bankstown and Hurstville.[4] Although the national park did not lie on the Georges River, its visitors from the city saw the Georges River as they crossed it on the railway at Como. The national park contained a wide variety of sites, which rose and fell in usage as leisure activities altered over time.[5] Within it, accessible to walkers from the railway stations along the western perimeter, areas had been set aside for picnics with some 'amenities' while other areas had not been developed by Europeans in any noticeable way, allowing settlers to think of them as 'pristine'.[6] This first Australian 'national' park suggested an egalitarian 'nation' made up of working people, rather than defined by affluent visitors from far away. This vision of the 'nation' as local, working people, as well as the recognition of the value of native bushland, was attractive to many on the Georges River, for whom the national park to the south became a model of the hopes they held for their own river.

---

4   Harper, 'The Battle for the Bush'; Harper and White, 'How National Were the First National Parks'; James, *Cosmopolitan Conservationists*.
5   Its beaches, for example, were far less well utilised in the nineteenth century when ocean swimming was less popular than they were by the mid-twentieth century, when ocean swimming and surfing were more popular and transport technologies were more readily available. Caroline Ford, *Sydney Beaches*.
6   Australian Government, Department of Agriculture, Water and the Environment, 'Royal National Park and Garawarra State Conservation Area'.

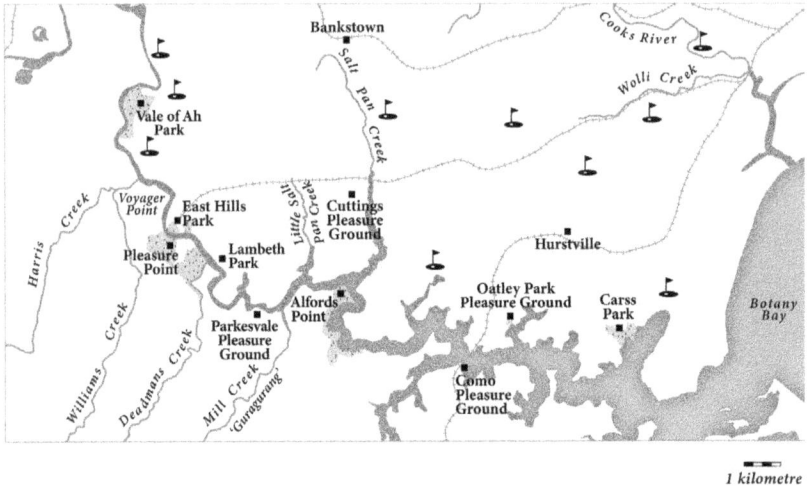

1 kilometre

Map 2.1: The Picnic River: pleasure grounds, parks and golf courses to 1950.

There were many parks along the Georges River, most with shops selling picnic food and hot water for tea. Those called 'Pleasure Grounds' might have additional attractions like dance floors and boats for hire. All had swimming areas, where nets protected swimmers from sharks, a very real threat in the river before pollution problems after World War II (WWII) drove the sharks away. Golf courses were rare in southern suburbs before WWII because golf was at first considered an elite sport, with most courses in the northern suburbs. The few along the Georges River were in low-lying areas, reshaped only with heavy labour. After the war, however, golf courses on the Georges River began to increase, contributing to the pressure for reclamation.[7] Cartography: Sharon Harrup.

There were many smaller parklands set up on the Georges River itself, some on Crown land but much on land that had originally been granted as freehold but that had been undeveloped because it was swampy or had such poor, sandy soils. Some land near the water had been 'improved' with the addition of a toilet block and some infilling on the edges of the swampy land or a locally built jetty allowing rowboats or ferries to stop. Other sandstone lands were undeveloped in any way, whoever the owner might be, and later aerial photography showed them to be crisscrossed with tracks, which allowed everything from 'blooding' greyhounds to clandestine meetings for illicit sex.

Wherever they were located, social gatherings might range from these secret assignations to Sunday school picnics and council picnics through to family picnics. Around the turn of the century, entrepreneurs began to offer spaces for such picnics – at a price – in larger or smaller 'pleasure grounds' with more 'improvements'.

---

7   Molloy, *A History of Padstow*; Molloy, *The History of Panania*; Molloy, *The History of Milperra*; Earnshaw, *The Land Between Two Rivers*; Innes, *The Story of Golf.*

One park for which there is an extensive photographic record is East Hills Park, in a rich archive conserved by local resident Esme Clisby.

Figure 2.1: The 1920s entrance to East Hills Park.

This was marked out as a park in the earliest British land grant over the area, made to James Watson in 1838. Many people who later formed the Picnic Point Regatta Association to campaign for the national park remembered the river parks as picnic places. Esme Clisby, interviewed for this project, conserved the history of this picnic river through her archive of photographs of East Hills Park in the 1920s, many reproduced by Andrew Molloy in *The History of Panania, Picnic Point and East Hills*. Photograph contributed by Esme Clisby.

Figure 2.2: Swimmers and picnics at East Hills Park, c. 1920s.

East Hills Park was popular throughout the early twentieth century for informal picnics and swimming. The area was netted to protect swimmers from the sharks rumoured to frequent the river. Photograph contributed by Esme Clisby.

Figure 2.3: Rowboat picnic group at East Hills Park, c. 1920s.

Rowboats were commonly used along the river throughout the first half of the twentieth century for fishing, travelling and to take part in social events, like this small group coming for a picnic at East Hills. Photograph contributed by Esme Clisby.

Figure 2.4: Sunday school picnics at East Hills Park, c. 1920s.

As well as informal social groups, there were often group picnics, particularly those organised by churches and Sunday schools, like this group walking into East Hills Park. Photograph contributed by Esme Clisby.

Figure 2.5: Buses at East Hills Park, c. 1920s.

Larger groups, like the Sunday school and church picnic groups, might come in chartered buses, but buses also ran from the railway stations at Bankstown and other larger townships, bringing visitors from the inner city out to the picnic river. Photograph contributed by Esme Clisby.

Figure 2.6: Refreshments at East Hills Park, c. 1920s.
The refreshments were basic – hot water for tea and freshly made sandwiches and cakes from the shop on the hill above the picnic ground, which also sold groceries for the scattered houses among the bush at East Hills. Photograph contributed by Esme Clisby.

Figure 2.7: Parkesvale, 1906.
Parkesvale – named after Sir Henry Parkes – was much more grand. At 50 acres, this highly publicised commercial pleasure ground on the Sutherland side of the river advertised itself as 'The Ideal Holiday and Tourist Resort'. It offered not only camp sites and a speedy motor launch to ferry visitors from the railway station at Como, but also 'boating, fishing, dancing, bathing, swings, merry-go-rounds' and even a 'razzle-dazzle'. As well, 'genuine travellers' – those who had travelled from the inner city – could consume alcohol along with their other activities. Photograph courtesy of Bankstown Historical Society.

Access to transport was a crucial factor in the siting of such pleasure grounds, as it was in choices about land purchases. Train lines, like that near Como, allowed the movement of crowds from the inner city to the Georges River, and subdivisions in the 1920s were often motivated by new railway building – or by rumours of future construction! From the railway stations, buses as well as boats and ferries would transport picnickers to the pleasure grounds, reflecting the common use of watercraft for everyday transport as well as for fishing, competition or leisure.

The best known was Parkesvale, upstream from Alfords Point on the southern, Sutherland side of the river, opening in 1905, which could be reached by paddle steamer (see Figure 2.7). The Como Pleasure Ground, close to the railway line, had opened earlier, in 1895, while Oatley Park was earlier still, in 1887. As the advertisements for Parkesvale suggest, pleasure grounds catered for all ages and offered many different types of pleasures, from razzle-dazzles to boating to dancing.[8] What made such establishments on the Georges River so attractive as Sunday picnic sites for city dwellers was that alcohol could be purchased there for 'genuine travellers', while the dance floors at Parkesvale and other pleasure grounds were used for local social gatherings as well as for people from further away.[9]

These larger pleasure grounds had mostly fallen into disuse by WWI, but there were smaller picnic grounds that continued to operate until WWII, shown in Figures 2.8–2.12. Some, like Carss Park, set up in 1924 on Kogarah Bay, and Sans Souci on Botany Bay, continue to exist as parklands, with just tiny kiosks as a reminder of their former glory.

Whether large or small, these pleasure grounds made their money from selling cakes, tea and alcohol, and by renting out rowing boats and dance halls. Later still, some swamp areas were 'improved' again to become golf courses: filling in a bit more of the swamp to create landscaped fairways and greens allowed groups of people to play this social and competitive sport. Golf courses, although they offered trees and greenery, brought their own problems. The greens and fairways needed fertilisers that washed into the creeks and rivers, acting as a contaminant and nutrient that encouraged troublesome growths like algal blooms. The course also

---

8   A 'razzle-dazzle' was a common and popular piece of circular play equipment in Australian children's parks in the early twentieth century. Although seldom seen more recently because it was believed to be dangerous, it was popular precisely because of the speed that could be achieved as it was pushed by children riding or running alongside. Larger versions, like that at Parkesvale, were suspended from a central pole.

9   Elliott Goodacre, interview. Elliott, a Picnic Point resident when interviewed in 2002, recalled his father's accounts of his youth along the Georges River. Earnshaw, *The Land Between Two Rivers*, gives vivid accounts of the pleasure grounds at Oatley and Carss parks.

needed frequent watering, particularly through hot and dry summers, and the water itself contributed to altered watertables beneath the course, as well as aiding the flow of fertilisers into the natural waterways.[10]

Figure 2.8: Hollywood Park on Prospect Creek, north of Milperra, c. 1920s.

This was one of many small parks along the river known as 'pleasure ground' with netted baths and hired boats. Photograph courtesy of Bankstown Historical Society.

Figure 2.9: The Vale of Ah Park, c. 1920s.

Another popular park with large netted baths, just downstream from Milperra and close to Kelso Swamp. Photograph courtesy of Bankstown Historical Society.

---

10   Simpson and Newsome, 'Environmental History of an Urban Wetland', 8.

Figure 2.10: Lambeth Street Wharf Pleasure Grounds, c. 1920s.
Another substantial commercial holiday and 'pleasure ground' was at Lambeth Street Park, downstream from East Hills and opposite what is now Sandy Point. Visitors arrived on buses from Bankstown station and could stay in sturdy cabins built on site. Photograph courtesy of Bankstown Historical Society.

Figure 2.11: Lessons at the Oatley Pleasure Grounds pool, 1928.
In the lower estuary there were more pleasure grounds. The largest was Como Pleasure Grounds, on the southern shore, with a grand building on a promontory visible from the railway line crossing the Georges River. Across the river in the Hurstville area was Oatley Pleasure Grounds, on the western side of Oatley Bay, and here too was a safely netted swimming pool and swimming lessons were held regularly. Photograph courtesy of Oatley Amateur Swimming Club and the *Dictionary of Sydney*.

Figure 2.12: Flying fox at Cuttings Pleasure Ground on Salt Pan Creek, c. 1920s.

All of these smaller pleasure grounds offered netted pools, picnic grounds and a shop, and most had playgrounds – just for fun – like the razzle-dazzle at Parkesvale and this flying fox at Cuttings Pleasure Ground on Salt Pan Creek. Photograph courtesy of Bankstown Historical Society.

Even before the golf courses, local councils had established rubbish tips in a few of these low-lying areas, which eventually allowed them to be covered over to be grassed and made into picnic grounds and a few into playing fields, like the Kelso Swamp area near the Vale of Ah (see Chapter 7). A similar attempt was made with Renown Park on the west arm of Oatley Bay but, as we shall discuss in Chapter 12, this 'reclamation' failed and the surface of the 'park' remained so unstable and toxic that much could not be used. Such 'reclaimings' were, however, occurring only at a modest pace and, as late as the 1950s, swamps were characteristic elements of the landscape around people's homes and remain so in people's memories.[11] Kevin Jacobsen (born 1934) is one for whom the swamps around East Hills still hold a place in childhood memory:

> We used to play there. The swamp's not there anymore – but we used to skate on the mud on the swamp. And we'd catch little swamp things. And we used to go rabbiting too.[12]

Such sociality 'beyond the fence lines' continued along the river despite the increasing subdivision of farming blocks from the 1920s in anticipation of the railway. Sociality, picnics – whether commercial, church or family – fishing and other leisure activities 'enculturated' the open spaces as highly valued elements of the identity of these working-class areas and the residents who lived in them. The types of sociality were shaped by historical periods and norms. Multi-generational family picnics or fishing expeditions were common among Anglo-Irish local residents in the 1920s and 1930s, but there were also picnics organised by church fellowships or Sunday schools. After WWII, picnics might be organised by the companies that owned the new large factories sited along the river, assembling 'modern' electric white goods, and seeking to foster corporate loyalty and bonding among employees. So while the householding communities of the Georges River were, by the 1960s, 'suburban' in the sense of valuing private and freestanding house blocks, on which they may have their own gardens, they did not see this as isolating them from the local, public and 'wild' spaces of the area's riverbanks or from the water of the river itself.

Nor was Indigenous sociality a thing of the past: Aboriginal people continued to live in secluded areas along the Georges River, with long-established Indigenous communities on Prospect, Harris and Williams creeks valuing the social networks they offered as they continued to fish,

11 PPRA, interview, 22 March 2006.
12 Kevin, Colin and Carol Jacobsen, interview, 12 July 2006.

prawn and share meals together. Denis Foley's grandmother, for example, had grown up and been living on Prospect Creek for many years, upstream of its junction with the Georges River at Chipping Norton.[13]

After Biddy Giles returned to the Georges River in the 1860s, one of her daughters, Ellen, followed her, only to be forced by the New South Wales Aborigines Protection Board in 1883 to go to Cummeragunja Station on the Murray River. Ellen married Hughie Anderson there, a Yorta Yorta man, and they returned to the Georges River in the 1920s, purchasing a block of land on the eastern side of Salt Pan Creek. Ellen was herself to have a role in the shaping of the floral symbolism of Australian nationalism. Her knowledge of Dharawal environments was drawn on by C. W. Peck in his long (fruitless) campaign to have the waratah replace the wattle as the national icon.[14]

Ellen and Hughie were joined there by William Rowley, who had been born around the mid-nineteenth century at Pelican Point on the promontory known as Towra Point, where the Georges River flows into Botany Bay. After working for some time as the overseer at Thomas Holt's oyster farm at Sylvania, and living and marrying at La Perouse, Rowley had moved upstream too in the 1920s, purchasing the block next to Ellen and Hughie on Salt Pan Creek.[15]

The Anderson and Rowley families each formed the hub of extended family and visitor camps on these blocks.[16] By this time, along with the Anderson and Rowley families at Salt Pan Creek, there were well-documented Aboriginal communities living on Prospect Creek near Chipping Norton, on Williams Creek, at Voyager Point on Mill Creek and at Kogarah Bay, along with many other small family groups along the riverbanks and islands, as well as in a number of encampments around Botany Bay itself.[17] The Salt Pan Creek community – the Anderson and Rowley families and many visitors – lived there during the Depression, and a number of people have remembered their times there fishing and prawning together in the creek below the blocks.[18]

---

13 Foley, *Repossession of Our Spirit*; Gapps, *Cabrogal to Fairfield City*.

14 Goodall and Cadzow, *Rivers and Resilience*, 133, fn. 43.

15 McKenzie and Stephen, 'La Perouse'.

16 Goodall and Cadzow, *Rivers and Resilience*, Ch. 6; Irish, *Hidden in Plain View*.

17 Foley, *Repossession of Our Spirit*; Gapps, *Cabrogal to Fairfield City*; Goodall and Cadzow, *Rivers and Resilience*; Foley and Read, *What the Colonists Never Knew*.

18 Campbell and Thomas, interview, 24 September 1980; Campbell, interview, 14 July 1982.

Figure 2.13: Younger members of Anderson family, Salt Pan Creek, 1925.
Younger members of Ellen and Hughie Anderson's family, two of their grandchildren, Ellen and Tom Williams (Jnr) (the two youngest children, centre), on the shores of Salt Pan Creek, c. 1925. Courtesy of State Library of New South Wales. Source: PXA 773/Box 1, Series 03 Box 1: Australian Indigenous Ministries pictorial material: pre-1960 photographs, part 2, item 78.

Figure 2.14: Bocce at Horsley Park, 1952.
A game of bocce being hosted by the Crestani family at their home at Horsley Park around 1952. Photograph courtesy of Fairfield City Library and Museum Photographic Collection.

The very public picnicking of British and Irish settlers along the Georges River paralleled the social gatherings of Italian or German settlers taking place at the same time, although these tended to be occurring in more private spaces, like homes and market gardens that remained at a greater distance from the river. Members of the Italian community, like the Italian workers who tended the grape vines on Williams Creek and at Fairfield in the 1880s, used the market garden spaces they rented to have bocce games, while families in the 1950s, like the Crestanis at Horsley Park, hosted community gatherings at their home.[19] The Germans at Lugarno and Holsworthy had social musical gatherings, playing zither and guitars, in the spaces of private homes, rented or owned, in the 1910s.[20] So although the most public sociality along the river was in the gathering of Anglo-Celtic settlers in parks and picnic grounds, the many remaining spaces and interstices along the river – the 'wastelands' – meant that there were other less visible social events taking place in less public settings.

Soldiers and Swamps

A proportion of these 'wastelands' served military purposes. Military training grounds had been established in 1899 at Artillery Hill near Grey's Point within the 1879 national park at Sutherland. Then, in 1912, the federal government established the large Holsworthy training facility, compulsorily acquiring grape farms along Williams Creek (where Aboriginal farm owners and Italian vine workers had been living) and other farmed land as well as unused spaces across a large area right up to the southern shore of the Georges River.

The military role was expanded during WWI with an internment camp as well as increased training facilities for Australian troops.[21]

---

19   Gapps, *Cabrogal to Fairfield City*, 293, 342–45.
20   Blewett, *Ferries and Farms*.
21   McKillop, 'The Royal National Park Line'.

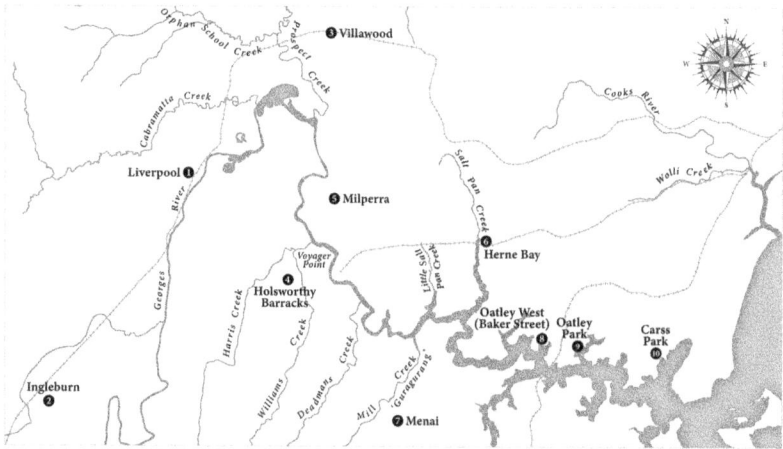

1 kilometre

1 Liverpool
Internment Camp from 1939.
Extended for 17th Australian Camp Hospital,
Australian Army.

2 Ingleburn
16th, 68th and 72nd Australian Camp Hospital,
Australian Army. Training Camp from 1940.

3 Leightonfield Munitions Factory
previously called Villawood Munitions Factory, 1941.

4 Holsworthy Detention Barracks
Training, from 1912. Detention Barracks,
WW1 & WWII.

5 Milperra
Soldier Settlement 1917.

6 Herne Bay
118th General Hospital, USASOS, 1942.

7 Menai
Lucas Heights HIFAR reactor 'Critical' (turned on)
in 1958.

8 Baker Street Oatley West
Oatley Anti-aircraft Searchlight Unit Camp.

9 Oatley Park
Tasmanian Battalion campsite
Campsite and training area for 26 Field Company
Royal Australian Engineers (RAE).

10 Carss Park
1 Division, 26 Field Company RAE used the
Ambulance Room of the St George and Sutherland
Ambulance as an Orderly Room during WWII.

Map 2.2: Locations of military sites along the Georges River.

This map indicates the impact of WWII on the Georges River. Older military sites like Holsworthy expanded while new military installations proliferated, often built on low lying areas and usually discharging sewage and other waste directly into the river. Cartography: Sharon Harrup.

Figure 2.15: Panorama view of Holsworthy military camp and training ground, 1914–18.

As a major training ground and barracks for Australia's military until after WWII, Holsworthy remained a secretive and mysterious place to local residents who were not allowed entry. Set aside first in the 1880s, this military site covered 50 acres by the early twentieth century. Photograph reference number: H02147−1. Reproduced courtesy of Australian War Memorial.

Figure 2.16: German internees in 1916 on pick and shovel work.

During WWI and WWII, Holsworthy not only held captured enemy troops but also naturalised Australian citizens originally from countries then at war with Australia and Australian-born citizens whose ancestors had migrated from enemy countries like Germany and Italy.[22] Photograph reference number: H17640—2. Reproduced courtesy of Australian War Memorial.

Even before that war ended, lands near Milperra became soldier settlement cooperative allotments from August 1917, planned to be poultry farms. The intensive clearing needed was impossible for many recipients, who had been selected to compensate them for wounds sustained in the war.[23] Most of the original returned servicemen had left the settlement by the later 1920s, leaving much of this land unused again.

Once again, in WWII, lands labelled as 'unused' along the Georges River were taken up for military camps, training grounds and more internment and prisoner of war jails. In 1943 these sites were extended even further to accommodate US troops who retreated to Australia during the Pacific War. Bushland, golf courses and pleasure grounds were all erased by

---

22 National Archives of Australia, 'Wartime Internment Camps in Australia', accessed 11 January 2021, www.naa.gov.au/explore-collection/immigration-and-citizenship/wartime-internment-camps-australia.

23 Much soldier settlement analysis is based on Victorian settlements. Glenys Allison has undertaken detailed research in the New South Wales Closer Settlement and Soldier Settlement files. See Allison, 'Bankstown Soldier Settlement Milperra'.

military camps and army hospitals. The largest was at Herne Bay near Salt Pan Creek, where a huge US Army hospital was built in 1943 on a golf course previously 'reclaimed' from saltmarsh swamp in the 1930s – with much heavy labour – by the Levingston family.[24]

Later in the twentieth century there would be further impacts of warfare and military personnel, technologies and experiences on the Georges River that negatively affected environmental conditions. Military technology, emerging in the 1930s and expanding during WWII, was to shape the way the changes in the more-than-human world of the river were seen.

Figure 2.17: National servicemen march past at their passing out parade at Holsworthy, 1954.

Young men undertaking their compulsory period of national service – known as 'conscription', 'nasho' or, in the later American term, 'the draft' – were trained for part of their service time at Holsworthy. So, although a restricted and mysterious place, Holsworthy was a constant reminder for young men in the area that their time might come. Photograph reference number: DUN/54/0257/EC–2. Reproduced courtesy of Australian War Memorial.

---

24 Madden, *Hernia Bay*; US National Library of Medicine, 'Collections', accessed 11 January 2021, collections.nlm.nih.gov/.

Farming the Water: Oysters and Growers

Settlers slowly began to value oysters for eating, not just for burning their shells for lime. Oysters were abundant, so early settlers could simply harvest naturally growing shellfish on the rocky shores along the Georges River. Thomas Holt attempted unsuccessfully to cultivate oysters during the 1860s, but more successful farming began on the Georges River during the 1870s, initially by dredging in mud near the shores and, by 1900, by catching oyster spawn (spat) on mangrove sticks, initially from the Georges River and later from south coast areas like the Minnamurra River. The young oysters were laid out in netted trays or racks where they would fatten until eventually gathered for market, either unshelled or in bottles.[25]

The oyster farming families lived locally, forming part of the slowly growing communities along the shorelines. Many members of the oyster farming Drake and Derwent families, for example, lived in Wyong Street, which ran down to Neverfail Bay, between Gungah Bay and Oatley Bay. Members of the family lived on this street or nearby for all of the twentieth century and into the twenty-first. Tending the maturing oysters in their trays in the bays and then preparing the harvested oysters for market was labour-intensive work. The industry produced a luxury gourmet product, and yet these remained small family concerns, drawing largely on family labour and producing only a modest return. Until the 1980s, as will be discussed below, the industry required high levels of environmental knowledge about the estuary and surrounding coastal areas but produced little surplus capital to enable advanced technical or scientific support.

In the early years of the twentieth century, oysters were cultivated in Lime Kiln Bay and other areas between Lugarno and Oatley Bay, but by the 1930s many farms had moved down river, setting up trays in Gwawley Bay and in the Woronora River, closer to the junction of the Georges with Botany Bay. However, Neverfail Bay remained an important base for the industry; it was close to the areas where the farming families continued to live, so their equipment was stored in sheds and their punts and other vessels were moored there.

---

25   Jackson and Forbes, 'Oysters on the Georges River'; Nell, 'The History of Oyster Farming'.

Oyster farmers were in a very specialised industry – they were farming the waters of the Georges River – so their industry was sensitive, and particularly vulnerable, to changes in the water quality, an issue that was to rise in urgency in the period discussed in later chapters. Yet, at the same time, oyster farmers and their extended families were all local residents in the suburbs along the river, and were interested in, and sometimes very actively involved in, campaigns about environmental issues on land like reclamations and dumping of garbage and dredged material, as well as about water quality.

Hopes and Disappointments

Before WWI, the building of railway lines seemed to offer the hope of economic expansion as had occurred in the UK and the US. Yet in Australia the population was simply not large enough to allow rapid expansion simply because there were whispers of a line. This proved to be the case during the 1920s, when hopes for a railway extension from Kingsgrove to East Hills through the Georges River area led to extensive subdivisions. The line eventually opened – with one track only – in 1931. Alas for the land developers, by then the Depression had hit and the blocks for which they had hoped to gain enormous profits lay pegged out but unpurchased. Peter Spearritt estimates that the amount of subdivided land in the Bankstown municipality more than trebled during the decade of the 1920s, at a time when the number of occupied properties in the area barely doubled, while in the adjacent easterly municipality of Canterbury, the number of occupied properties actually fell, years before the Depression hit.[26]

Nevertheless, the overcrowding in inner-city areas was already urgent by the end of WWI. An attempt to address the problem had been made with the establishment of a Government Housing Commission, in existence from 1919 to 1924, until it was abruptly dismantled by a conservative government.[27] Overcrowding only became worse during the 1920s and then the Depression interrupted any building at all. Dr J. S. Purdy, Sydney's metropolitan medical officer, pointed out as early as 1920 that the alarming rates of severe inner-city overcrowding were a major health

---

26   Spearritt, *Sydney's Century*, 50–52. The final extension from East Hills did not happen till 1987!
27   Spearritt, *Sydney's Century*, 21.

hazard.[28] Yet even with the failure of speculative subdivision towards the river, the population of the Bankstown areas closest to existing stations rose through the decade. In fact, Canterbury and Bankstown had the greatest proportional increase in population across the city.[29] So the expectation of future increased building expansion in the Georges River were clear. Dr Purdy was extremely critical of the area, pointing out in 1924 that Bankstown had reserved less than 10 per cent of its area for parks and recreation. He foresaw that the area would fall 'into the condition of the older portions of the city' unless it purchased land 'on the periphery as playing areas in advance of population'.[30]

Depression Camps

The military presence on the river lands still left much unused and apparently 'wasted' space, particularly along the uneven, steep or boggy riverbanks. This land was needed in the economic depression of the 1930s, when many workers were made homeless by unemployment, evictions and foreclosures. Areas with high proportions of working-class residents like Bankstown were particularly hard hit and there were many battles over evictions, reflecting the active network of political organisations even if, as Nadia Wheatley has pointed out, they could offer few long-term solutions.[31]

Andrew Molloy has gathered many oral histories of the unemployment camps. For example, Ray Parker, a delivery boy from the butchers at Padstow, remembered the 'Happy Valley' where:

> About 8 families lived in mostly bag humpies … they were good men – many who had never been out of work in their lives before, but who had just fallen on tough times like so many people.[32]

Other memories were much more grim. Molloy's interviewees recalled families damaged by poverty, isolation and ill health, then scarred by domestic violence. These camps made few calls on the riverbank

---

28 Purdy, 'Metropolitan Health Officer's Report for 1920', 45; 'Housing Problem', *Daily Telegraph*, 7 October 1920, 6.
29 Spearritt, *Sydney's Century*, 38.
30 Purdy, 'Metropolitan Health Officer's Report, 1924', 112; 'More Parks: Dr Purdy's Plea', *Daily Telegraph*,14 April 1925, 5.
31 Wheatley, 'Meeting Them at the Door'.
32 Molloy, *A History of Padstow*, 99.

environment; while they might have timber frames, the walls were hessian bags washed with lime but few had any access to water, so they were, like most of the rest of the area, unsewered and unserviced with any sanitary collection.[33] All of these camped families would have hunted small game and birds along the shores and harvested fish, prawns and oysters from the river.

There were unemployment relief projects in the area too during the Depression, referred to ruefully as 'The Susso', and these included building sections of Henry Lawson Drive (near Georges Hall, Milperra, East Hills and Picnic Point) and less practical sandstone 'Oatley Castle' inside Oatley Park, used, at least for a time, as a kiosk. On the southern side of the river, in 1932, the Reverend Robert Hammond set up an Anglican relief project, Hammondville, just upstream from Voyager Point, offering small blocks to unemployed Christian workmen who could demonstrate their sobriety. Given the sandy and saline soil there, it was unlikely to offer rewarding farming, but the blocks were taken up by some.[34] (It persists today as an Anglican Church–owned retirement village.) Locals would invariably have been employed on all the heavy work of these relief projects, much of it, like the eccentric Oatley Castle, frustratingly impractical, thus further influencing attitudes to the Georges River.

The More-than-Human World

There were environmental effects from all these low key uses but these were not striking in the later nineteenth and early twentieth centuries. There was evidence of a very limited mangrove presence in the downstream estuarine regions in the reports of the early British botanist Joseph Banks in 1770. It was the non-botanist, James Cook, who noted mangroves at 'the head' of Botany Bay in 1770, but Banks made no mention of them. Hunter noted extensive mangroves in the Hawkesbury but was silent about any mangroves on the Georges River or Botany Bay shores even though he was camped there for weeks in 1788.[35]

---

33   Ibid., 98–104.
34   Lake, 'Hammondville'.
35   Australian Botanic Garden, 'Banks and Solander Species List', accessed 11 October 2020, www.australianbotanicgarden.com.au/science/the-botany-of-botany-bay/plants/banks-and-solander-species-list; Hunter, *An Historical Journal.*

When observers in the later nineteenth and twentieth centuries saw mangroves expanding, they often assumed that mangroves must have been abundant at the time of colonisation but had been depleted by early colonisers. One reason for this assumed depletion was the very early use of mangroves or saltmarsh for soap making, which was mentioned in a number of secondary sources. However, the amounts of estuarine vegetation that were harvested were not recorded; nor is it known whether the source was trees such as *Avicennia marina* or some varieties of saltmarsh. In fact, the most frequently cited article, Juliet Bird's 1978 study, is not based on evidence from Sydney but rather from Westernport Bay in Victoria.[36] Soap manufacturing around Sydney had petered out by 1850.[37] However, even if more mangroves had been used in the manufacture of soap than the evidence suggests, there was little regrowth; most documentary sources from the later nineteenth century and most art and photographic sources from the nineteenth and early twentieth centuries suggest there were few mangroves in the sheltered estuarine bays along the lower Georges River. While not definitive, this is consistent with Lynne McLoughlin's studies of the Lane Cove River in Sydney's north and the Parramatta River in the west. She dates the expansion of mangroves there to around the 1880s.[38]

Another use, although much later in the nineteenth century, was that of oyster farmers who used mangrove wood in stands to attract attachment by oyster spawn (or spat) as it drifted through the waters. Yet the Georges River mangroves were depleted already by the turn of the century. Instead of local mangrove stands, oyster farmers who had added leases on the coasts north or south of Sydney would gather mangroves – like the red mangroves of Minnamurra remembered by Laurie Derwent – to be used for catching spat. By 1950, mangroves were unavailable and instead sawn hardwood, tarred to avoid rot, was being used by the industry, generating still further environmental debates.[39]

Another source of information about mangroves arose because observers were aware of the increased siltation of creeks and rivers because of upstream clearing for agriculture. Where they saw mangrove growth, they assumed the vegetation was expanding opportunistically because the new accumulations of silt were making 'islands'. This was the source

---

36   Bird, 'The Nineteenth-Century Soap Industry'.
37   Ibid., 40.
38   McLoughlin, *The Middle Lane Cove River*; McLoughlin, 'Mangroves and Grass Swamps'.
39   Derwent, interview.

of reports such as that in the *Sydney Morning Herald* of 1885, which noted that a recent government inspection party on the lower Cooks River had found an 'island' of mangroves, which had appeared over the previous 16 years.[40] Only with evidence emerging from WWII was this assumption of opportunistic expansion (i.e. whenever a silt bed collected) shown to be inadequate.

This evidence came as a result of rising anxieties during the interwar years that led the Royal Australian Air Force (RAAF) to develop its capacity to make use of photography. From 1930 the RAAF began to take annual aerial photographs in strips and in very high resolution, covering the whole of the Australian continent. These photographs confirm that the expansion on the middle reaches of the Georges River estuary may have been a little later than on the lower Cooks River. Comparisons of Georges River photographs from 1930 to the 1980s demonstrate few mangroves present in 1930 but substantial mangrove expansion in later decades. The mangrove expansion at Oatley Bay was landwards only, at the expense of the saltmarsh. But in Salt Pan Creek, mangroves also expanded into the creek. Silt had accumulated as mud flats from clearing for agriculture and timber upstream around Bankstown, but the mangroves had not expanded simply because the mudflats came into being. In fact, many mudflats had stood bare for decades, as can be seen in photographs of the US Army Hospital at Herne Bay taken in 1944.[41] In the first decade from 1930, any mangrove expansion seems to have gone largely unnoticed, and, where it was noticed, it added to the approval of council work that uprooted mangroves to 'reclaim' riverbanks for parkland.

But, after WWII, the mangrove expansion began to attract attention.

---

40   'The Cooks River Mud Flats', *Sydney Morning Herald*, cited in Tyrrell, *River Dreams*, 87.
41   Haworth, 'Bush Tracks and Bush Blocks'; Haworth, 'Changes in Mangrove/Salt Marsh Distribution'; Canterbury and District Historical Society, photograph, 'I Grew Up in Mortdale', Facebook, accessed 5 May 2020, @igrewupinmortdale2223.

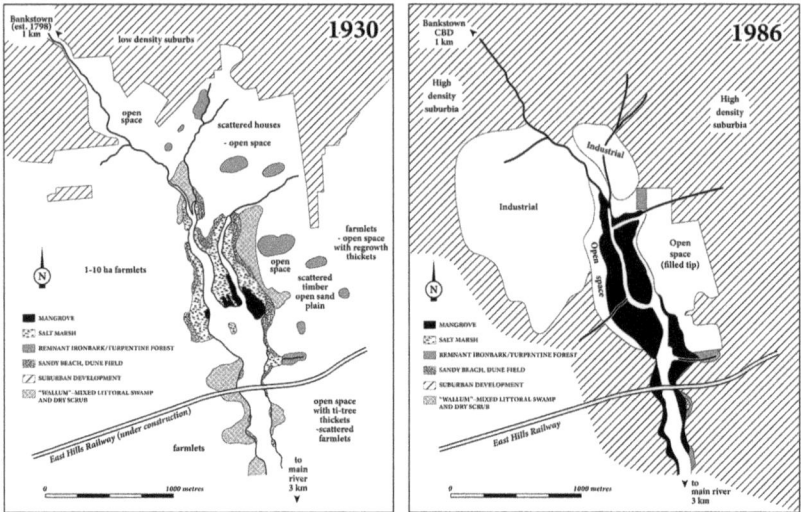

Map 2.3: Mangrove expansion on Salt Pan Creek, 1930–86.

These maps, derived from RAAF aerial photographs, indicate the areas where siltation had been occurring from agriculture and urbanisation for decades before 1930, creating islands, on some of which saltmarsh was growing. Despite this long period of siltation, mangroves had not expanded onto these silt flats or shallow creek areas. Between 1930 and 1986, however, mangrove expansion occurred, leading to the rapid colonisation of all the exposed islands and much of the shallow, silted bed by mangroves. Diagrams redrawn from Goodall, 'Frankenstein, Triffids and Mangroves', based on drawings in Haworth, 'Changes in Mangrove/Salt Marsh Distribution'. See Chapters 10 and 11, this volume. Cartography: Sharon Harrup.

Part II:
Initial Shock

3

Hope, Fear and Planning

Even by the outbreak of World War II (WWII), the Georges River was still seen as a place for picnics as well as a place with many 'wasted' spaces. But WWII changed the way Sydney saw its Georges River. Although the end of the war was celebrated, the changes it had brought had already sounded the death knell of the Picnic River.

With the country at war, its empty spaces offered more land for military training and internment camps, and once the Americans were forced to retreat from the Pacific, there was room for them too. The war had come very close after the rapid advance of the Japanese across South-East Asia and the Pacific, the bombing of Darwin in February 1942 and the intrusion into Sydney Harbour by Japanese submarines just months later in May. This made all the coastal rivers seem vulnerable. East Hills people remember the army coming down the river and ordering all the boats – no matter how small or old – to be 'smashed up' to stop them being used by any future invaders.[1] In this nervous atmosphere, the Americans were welcomed and the Georges River became one of a series of key locations for US Defense installations.

There had already been much disturbance along the Georges River as discussed in the last chapter. Salt Pan Creek was an example, including the swampy land at Herne Bay, on the eastern shore. During the 1930s, the landowning Levingston family had cleared much timber and filled in the swampland to build a golf course.

---

1   Colin Jacobsen, interview, 12 July 2006.

Figure 3.1: Levingston family golf course, undated c. 1940.
Constructed during the 1930s at Herne Bay by reclaiming swampland and clearing much timber. This photograph looks across the golf course to Salt Pan Creek. Negative number 100869. Courtesy of *Pictorial Canterbury*, Canterbury-Bankstown City Council, Local History Photograph Collection.

Figure 3.2: Herne Bay Military Hospital, 1944.
Aerial view looking west, towards Salt Pan Creek, of the massive US Army Hospital built over the Levingston Golf Course at Herne Bay, opened in 1943. This photograph shows the rail line across Salt Pan Creek at the left of the photo. The image also shows the large area of open waters of the creek at the rail bridge relatively free of mangroves in 1944. Source: Canterbury and District Historical Society, photograph, 'I Grew Up in Mortdale', Facebook, accessed 5 May 2020, @igrewupinmortdale2223.

This simply looked like empty space when wartime military needs prevailed, so the Levingston Golf Course at Herne Bay was turned into a huge US Army hospital.

Postwar Planning: The County of Cumberland Plan

As the tide of the war turned and it appeared victory would be possible, governments in Australia began planning for a future peace. The Australian Government had come to the conclusion that reconstruction after the war must achieve greater industrial independence so that the country would not risk being cut off from vital supply chains as had occurred during the war. Increasing secondary manufacturing was a priority and, for this, space was going to be required.[2] Yet, for the State of New South Wales, there was an even more urgent priority: the housing shortage. This had been brewing in Sydney from the 1920s but the Depression and then the war had delayed any hope of providing enough homes for the city's growing population. In this period, the profession of urban planning was rising and it was seen as an important vehicle for delivering both goals in the same process.

This led to the plan for the whole of Sydney, which technically was located in the little-used administrative area known as the County of Cumberland. The planning, begun in 1949, was therefore known as the County of Cumberland Plan (CCP) and was released to the public in 1951. Its goals were to be largely fulfilled through regulation by creating 'zones' for particular types of development. Its other regulatory tools were to be 'suburban employment zones, open space acquisitions and the Green Belt', the latter being a strategy for containing urban sprawl by reserving areas through zoning as either 'rural' or 'green space', ensuring that this land would remain undeveloped and, in the case of 'green space', as publicly accessible parks, incorporating bushland for unstructured recreation.[3] While there was no consideration given to conservation of the 'bush', there was an expectation that natural, native bush would remain. All this planning instrument related to land-based locations – there was no regulation over use of the underwater land like the beds of rivers. Denis Winston called it 'Sydney's Great Experiment' in his 1957 study, regarded as the classic exposition of the plan's goals.[4]

---

2   Macintyre, *Australia's Boldest Experiment*.
3   Ashton and Freestone, *Town Planning*.
4   Winston, *Sydney's Great Experiment*.

Figure 3.3: 1945 poster for the coming County of Cumberland Plan, showing the inner city as crowded and polluted – and dangerous.

The plan is shown to be ushering a suburban future for the (nuclear) family that is ordered and neat, as are the green spaces shown. No wild bushland there! *You and the County Plan* (ref 2020/503368) reproduced courtesy of City of Sydney Archives.

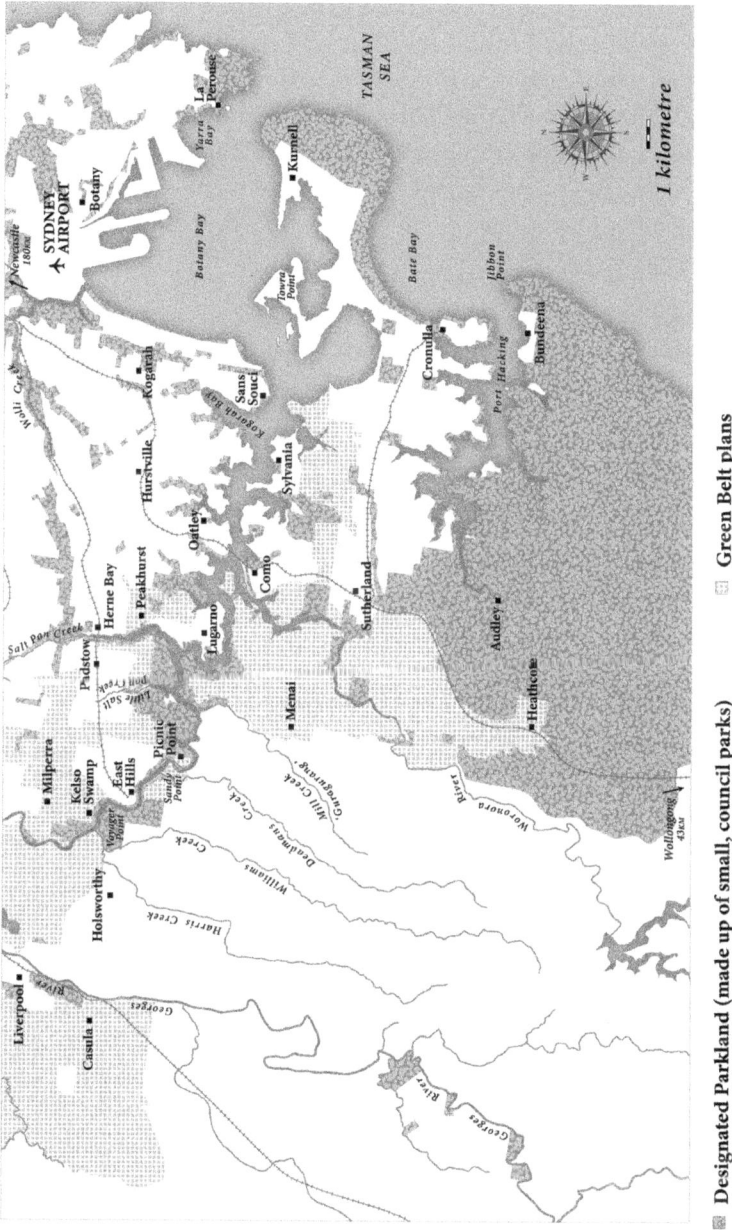

Map 3.1: County of Cumberland Plan section showing proposed green belt from Royal National Park to Georges River.

The area proposed by the Cumberland County Plan to be retained as 'green belt', published with the plan in 1951. This map fuelled the hopes of residents of the Georges River that the bushland along their river would be recognised and protected. Most of the areas shown as green belt on this map were later subdivided and developed as residential suburbs. Cartography: Sharon Harrup.

The CCP offered an exciting possibility for those Georges River residents who loved the wildness of the riverbanks and wanted to see their river recognised as valued and iconic 'bush' in the way the 1879 national park at Sutherland had been recognised. The map of the CCP showed the proposed green space to stretch all the way from the Sutherland national park up to the Georges River itself. This was the hope that the CCP offered: that the Georges River would finally be recognised as truly Australian bushland, to be valued and celebrated forever.

Yet this hope was futile. The plan was unsuccessful in its attempt to conserve what is now highly valued green space in order to consolidate the city's unchecked expansion. The assumption is that it was defeated by rapacious land developers and local government councils hungry for rates.[5] However, opposition to the green belt was not just from developers. Despite their hopes, some local residents had deeply mixed feelings about the plan. While many local communities wanted more open space, the CCP raised lasting anxieties among the general population because, although it aimed to conserve 'green space', it expected to do this through the contradictory process of allowing increased density of population within the areas zoned 'residential'. While still expecting freestanding homes to be widespread, the CCP endorsed increases in low blocks of flats and multiple tenancies in those inner suburbs, as well as supporting the goals of the newly established state Housing Commission, which sought to solve crowding and disrepair in inner-city housing by moving people to the suburbs, initially into hostels and later into newly built homes.[6] This contradiction left many in the Georges River area uneasy, fearing that they were about to lose the spaciousness that they so valued.

The oral histories of Georges River residents confirm that there were different strands in local ambivalence to the plan. As the CCP showed, green belt reservations from sale were planned for much of the shoreline of the Georges River, with additional restrictions for agricultural reservations (zoned 'rural') in Lugarno and on the western shore of Little Salt Pan Creek. These reservations were opposed by land developers, who had lost money in the 1920s after the rumours of railway development failed to materialise. They still had many unsold subdivisions and so were eager

5   Allport, 'The Unrealized Promise'; Ashton and Freestone, *Town Planning*.
6   Spearritt, *Sydney since the Twenties*; Spearritt, *Sydney's Century*; Allport, 'The Unrealized Promise'; Ashton and Freestone, *Town Planning*.

to expand housing areas, not have them further restricted by a green belt. Similarly, some individual landowners, like commercial speculators, were hoping to subdivide and sell their farming land, so for them, the green belt and agricultural zoning presented unwanted restrictions.

Yet many local residents nurtured the hope offered by the CCP that the bush – and particularly the river foreshores – would be protected as green zone for picnics, hunting or other, less legal, pleasures. The Picnic Point Regatta Association and the residents of East Hills, for example, feared that the increasing density of the residential areas would spill over into the open space, leading to more and more private development of the river foreshore. Their concern was that the green zone plan could not be implemented, leaving their highly valued open space vulnerable to development.

The Postwar Population Explosion

Despite the best efforts of those who developed the CCP, it had assumed that orderly expansion and the retention of green space could occur without any effective mechanisms to deliver them. In fact, the rise in population far outstripped the 1949 planners' expectations.

By 1954 the increase in Sydney's population was already double what had been predicted in 1948.[7] From 1946 to 1961, it was the adjacent Bankstown and Fairfield local government areas, already densely settled, that faced the greatest absolute increase in population across the whole of Sydney, from a base of 69,599 to 232,958 people, a rise of over 160,000 people or 240 per cent. The population of Sutherland, with a much larger area on the southern side of the river, also rose steeply, adding 82,562 people to rise by 282 per cent, although with less densely packed results. While some outlying areas like Blacktown and Hornsby had a comparable proportionate increase, their initial population was far smaller so their absolute numbers remained lower. It was only the three Georges River districts that faced such a massive rise in real numbers.[8] All these people

---

7   Spearritt, *Sydney since the Twenties*, 93, citing 1954 Census; Kass, 'Cheaper than Rent'.
8   Allport, 'Castles of Security', 103.

needed housing, for which timber, fibro (often asbestos fibro), tiles and cement were required. Riverbeds were a source of sand for cement and were close at hand to where the greatest need was being felt.[9]

Zoning and Factories

But a major weakness in the CCP was the existing lack of land zoned 'residential only' in the working-class south-west. Decisions for 'residential only' zones had to be ratified at state government level and any new large factory developments could only be located in areas that were not zoned 'residential only'. During the interwar years, the vast majority of the 'residential only' zones approved had been those in high land-value areas like the North Shore and the Eastern Suburbs, from where wealthier and higher status interest groups could exert more pressure. Proposals for 'residential only' zones for low land-value areas like the Cooks and Georges rivers areas were more usually rejected.[10]

A zoning of 'industrial' was more readily approved by the state parliament after WWII for the Georges River, as Arthur Gietzelt, then president of Sutherland Shire, recorded in his autobiography. Gietzelt described a strategy of increasing open space for recreation in 1962 by gaining a zoning of 'industrial' over a large area, some of which could then be sold to industry while the rest was used for public open space.[11] Such strategies resulted in the concentration of new factories in the council areas along the Georges River. From 1945 to 1965, the proportion of all factories located in the inner city declined from over 68 per cent to 32 per cent, while those in the 'South' region – predominantly Bankstown – increased from 9 per cent to 20 per cent, an increase greater than in any

---

9   According to the geological history of the coast at Botany Bay, the earth's crust there has risen in the past, so that the lowest points in the Georges River are around Liverpool, where much of the river's burden of silt was therefore dropped, until, over millions of years, the river could cut its way through the Woronora Plateau to the sea. While this left lower reaches with sandy beds, more suited to building materials, there were also higher concentrations of acid sulphate soils in the riverbed as a result of bacterial and chemical interactions around past and present riverine vegetation. The riverbed materials below Liverpool, therefore, seemed more suited to building, but carried substantial risks to environmental health, to be discovered later. Haworth, Baker and Flood, 'Predicted and Observed Holocene Sea-Levels'; Haworth, Baker and Flood, 'A 6000-Year-Old Fossil Dugong'; Baker, Haworth and Flood, 'An Oscillating Holocene Sea-Level'; Baker, Haworth and Flood, 'Inter-Tidal Fixed Indicators'.

10   Coward, *Out of Sight*, 240–42; Butlin, *Sydney's Environmental Amenity*, 133.

11   Gietzelt, *Sticks and Stones*, 189–92.

other area. This led to major industrial pollution of the air and soil, as well as of the river waters themselves, leading to severe health hazards for local residents.[12]

The high number of factories in the area led the government to locate most of its new migrant worker hostels and low-income, city-relocation hostels in this area to provide workers for the factories. The unpredicted increase in the population overall was, therefore, compounded in the Georges River area. This in turn meant that public housing services like curbing, guttering, public transport, parkland and even public schooling all fell far behind the rate at which people were dumped onto the hostels and estates along the river. Sewerage infrastructure was already far behind demand in the 1920s.[13] As the postwar population soared, the government's main anxiety was about safe drinking water, particularly after a prolonged drought from 1936 to 1942. So, government spending was focused on providing adequate piped drinking water into the thousands of new houses. Capital works of the Water Board prioritised water storage and dam building, which was continuous from 1918 to 1960. There was far less focus on the disposal of liquid wastes and virtually none at all on sewerage infrastructure, leaving most of the new estates unsewered for many years after their development.[14]

Although plans had been well advanced in 1911 to provide sewerage across the city, World War I (WWI), the Depression and then war again had blocked any progress at all. This meant that repairs and maintenance fell behind, and people in areas already sewered had many complaints. Things were much worse along the Georges River, as it was already under pressure from its major disproportionate population increase and lag in house construction. This led to sewerage infrastructure, particularly in the least affluent and, therefore, less politically influential areas, falling ever further behind the expansion of population and the extent of housing, both private and public.[15] By 1959 Bankstown Municipality had the lowest rate of houses connected to a sewerage system (31 per cent) of any major residential area in Sydney.[16] This major delay led to a long backlog of sewerage networking, which meant that alternatives had to be found,

---

12 Coward, *Out of Sight*, 233.
13 Spearritt, *Sydney's Century*, 20.
14 Coward, *Out of Sight*, 249; Butlin, *Sydney's Environmental Amenity*, 139.
15 Coward, *Out of Sight*, 248–52.
16 Ibid., 251. Coward drew his figures from the New South Wales Statistical Register, which cited the Metropolitan Water Sewage and Drainage Board, 1960.

such as continued or expanded use of septic tanks. Often, however, the expansion of housing into previously non-residential bushland meant that such temporary septic disposal systems were located in unsuitable soils. This led to frequent overflows and run-off finding their way into rivers. Even more directly, distrust in the known inadequacies of the disposal infrastructure led to raw or minimally treated sewage being dumped straight into rivers.[17]

Bankstown Council pleaded with the Metropolitan Water Sewerage and Drainage Board for an extension to enable flush toilets to be used at Bankstown School, achieved in 1951, but, as W. V. Aird's 1961 study of sewerage infrastructure in Sydney shows, the rest of the areas to the west of Salt Pan Creek – and much of that to its east – could not be served with flush toilet infrastructure until long after.[18] Aird points to the striking absence of effective waste disposal in any of the areas that drained into the Georges River in 1961. (See Chapters 5 and 6 for the continuing effects of these decisions.) The reason for the failure of the state government to extend sewerage infrastructure to these areas was cost. As Aird explained, it was simply too expensive to consider sewerage infrastructure when the priority had to be to provide potable water to the expanding population. The populations along the Georges River, even when the Labor Party was in power, did not have enough political clout to intervene in the state government's prioritisation of expenditure.

By every measure, the working-class environments of the Georges River area came off worst – although sometimes jockeying with the Cooks River, infamous for its fumes, pollution and heavy metal contamination, for the wooden spoon.[19] There were more factories and so more unregulated industrial pollution. And there were more and more incoming people and so there was more pressure to build houses on scarce land. This meant there was even less sewerage infrastructure being built than anywhere else in the city and so the area had the worst run-off into the river. Put simply, the heaviest environmental cost of Sydney's postwar modernisation was paid by the Georges River.[20]

---

17   Ibid.
18   Aird, *The Water Supply*; 'Twenty-Year-Long Struggle Brings Sewerage at Last to Bankstown School', *Tribune*, 24 October 1951, 4.
19   Tyrrell, *River Dreams*.
20   Butlin, *Sydney's Environmental Amenity*, Ch. 3.

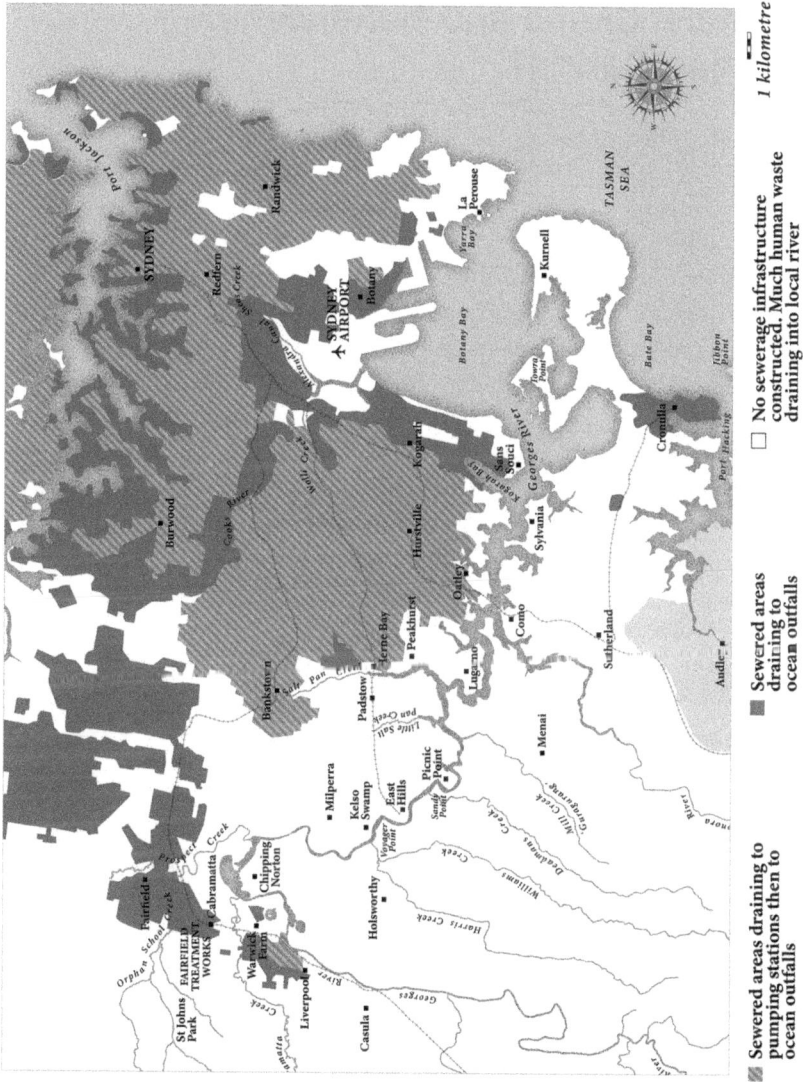

Map 3.2: Sewerage infrastructure, southern Sydney, 1961.

W. V. Aird's history, *The Water Supply, Sewerage and Drainage of Sydney*, showed that, in 1961, a very large proportion of Sydney's population – all those living in the unshaded area on this map – had no sewerage infrastructure at all, other than septic tanks, the overloaded treatment works at Fairfield and a few smaller treatment ponds. Across this unshaded area, most human waste, septic tank overflow and stormwater run-off flowed directly or indirectly into the Georges River. Cartography: Sharon Harrup.

Hostels, Slums and Subdivisions – Shifting Sands?

Although various housing settlements and plans had been attempted before WWI, there had been little general success and no appetite for public housing schemes, even in the Depression. The New South Wales Housing Commission was established in 1941 by the McKell government to respond to the continuing severe shortage of housing. Later, with demobilisation and the hopes many young couples had for beginning families, the need for housing became acute, leading the federal government to become involved in what became social housing.[21] Added to these sources of population increase, there were Aboriginal families from rural New South Wales who refused to continue to put up with the discrimination they faced in country towns. The trappings of modernity such as indoor picture shows and Olympic pools had increased the opportunities for segregation and many Aboriginal families decided that, with work more prevalent in the cities, they could get better schooling and health care if they moved. These rural families therefore moved into Redfern, often sharing accommodation, such as the Smiths from Wellington who lived with relations in overcrowded Caroline Street, hoping to move eventually into a home of their own.[22]

Despite the fears of Georges River residents and the hopes of land developers that land sales to private owners would increase rapidly, it was in fact the New South Wales Housing Commission's social housing program that first impacted the river population and environments.[23] The federal and state governments, eager to respond rapidly to the housing crisis, turned first to the most readily available and cheapest sources of land and accommodation. These were offered by the military establishments dotted all over the city, many of which, as discussed earlier, were located along the Georges River in areas dismissed in previous decades as 'wastelands'.

While the federal government was interested in hostels for assisted migrants and displaced people, the state government's Housing Commission focused on inner-city crowding and postwar needs. In the midst of a rash of headlines about poor quality housing and 'slum conditions' in the inner

---

21   Allport, 'Castles of Security'; Spearritt, *Sydney's Century*, 19–21.
22   Flick and Goodall, *Isabel Flick*.
23   Davies, Mulholland and Pipe, *West of the River Road*, 49.

city, the state government's Housing Commission planned to offer needy families temporary accommodation in hostels prior to moving them to the houses that the commission would build in the future. To make this proposition attractive to people who might otherwise have chosen to stay close to family and work, even in crowded conditions, the rental of hostel flats was very low and they were available immediately.

The first and largest hostels were set up at Herne Bay, close to Salt Pan Creek, and at Hargrave Park, near Liverpool, not far from Chipping Norton. There were a number of other hostels set up soon after, with only a very few on the more northerly side of the city, where the largest was Bradfield Park.[24] This hostel was closer to 'white-collar' job opportunities and Spearritt has argued that it was 'the main centre for white-collar workers, an appropriate setting given its location in middle-class Ku-ring-gai'.[25] Most hostel residents were brought to facilities in working-class areas.

The Herne Bay hostel was housed in the sprawling US Army Hospital and, by 1954, it could house 6,000 people. They lived in weatherboard barracks, each building divided into three, with no soundproofing between families.[26] They did at least have kitchens inside each family's flat, allowing people to cook for themselves, although residents often had to share bathing facilities as well as laundries.[27]

The mainstream press commentary was overwhelmingly negative. Hogan cites the response from the *Truth* in 1956 to the Commonwealth's introduction of the Colombo Plan, which was to bring students to Australia for higher education in an attempt to distract attention from the country's 'White Australia' immigration restrictions. The *Truth* argued that Australia had its own Third World, and asked the foreign minister in banner headlines: 'What about the horror of Herne Bay, Mr Casey?'[28] For the earlier Georges River residents, the rapidly expanding hostels added to the sense that spaces were closing down.

---

24 Hogan, 'Postwar Emergency Housing in Sydney'.

25 Spearritt, *Sydney since the Twenties*, 101.

26 Interviews conducted among Aboriginal residents for this research included Judy Chester, Janny Ely and John Lennis. Other Aboriginal families there included John Kinsela's family, the Madderns and Captain Reg Saunders, whose family was the second to live at Herne Bay. See Glenda Humes's account in Sykes and Edwards, Murawina.

27 Hogan, 'Postwar Emergency Housing in Sydney', 12–15; Hogan, *Almost Like Home*; Madden, *Hernia Bay*.

28 Cited in Hogan 'Postwar Emergency Housing in Sydney', 18, from *Truth*, 10 June 1956, 3.

Figure 3.4: Clothes lines at rear of flats, Herne Bay hostel, June 1946.

The long weatherboard and fibro wards of the US Army Hospital were converted in 1945 into the Herne Bay hostel for families from the inner city by the New South Wales Housing Department. Each long hut was partitioned to allow self-contained living units for three families, each with cooking facilities, but with shared bathrooms and toilets. This photograph shows the rear of a hut at the Herne Bay hostel, with clothes lines and fences dividing family living spaces. Photograph reference number: 129560—1. Reproduced courtesy of Australian War Memorial.

Figure 3.5: 'Wet Day at the Herne Bay Hostel', 1950.

Published originally in *Sun Herald*. Courtesy of Nine Publishing.

Figure 3.6: Herne Bay hostel nursery school, 1947.
Sydney Day Nursery was called on to set up a day care centre as soon as possible. This was built in 1946 and opened in January 1947. The Herne Bay hostel brought the first postwar influx of population into the areas surrounding the Georges River. This was closely followed by further independent building, as young owner-builders – both returned servicemen and others from the inner city – expanded the suburbs around the railway lines. Then still more hostel accommodation was needed for the many assisted immigrants, often brought to be workers in the river's new industrial areas. The rapid rise in population included many children born in the 1940s and 1950s, later known as 'baby boomers'. Courtesy of Archive of Sydney Day Nursery Children's Services.

Factories and Workers: 'Poms' and 'Reffos'

The fears of local residents about the weakness of the CCP's zoning recommendations were well founded. A far more dangerous threat than any council and local developer pressure was the desire by industries to expand their factories or open new ones. Not only had the federal government decided that it would support industrial expansion, but state governments were eager to increase employment possibilities. State governments were, at the same time, reluctant to locate industrial development in politically powerful, middle-class areas. Noel Butlin's study of the Botany Bay area pointed to the tendency in New South Wales Government decisions to reject applications for 'residential only' zoning from councils in working-class areas and, particularly, from those along the Georges River where population was relatively sparse. Dan Coward's intensive analysis of state government decisions confirmed this pattern, demonstrating that far more 'residential only' zonings were approved for high land-value areas than in low land-value areas.[29]

In the postwar period, the emerging economy of consumption, particularly of white goods, required very different types of land use than the heavier industries like steelmaking, which had characterised pre-war factories. Instead, after WWII, industries needed flat land in large amounts to develop 'assembly line' factories, in which 'process workers' assembled the many new electrical goods that were finding places in homes and businesses.[30] Such large areas of flat land were exactly what the Georges River wastelands offered.

These factories required workers and the 'wasteland' areas along the Georges River that were not filled up with industrial sites seemed very available for workers homes. So, added to the already-increasing population of owner-builders taking up subdivisions and the role of the Housing Commission in bringing inner-city residents out to hostels and then to newly built houses, the federal government escalated its assisted migration policies. Some 'displaced people' were included in the migrant intake, dislocated by WWII and the subsequent imposition of Cold War polarisation in Eastern Europe. The majority, however, were intended to be from the UK, where Australia was advertised as offering attractive climates, abundant jobs and ready homes. In fact, these assisted migrants were located in a series of barrack-like hostels revealingly called 'migrant *worker* hostels' – most located on military land, as it was again the least expensive option. Some were carved out of the Housing Commission hostel areas like Herne Bay, but others were standalone establishments, like the East Hill migrant workers' hostel at Voyager Point on the southern bank and Villawood near Fairfield on the northern side of the Georges River.

The conditions for migrant workers in these Commonwealth hostels were even worse than for the Housing Commission hostel residents. The Commonwealth government had decided to save funds on its emergency housing by building different facilities for migrants and displaced people, even though many were also housed in former military establishments and alongside the Housing Commission hostels. The migrant workers and displaced people were not only in crowded and poorly soundproofed

---

29 Butlin, *Sydney's Environmental Amenity*; Coward, *Out of Sight*.
30 Spearritt, *Sydney's Century*, 116; Logan, 'Suburban Manufacturing'.

dwellings but also were forced to eat in canteens, as they were denied private cooking equipment in their flats, and they had to share ablution blocks as well.[31] This was a far cry from the glowing advertisements that had enticed many families to leave war-damaged Britain to come to Australia, and many protested. For local river residents, often building their own fibro homes at weekends, these assisted migrants soon acquired the label of 'whingeing Poms' while the displaced families from Eastern Europe were even more denigrated as 'reffos'. Many of the British migrants returned to the UK, but for the displaced people there was simply nowhere to which they could return. These years along the river saw not only rising populations and diminishing space, but also rising social tensions and a retreat into ethnocentrism that marked the Georges River suburbs for many years to come.

Bodgies, Widgies and Delinquents: Fears of and for Working-Class Youth

Three elements in the population increase were felt more heavily and more rapidly in the Georges River area than anywhere in Sydney: the expansion of Housing Commission social housing and inner-city slum clearance, along with the housing of assisted migrant workers and displaced refugees. These were all related to the increasing location of industrial sites onto the readily available military or 'wasteland' sites on the river. Together, these elements led directly into the first of the recognisable environmental campaigns on the Georges River – the call for a national park – which was driven by anxieties about crowding as well as the fear (well founded or not) of toxic industrial discharges. Further, there was a delayed element of the population increase that had very real environmental implications: as children were born to the new families in the area, it became clear that there would be a rising generation of working-class adolescents in the Georges River area. This caused a great deal of anxiety, as seen in headlines across the 1950s and into the 1960s, which was felt during that first environmental campaign that was conducted largely during the 1950s. This anxiety was to rise even further in prominence as these children grew, becoming a driving element in the second cluster of environmental campaigns from 1965 to 1975. As it is relevant to both, it should be outlined here.

---

31   Hogan, 'Postwar Emergency Housing in Sydney', 12–13.

The influence of American popular media (like film and music) had already been felt – and criticised – during the interwar period. After the stationing of US troops in Australia from 1943, during which social tensions emerged (of the 'over-paid, over-sexed and over HERE!' variety), there had emerged deeply ambivalent postwar attitudes across many groups in Australia towards American cultural influences. From both the UK and the US, there were signs of adolescent discontent emerging that fuelled these attitudes.

As the Georges River area – particularly from Liverpool to Bankstown and Peakhurst – had seen such a rise in the number of working-class jobs and families, and, consequently, of adolescents, these fears fell heavily on both elites and on working-class parents in these suburbs. Parents feared for their children's future in a period when training for apprenticeships and tertiary education was expensive and, for many, simply unattainable. For political and social elites in other parts of Sydney, working-class youth posed a threat – a menace of violence driven by envy – that must be controlled and contained.

Early headlines in Sydney put such fears into very public circulation: 'Juvenile Delinquency Begins in the Wrong Type of Home', one headline shouted 1945.[32] Parents – and particularly mothers – who went to work in the new factories and were not 'at home' were a cause of such threats, while 'broken homes' and a rising social tolerance for divorce was another source of parental guilt. In any event, the outcome was the threat of violence for the general public, as this *Sydney Morning Herald* headline made clear: 'Wolf Packs on the Prowl'.[33] In the Georges River area, this sense of threat was compounded by the xenophobia around incoming assisted migrants and refugees. An article in 1957 in a local Fairfield newspaper explicitly linked allegedly knife-wielding 'bodgies' and 'widgies' on buses in the area with a 'New Australian' who had – in a completely different incident – 'produced a knife'.[34]

---

32 *Sydney Morning Herald*, 5 September 1945, cited in Powell, *Out West*, see 'Menacing Youth'.
33 'Wolf Packs on the Prowl', *Sydney Morning Herald*, 27 September 1955, 29.
34 'Bodgies and Widgies in Fairfield', *Biz*, 27 February 1957, 7.

One of the new suburbs into which the Housing Commission resettled the residents of its hostel at Herne Bay was Green Valley, a housing estate just west of Liverpool. Between 1961 and 1966 its population increased from 1,000 to 24,000 people, and in 1966 around 60 per cent of that population was under 20 years of age. As Gabrielle Gwyther points out:

> The mere concentration of such large numbers of youth in the area meant that 'delinquency' was an observable problem and consequently newsworthy. The media unfairly dubbed the suburb 'Dodge City' in reference to the mayhem of the American wild west.[35]

Gwyther might have added that it was the economic and social class of these concentrated numbers of young people that was of such concern, while the assumption of mayhem on the American frontier was a reflection of much of the popular culture then flowing from the US.[36]

Such headlines and reporting continued, and many authorities offered 'solutions', most of which, while blaming parents and particularly mothers, proposed outcomes that were spatial. A clear statement of this spatial approach to solving the 'problem' was the 1962 address to Rotary (a charity and social organisation of businesspeople) in nearby Parramatta by Sergeant Con Hansen in an article headlined 'Terrifying Increase in Delinquency'.[37] As well as criticising 'films and literature emphasising sex and crime', Hansen identified 'inadequate home life, lack of home training and broken marriages' as the causes of this 'terrifying' increase in the area's crime by juveniles. He proposed four solutions: 1) social resistance to easier divorce laws in order to hold homes together; 2) increased parental interest in both school and organised youth sport; 3) the provision of more playing fields on which to hold such organised sports; and 4) greater support for youth assistance organisations, particularly 'Boy Scout movement, youth and church clubs'.[38] It is notable here that Hansen's conception of this social disorder (in common with the views of many other authority figures) was gendered. While young women (as 'widgies') might misbehave, this postwar menace was overwhelmingly seen to be

---

35   Gwyther, 'Western Sydney'.
36   Ibid.
37   '"Terrifying" Increase in Delinquency', *Cumberland Argus*, 28 March 1962, 3.
38   Ibid.

caused by young working-class males, an interesting shift from earlier decades of the century when it was the menace of young working-class women's sexuality that was identified as a social threat.[39]

Most notable in Hansen's proposed solutions was the importance of spatial strategies to counter this 'threat' – through the provision of more organised sports (with parental 'interest') that required more playing fields. Fears for their children as well as interests for themselves can be seen in the motivations of the campaigners who advocated for a 'national park' at East Hills (1947–61). However, by the mid-1960s, when 'top-down' council actions precipitated a series of environmental campaigns (1965–75), it was fears *of* young working-class men held by councillors that dominated. The goal continued to be to use spatial strategies to address social conflicts.

---

39   Goodall, 'Assimilation Begins in the Home'.

4

A Tale of Two National Parks

The first Georges River National Park only existed from 1961 to 1967, but it was a powerful expression of what the river and its foreshores meant to suburban communities. It left a persistent memory of the goals to be won and the threats to be fought off.

For decades, the Georges River communities had had Australia's first national park, the 'Royal', on their doorstep, just to the south, covering a large and varied area in Sutherland Shire from Audley and Waterfall eastwards down rugged escarpments to the coast. While this national park had been established in 1879 as a site for healthy recreation, its area included picnic grounds, boating and ocean swimming sites, as well as bushland recognised as endemic 'bush', iconically Australian and so a welcome contribution to popular floral nationalism.[1] This Sutherland national park encouraged people across the region to see their own environment more positively.

Discussions about a new national park on the Georges River began in the community and between local government councils from as early as 1944. Local newspapers reported suggestions from aldermen from Bankstown, Liverpool and Sutherland councils from 1944 to 1946.[2] A Bankstown-based parks association existed over this time among residents who feared the river shores might be built out and lost to the public.[3] The discussion

---

1   Goodall and Cadzow, *Rivers and Resilience*, 132–34.
2   'Another National Park: Proposed Georges River Scheme', *Propeller*, 23 March 1944, 1; 'Proposed National Park', *Propeller*, 5 December 1946, 1; 'Georges River Development: Conference of Councils', *Biz*, 13 September 1945, 2.
3   'Georges River Banks May Soon become One Big Park Area', *St George and Sutherland Shire Leader*, 12 October 1961, 7.

seemed to fade for some years but was reactivated again around 1950 among working-class people living on the northern and southern river shores near East Hills and Picnic Point. Their vision had a particular focus on the river.

The Picnic Point Regatta Association (PPRA) had formed initially to support the rowing regattas held before the war on the straight stretch of the river where sculls, fours and eights would be raced. Most of the residents around the river owned rowboats for fishing for food as well as relaxation. Visitors would come from Bankstown or further afield and – as well as picnicking – would hire rowboats from the many boat sheds along the river. Dances were held in the boatsheds and soldiers from the Holsworthy barracks are remembered to have whistled from the south side of the river to get a boat to come across to bring them over for the dance.[4]

During World War II (WWII), the army destroyed or confiscated many of these local boats, fearing, after the intrusion of Japanese submarines into Sydney Harbour in 1942, that the boats could be used by an enemy if there was an invasion along the river.[5] After the war, fishing still required rowboats but powerboats began to travel the river too, mainly from further downstream, but they contributed to the river being used once again. The new technologies of the war were making themselves felt on the river. The word 'regatta' came to include powerboat races and, soon after, to include water skiing, initially as a theatrical spectacle for audiences but later more competitively.[6] Both powerboat races and water skiing required straight, deep stretches of water, a condition that was to shape later conflicts. But, in the 1950s, such concerns were still in the future.

None of the PPRA members had powerboats. In the 1940s they seem to have focused on East Hills Park with its picnics and swimming as much as on regattas. Many local people remembered the activities held in the East Hills Park in the interwar period, as recorded in the photographic archive so carefully preserved by Esme Clisby (see Chapter 2).

---

4   Alf Stills, Eileen Stills and Carol Jacobsen, interview, 22 November 2005.
5   Colin Jacobsen (aka Col Joye), interview, 12 July 2006.
6   'His Hobby is Breaking the Speed Limit', *Cumberland Argus*, 13 April 1949, 9; 'Warship at Big Yacht Regatta', *Sun*, 8 February 1953, 43.

Figure 4.1: Family picnic at the old East Hills Park, 1920s.
Photograph contributed by Esme Clisby.

So it was this wider array of activities that led the PPRA to spearhead the campaign from 1950 to have a large park encompassing both sides of the river. Drawing on the hopes they held from the southern national park, as well as the County of Cumberland Plan proposal to have a green zone stretching all the way to the Georges River, they wanted their Georges River parklands to be recognised *as* 'national' – that is, with a similar mix of purposes for recreation *and* enjoyment of the native bush – and set aside for the people – the living, embodied 'nation' – working-class, smallholders, river users and *local*.[7]

The big pleasure grounds had gone by that time but smaller ones like the Vale of Ah and East Hills Park had hung on. New ways of using the river lands for leisure had emerged with the adoption of golf as a sport. At East Hills, for example, the Bowers family 'improved' their low-lying lands with clearing, infilling and landscaping to create the East Hills Golf Course, without considering that they were destroying a wetland.[8] The whole area continued to be seen as a holiday location, and 'Picnic Point' well deserved its name. The older activities of swimming and fishing continued on the river itself as well as boating in all its forms, from the old rowing competitions to the newer powerboats with their water skiers attached.

---

7   PPRA, interview, 22 March 2006; 1958 Annual Report, Picnic Point Regatta Association Archive, Alf Stills Collection (hereafter PPRA Archive).
8   Molloy, *The History of Milperra*, 71–82, 95–104.

Figure 4.2: Esme Clisby, Eileen Birch, Joy Cornwell, East Hills activist reunion 2006.

Esme Clisby, Eileen Birch and Joy Cornwell share photographs and mementos of the East Hills Park and the Georges River National Park (1961–67) at gathering, Panania RSL, 22 March 2006. Photographer: Heather Goodall.

Figure 4.3: Eileen Stills, Carol Jacobsen, Alf Stills, Alan Parnell, East Hills activist reunion 2006.

Eileen Stills (left), Carol Jacobsen (George and Min Jacobsen's daughter), Alf Stills (secretary, PPRA), Alan Parnell, 22 March 2006. Taken at Panania RSL at gathering of East Hills residents and members of the PPRA to share memories of the parklands and the campaign to achieve national park status. Photographer: Heather Goodall.

Picnics at the East Hills Park and swimming enclosures before and after the war were a key motivation for Esme and many of those who gathered in 2006 to remember the 1950s campaign for the Georges River National Park.[9]

The lives as well as the memories of the key interviewees for this project give a glimpse of the motivations of these campaigners. Alf Stills had been born at Bankstown but when he married in the 1920s, he chose to live near the river because of the fishing. Although he did not row competitively himself, he became the secretary of the PPRA in 1950, as it was this wider use of the river that he valued.

Alf's wife Eileen had grown up on the southern shore of the Georges River opposite East Hills and her three brothers were commercial fishermen.

Figure 4.4: Alf Stills, East Hills activist reunion 2006.

Alf Stills with Bankstown souvenir book, 22 March 2006. Alf brought his archive of PPRA membership and correspondence files to contribute to this project. Photographer: Heather Goodall.

Figure 4.5: Eileen Stills, East Hills activist reunion 2006.

Eileen Stills with map showing East Hills Park and her childhood home on the southern side of the river, opposite the park as well as the Jacobsen's home, 22 March 2006. Eileen's three brothers were all commercial fishermen on the Georges River. Eileen remembered that she often heard music echoing across the river from the Jacobsen home – sometimes because Min Jacobsen was singing through the day or playing the piano for family or community singalongs or later as the family's sons, Col Joye and the Joy Boys, practised for performances. Photographer: Heather Goodall.

---

9   PPRA, interview, 22 March 2006.

The other key campaigner was George Jacobsen (c. 1905–1994), who had grown up on another river, the Parramatta, in a childhood he described to his children as being all 'swamp, reeds and fishing'.[10] George became a cabinet-maker working in the inner city but brought his family to the southern bank of the Georges River in the Depression, then floated his house across the river to set it up at East Hills during the war. He had been on the Bankstown-based parks association initially, in the early 1950s, aiming to expand parkland on the river, but had joined Alf, Eileen and others in the Regatta Association in 1956 as they sharpened their focus on gaining a national park.

George Jacobsen's three sons became well known in the 1960s under the stage name Col Joye and the Joy Boys. Col and Kevin were interviewed with their sister, Carol, and offered valuable insights not only about their father and his campaigning but also about how they remembered growing up on the Georges River.[11] As Kevin explained his father's commitment:

> He was always 'community'-minded … we didn't realise what it was. But when you think about it, it was the Labor Party in those days used to talk about the local community. But it wasn't *politics* politics. It was 'what could be done for East Hills?' And then the Progress Association was a similar thing which led to the Picnic Point Regatta, which led to the Georges River Trust. And I remember him going to fight some developers that wanted to develop all along the river.[12]

All the kids spent their spare time on the river. Carol remembered the pool at East Hills Park, a netted tidal enclosure in the river where the small, local community gathered on the intolerable nights in summer when it was too hot to lie on the sheets, too hot to sleep. Col and Kevin both recalled fishing, catching crabs – 'the big mangrove muddies' Col said – and prawning in the creek. George's link to the bush was his racing dogs and his dedication to the parks: Kevin remembers walking his father's greyhounds each day.

---

10   Kevin, Colin and Carol Jacobsen, interview, 12 July 2006.
11   Ibid.; Connell and Seitch, interview, 5 May 2006.
12   Kevin Jacobsen, interview, 12 July 2006.

Figure 4.6: George Jacobsen with his racing dogs, in the backyard of his East Hills home, undated c. 1960.

Photograph courtesy of Carol Jacobsen.

The boys learnt from George's father, William, how to shoot birds and rabbits. Col remembered his grandfather as a hard, solitary man, an old railway worker and staunch unionist who had held solid for the union on a three-year strike. William treated people as rogues until they had proved themselves to be otherwise. He never allowed the boys to hunt without reminding them about Aboriginal approaches to the bush:

> The mad whitefellas'll end up ruining the world … You have to look at what the blackfellas did, the way they treated the land. If you catch a bird and kill it, you've got to eat it, no matter what.[13]

---

13   Kevin, Colin and Carol Jacobsen, interview, 12 July 2006.

Underlying everything, his family felt that George was committed to the *people* of East Hills. George wasn't alone in this; he was one of many in these working-class suburbs who were trying to make a community for themselves and their children out of the rubble left after the Depression and the war.

The orientation to the surrounding community was one that George shared with his wife Min. Carol Jacobsen recalled her mother was their 'Rock of Gibraltar'. She was always with the children and didn't go to meetings, unlike George, who was always at one meeting or another. Instead, Min drew all the community into their home and did her community work through her domestic role:

> We had a pianola at our place. The thing was to have nights and have everybody around and all sing around the pianola. My mother was the major instigator, even though my father, once you got him up you'd need a crook to get him down, because he wouldn't stop. He was shocking!
>
> But Mum was the one to keep the music going. We always had music in the house. My mother sang every day, all day, as long as I could remember, she never NOT sang, all day.
>
> She always had the house open. We had the cricketers, Mum would have the big bowl of soup and the bloody cricket kids would come home and the soup would be there for them, they'd all be fed. And the footballers.
>
> She had this big industrial sewing machine because she basically made – especially in our area – she made everyone's clothes. She cut everyone's hair, she did everything.
>
> She even used to sew the doubles, made out of cardboard. So you would write the doubles in and then she would sew around the doubles. You'd have to rip it up to see if you'd won. And that's how they helped to get money for the football club.[14]

The local community was at the forefront of the Regatta Association's campaigning, which was focused on trying to regain public ownership of the lands along the river from an early freehold tenure, known as the Lewis Gordon Estate. Although the foreshore had been freely used by

---

14   Carol Jacobsen (during a conversation with Alf Stills), PPRA, interview, 22 March 2006.

the public, much of this land, as discussed in earlier chapters, had been granted freehold in the early years of the British colony but was regarded as 'wasteland' so it had never been developed. The PPRA wanted to secure both the section on top of the escarpment to make a sports ground and the section at the foot of the escarpment, the actual river frontage, to ensure it remained as permanently open, public space. What they feared was that the sale of the high area and the lowland would mean that the everyday, working people along the river would be excluded.

The campaigners, like those they spoke for, had *chosen* to live there: they valued the spaciousness, the sense of freedom from rules and surveillance that access to the river and its environment gave them. George in particular valued the *bush*; however, although the fact that it was 'native' was important to him, he also made the dusty patches more inviting by planting as much kikuyu grass as he could convince his sons to water – this was an aggressive, exotic grass that, as Colin said, would 'grow up your leg while you stood there'.[15] The Stills and Jacobsen families' reasons for living in the area were an attachment to the wider landscape of river and bank, rather than of attachment only to their own freehold blocks, even though this was an area that was becoming suburban through these years. Kevin Jacobsen, for example, born in 1934, recalled growing up at East Hills and using the river frequently for fishing, swimming and, particularly, netting prawns in Salt Pan Creek to the east, which he remembered to have been much more accessible in his youth before 'it was all mangroves'.[16]

The engagement with local places, whether land or water – riverbanks, fishing holes, camp sites, dance halls and swimming enclosures – were expressions of their community network, their sociality. Alf and Eileen Stills explained how the long struggle to gain public ownership of the Lewis Gordon Estate had been closely linked to a whole range of community groups who wanted to use the areas or did so already, like the Scouts and Guides. The PPRA had set up a funding stream, raising money by holding dances, running bingo nights and selling the sand that was being dredged from the riverbed after the council had granted them power to lease to sand miners. They planned to use these funds to make 'improvements' on the riverbanks to enable picnics, as 'to have a picnic ground you have to

---

15 Kevin, Colin and Carol Jacobsen, interview, 12 July 2006.
16 Ibid.

have toilets'.[17] But the state government prevaricated about the transfer of the land title, despite it being designated 'green space' under the County of Cumberland Plan. For eight long years, there was no certainty about the transfer. In the meantime, the PPRA disbursed the funds it raised to local organisations, ensuring that, even if the land was not as available as early as they had hoped, the organisations would be healthy enough to take advantage of it when it finally came.[18]

While these were the motives for those who had chosen to live close to the river, like Alf Eileen and George, others who came had had no choice of their own. These were the people 'slum cleared' from the inner city, the assisted migrants and the displaced people. But they also engaged beyond their fence lines to relate to the river and the spaces around it. Judy and Janny Smith came as children to the Herne Bay Housing Commission hostel on the eastern side of Salt Pan Creek when their family was 'slum cleared' from Caroline Street in Redfern. Their parents had decided to come to the city from Wellington in rural central New South Wales for better health care for their mother and better schooling for their kids. But, as Judy explained, coming from Wellington (inland), 'we were river girls', and they spent much of their time down on Salt Pan Creek swimming or fishing and then, when the family moved to a house constructed by the Housing Commission at Green Valley, off the river and upstream, the girls still travelled to the nearest swimming area on the Georges River at Liverpool.[19]

There were many people from crowded inner-city areas, Aboriginal and non-Aboriginal, who were moved to Housing Commission hostels. While most of them, like the Smiths, wanted better quality housing, they had little choice in where they were sent. There were three main hostels, one at west Linfield (Bradfield Park) and two on the Georges River: the one at Herne Bay was the largest and the other was upstream at Hargrave Park, near Warwick Farm. The historian Michael Hogan grew up at the Bradfield Park hostel, and has recorded many people's memories

---

17   PPRA, interview, 22 March 2006, unidentified speaker in group discussion.

18   Minister for lands to Joe Kelly, local member in state parliament (and one of the people Alf and George lobbied constantly), 16 February 1959. Kelly took up the PPRA demand on their behalf and made written representations to the minister. PPRA Archive, 1948 to 1968.

19   Goodall and Cadzow, *Rivers and Resilience*, 210–13. Similar experiences were recounted by WANA interviewees: Wafa Zaim, a Lebanese Sunni migrant, and Khali Bibi Hekmat, an Afghani Hazara woman refugee.

about all the hostels.[20] As a boy, he envied the young people growing up in Herne Bay and Hargrave Park, who seemed to have much more adventurous lives, but he realised as he grew older that the two Georges River hostels in particular 'had gained a bad public reputation' and were seen as much rougher places with more working-class residents and more unruly social environments.[21] Yet, just as it was for the Smith family, the close proximity of the river for fishing, prawning and swimming made the difficult circumstances of the hostel much more tolerable.[22]

Figure 4.7: Sally Smith with her children, Janny, John and Judy, 1963, soon after moving from the Herne Bay hostel to Green Valley.
Courtesy of Chester family archive.

The PPRA planned to turn the upper section of the Lewis Gordon Estate, a large area of flat, clifftop land, into a sports field and recreation area. They wanted the lower level of the estate, the strip along the riverbank now known as Burrawang Reach, to remain as 'natural bushland' and to be the 'bush' element of the national park. But the 'green belt' was not strong enough – just as local people had feared – to deliver the Lewis Gordon Estate to the people. Despite the PPRA undertaking long letter-writing campaigns and sustained pressure on state and federal politicians as well as local government, the upper flat area of the Lewis Gordon Estate was, in the end, turned over to the state Electricity Commission to build a substation to service the electricity demands of the modern, electrified homes of the postwar economy, leaving an ugly blank square in the middle of the map of the national park.

---

20   Hogan 'Postwar Emergency Housing'; Hogan, *Almost Like Home*.
21   Hogan, 'Postwar Emergency Housing', 16–17.
22   Connell and Seitch, local and Herne Bay residents, interview, 5 May 2006.

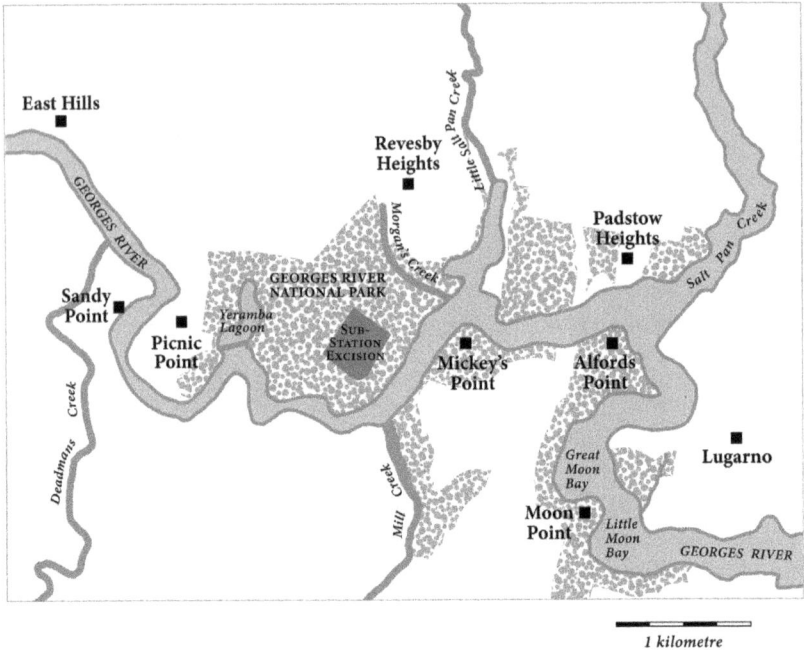

Map 4.1: Georges River National Park, 1961–67.
The area declared to be the Georges River National Park from 1961 to 1967, based on the Lewis Gordon deceased estate, but only after the excision of a large flat area on the escarpment for an electricity substation to service the expanding population. Three local government councils were involved (Bankstown, Hurstville and Sutherland) and the park was administered by a trust made up of council appointees and local residents. Cartography: Sharon Harrup.

Despite the disappointment of the loss of the upper section, the remainder of the Lewis Gordon Estate was declared as the Georges River National Park in February 1961, with a complicated management structure through a trust involving three large councils (Bankstown, Hurstville and Sutherland). It included areas in each of the three council areas, although most lay in Bankstown Council's jurisdiction. On the northern foreshore, it extended from Salt Pan Creek and Morgan's Creek upstream along the Picnic Point shoreline to Yeramba Lagoon, and on the southern shore it included Mickey's Point (opposite the mouth of Little Salt Pan Creek) and Alfords Point (opposite the mouth of Salt Pan Creek).[23]

---

23 'National Park Loses Status – and Finance', *Bankstown Torch*, 23 August 1967, 7.

Councils – whether municipal or shire bodies – were made up of representatives elected by citizens within divisions of the council area called 'wards'. Councillors were typically most responsive to local businesses, seen to have the potential to increase the area's – and the council's – income, and to local organisations that were seen as voicing collective goals.[24] Funded by state governments as well as by rate collection from landowners, councils were tasked with managing the area's development as well as providing services like road maintenance, sewage collection and garbage disposal. While state governments played a role in each of these processes, the recommendations of local governments were important factors in all such decisions. In the postwar decades, as the Georges River area suffered major population increases and industrialisation, councils could play major roles in environmental politics.

When the 'Royal' had been first set aside in 1879, it was not reserved as 'Crown land'. Instead, the state government had changed the title by vesting the land of the park in the actual individual members of the trust set up to manage it, with these members appointed by invitation from the state government. Trust arrangements for parks and other public places had varied over the years since 1879, and the 'trust' format was seldom used by 1961. Nevertheless, perhaps due to the sustained public campaign as well as the role of local politicians, the Georges River National Park was to be managed by a trust, although the parklands remained as Crown land and the trust had little real independence. It was to be comprised of representatives of the three local government bodies – two from Bankstown and one each from Hurstville and Sutherland – and officials of the state Lands Department and Planning Authority. There were only three local people appointed as members, one of whom was George Jacobsen who held that position into the later 1970s.

The PPRA collectively swallowed its disappointment at the loss of the potential sporting field, although Alf was still bitter in 2006 about what he saw as a broken promise. Once the national park was declared, the PPRA set about working actively to support the trust and make the remaining area into something that would approximate its aims of fostering sociality along the river. To achieve this, the land along the river needed to be remodelled – not just a toilet block and a few taps but more substantial landfilling and reclamation was needed. The two potential areas were the

---

24   Gietzelt, *Sticks and Stones*, gives detailed insight into the political pressures within and on Sutherland Shire Council during the 1960s.

narrow strip around the base of the escarpment – a strip that came to be called Burrawang Reach – and the rocky mouth of a small creek that flowed into Georges River just west of Burrawang Reach. This area was to be extensively 'reclaimed' to create grassed picnic areas and was called Cattle Duffers Flat, a romantic name that invented an entirely fictional history about the area having once been used, wild and untamed, to hide cattle stolen ('duffed') from nearby settler properties. Both these proposals involved uprooting and destroying stands of the expanding mangroves. This goal opened up a major rift in the PPRA, exposing an emerging concern for the non-human environment.

Alf Stills, still PPRA secretary, was one who wanted to push ahead with the mangrove destruction. Alf did not like mangroves. He had been one of the people who had noticed that they were expanding, explaining to me that, as a young man, he 'did prawning in Salt Pan Creek but it was all mangroves later on'.[25] He was driven by a determination that at least some of the Regatta Association's vision would be achieved and he had no qualms about digging up mangroves to do it.

As he described it:

> **Alf Stills:** Our main aim was from the beginning to start a sporting area up top. And we were going to develop from there ... but we couldn't develop the land. But where that picnic area is down there, there used to be a lot of mangroves. We had a lot of trouble developing it, because they reckon we shouldn't have got rid of the mangroves. Well we did, we finally got rid of them. Lot of them put that wall round the river and made it a grassed area. And you can't get near that place down there now, for people!
>
> **Interviewer:** So there weren't so many mangroves 50 years ago?
>
> **Alf Stills:** No, no.
>
> **Interviewer:** ... but the gum trees? Were you interested in keeping some of that around the recreation area?
>
> **Alf Stills:** Well they wanted to keep the bushland there, they didn't sort of want to chop it all down.[26]

---

25 Notes taken during PPRA, interview, 22 March 2006.
26 PPRA, interview, 22 March 2006.

Other members of the National Park Trust held similar views to Alf. Ed Byron was one; he became a trust member after the park was established in the early 1960s and remained on the trust for a decade. He was a town planner and spoke of the other members of the trust – whether from the council or the community – as 'dedicated, genuine, local people'. He was emphatic about the need to remove mangroves, saying: 'We had to destroy the mangroves because they took over everything. They thrive on rubbish, they get the run off and the mangroves thrive on it'. Of the trust's accomplishments, Ed was most proud of the facilities like toilet blocks and picnic tables that facilitated informal social gatherings. His wife, Noeline, interviewed at the same time, was strongly in support of his work on the trust and its focus on fostering family and social gatherings. Noeline, however, did not go to any public meetings. Like Min Jacobsen, she did not see such meetings as accessible to her. For her, the land and river management was all 'a bloke's world'.[27]

One of the people within the PPRA who opposed this mangrove removal was George Jacobsen, as his son Colin recalled:

> He was horrified they were taking out the mangroves … [I thought] What would you worry about mangroves for? I mean I must have been 12 because I can recall the mangroves. He said: 'They're not going to take the mangroves off'.[28]

George lost this battle. The Burrawang Reach and Cattle Duffers' Flat picnic grounds became reality and do indeed have many visitors to this day. But, as a member of the trust, George could keep on arguing his point, as his children recall him to have done. The next battle came up soon, when the final stages of Henry Lawson Drive, running parallel to the river, were completed with bridges over Little Salt Pan Creek in 1963 and then the larger and more easterly Salt Pan Creek in 1964. It was initially intended that all mangrove stands on the route would be removed, leaving grassed park on both sides of the road. As George's daughter Carol remembered, he was angered that this would remove the 'reeds, the rushes and the birds' as well as the mangroves, and he campaigned tirelessly through the trust to stop it happening. This time he was at least partially successful as Colin remembers: 'And finally he had to settle for mangroves [only] on one side. But the mangroves *remain* there!'[29]

---

27   Ed and Noeline Byron, interview, 31 May 2006.
28   Kevin, Colin and Carol Jacobsen, interview, 12 July 2006.
29   Ibid.

The Georges River National Park Trust was a difficult place for people with strong views, as George found out. So too did a number of council appointees who held views similar to George's. The trust members came under sustained pressure to allow parts of the national park – frustratingly curtailed as it already was – to be carved off, rezoned as residential or some other zoning form that would allow development. This pressure at times took the form of offers of bribes from land developers, as George's son Colin remembered:

> I recall him being evil-tempered – which the Jacobsens have a side to them of such – when he was on some committee and they offered him money to open up an area around Picnic Point, for building. And I can recall the times he stood against some kind of paint works down the end near Milperra. He said: 'They're not going to ruin that. They're going to kill our river!'[30]

At such times, the lessons from the damage to the Cooks River must have been starkly in the minds of Georges River residents like George Jacobsen. At other times, the pressure was less directed at individuals like George and more generally at the municipal council as a whole, which again found George battling to convince the council to purchase land being sold in order to incorporate it into the park, as Colin recalled:

> I remember my father in there hammering time after time after time, going to meetings, making sure that that land [was] retained, and I'm sure it was the council he convinced into buying that block of land. He said: 'We need all this open space' … The fact is that they realised that the land is all we've got, really. The earth is all we've got.[31]

* * *

It was not only the Georges River National Park that faced pressure during the 1960s. It was a hard decade for the Royal National Park too. But the Royal was regarded very differently to the Georges River.

Arthur Gietzelt was then a senior Labor Party councillor in Sutherland Council, where he was elected president from 1961 to 1963 then again from 1966 to 1971. By tradition, the New South Wales Government

---

30   Ibid.
31   Ibid. This appeared to be about Innan's household block and boatshed, eventually purchased by Bankstown Council.

invited each president of Sutherland Shire to sit on what had been renamed the 'Royal National Park' Trust after Queen Elizabeth's visit in 1954. Few former presidents had taken up this offer but Gietzelt did, becoming a trust member from 1962, a position that was independent of his shire role. He therefore continued as a trust member, whichever party held power in the shire council. For Arthur Gietzelt, the Royal National Park was important for both its social and its environmental qualities. He strongly endorsed the *St George and Sutherland Shire Leader* editorial:

> The preservation of the 40,000 acre park, the largest and most beautiful area of its type near Sydney, is an essential recreational need for the future of both the Shire and Sydney ... The park is a wonderful part of nature – a sanctuary for 233 species of birds, many marsupials and a wide variety of Australian flora.[32]

His tenacity was needed, as there were intense pressures on the trust and on the park during the 1960s. His membership of the trust brought Gietzelt directly into conflict not only with private freehold landowners, developers and coal miners but also with his own council, which was seeking to quarry gravel and allow housing expansions on the Royal National Park land. At times, when his own Labor Party was not in power at either state or local government level, Gietzelt drew on support from other trust members to negotiate with the more progressive conservative (Liberal Party) politicians at both levels of government in order to retain or even expand the park area.[33]

The trust not only had to grapple over this time with the intractable problems of freeholder, council and mining company demands, but had to resist pressure to allow a cemetery, schools, a public golf course, youth clubs and playing fields to be built on national park lands. Through each of these conflicts, Gietzelt defended the Royal, often at personal and political loss. He proved himself to be a fighter for the environment of the same stature as George Jacobsen, contributing significantly himself, and in concert with fellow Sutherland councillors like Kevin Skinner, to the protection of the Royal National Park from the many bodies that were seeking to eat away at its edges and undermine both its social and environmental value.

---

32 *St George and Sutherland Shire Leader* (hereafter *Leader*), 18 August 1965, 2, cited by Gietzelt, *Sticks and Stones*, 185–86.

33 Gietzelt, *Sticks and Stones*, 181–88.

Yet Gietzelt's attitude to the Georges River and its foreshores was very different to his attitude to the Royal. Over this same period, Sutherland Council had a core role in the Georges River National Park Trust, being one of three councils with responsibility for the park. In thinking about the northern and more densely populated area of the shire, adjacent to the Georges River, Gietzelt was most aware of that area's rising birth rate, calling it a 'generational' challenge: 'The post-war baby-boomer push for playing fields for their many children continued through the mid-sixties. It was a generational thing that many older councils rarely faced.'[34]

In 1966, the Labor Party was re-elected in Sutherland local government elections and Gietzelt was again shire president. His close friend and ally, Kevin Skinner, was chair of the Parks and Playgrounds Committee, and both Skinner and Gietzelt felt under pressure to provide a 'home ground' for every sports code in the shire.[35] The two men worked closely with the shire engineer and chief clerk to identify current shire council holdings that could be used to create such playing fields. They were all on the Georges River.

One example from 1966 that Gietzelt discusses at length was the creation of Kareela Park, which he describes as 'undulating topography'. This was a euphemism for the fact that this was the gully of a tributary of the Georges River, a small creek that ran northward into Oyster Bay. Gietzelt admitted that it was 'what some would call a wasteland' but to him and other Labor councillors it was land that 'could be made useful, indeed productive' by reclamation, by 'ripping out the rock' of the high ground and using it to level the steep gully sides and by removing 'degraded vegetation'.[36] The result was four playing fields, made ready with almost miraculous speed by the application of 'instant turfing', which had 'developed an unkempt and seemingly useless bit of land'. As Gietzelt saw it, 'humankind had indeed transformed nature'. Kareela was the model for the transformation 'several times' of similar 'useless' Georges River gullies and creeks into playing fields.[37]

Another example was the creation of a 'home ground' for the much larger sporting body, the Cronulla-Sutherland Rugby League team, known as 'the Sharks'. The site Gietzelt believed could be transformed to make

---

34 Ibid., 189.
35 Ibid.
36 Ibid., 190.
37 Ibid., 191.

'Shark Park' was at Woolooware Bay, on the Georges River, on land the shire purchased from a company that had fallen bankrupt and was eager to sell. The land had been zoned 'rural' and so was protected as 'green belt' under the County of Cumberland Plan, but Gietzelt negotiated with the state government Planning Authority to have the land rezoned 'industrial'. This allowed the shire to sell a portion of it to an industrial group to build a factory, which recouped the purchase price. The remaining land was initially to be made into 23 playing fields because it was 'suitable for reclamation' – that is, it needed to be 'saved' because it was 'only' a swamp – and so it was opened as a tip for 'non-putrescent, hard-fill' household waste, comprised of 'old beds, refrigerators, washing machines and other household discards'.[38] Over the following year, the plan was revised to turn these 23 playing fields into the Sharks' home ground. The club had initially been unhappy, wanting somewhere close to the shopping centre, but Gietzelt talked them round. By mid-1968 the club had paid a nominal price to the shire to take over the land, becoming the only club in Australia to own its own home ground.[39]

It was to be precisely these local government strategies for dealing with 'useless' Georges River land – rezoning and 'reclamation' after 'ripping out' unwanted rocks and 'degraded vegetation' and dumping garbage – that were to be protested against so vigorously in the later 1960s and early 1970s. Yet Gietzelt noticed little protest about the Georges River just a few years before. So perhaps the most valuable insight from his autobiography is the difference it shows between his attitudes to the Royal National Park and to the Georges River, both of which were within his responsibility as a Sutherland Shire councillor. While Gietzelt took courageous stands to defend and conserve the Royal National Park, he saw the Georges River and its bushland foreshores only as places to be 'transformed' from 'useless' and 'degraded' to 'useful and productive' to meet the 'generational' challenge.

***

Such attitudes seemed to the Georges River campaigners to be lurking behind the decision in 1967 to withdraw the status of 'national' from the Georges River National Park. It was known as a national park for only six years. In 1967 the New South Wales Government passed its first

---

38   Ibid., 198–99.
39   Ibid., 200–01.

National Parks and Wildlife Act, which established the National Parks and Wildlife Service (NPWS) and formalised a hierarchy of parks with the designation of only 12 as 'national'.[40] The Georges River was not on the list. The legislation enshrined 11 parks as 'national' in its new order, while 54 other parks were given the less imposing title of 'state park' or 'nature reserve'. There were three national parks in some proximity to the urban centre: Ku-ring-gai Chase and the Royal, along with the Blue Mountains National Park marking the far western limit.[41]

The explanation given by the government for demoting the Georges River from 'national park' to 'state park' was that the 'accepted world concept of National Parks was that they embraced spacious land areas'.[42] The smallest of the 12 newly recognised national parks was 15,400 acres, the smallest of the existing 54 state parks was 1,310 acres, while Georges River National Park was as yet only 426 acres. Even with its as yet still unsecured Lewis Gordon addition, it was only ever going to be about 700 acres.[43] Another category for protection was 'historic park', which denoted European 'history' not that of Aboriginal people. Kurnell qualified as 'historic' because it was the landing place of James Cook, but the Georges River parklands did not. The fantasy history invented about Cattle Duffers Flat had not impressed the state government.

The local reaction was shock. 'Bill Will Strip Park of Status' and 'Georges River Parkland Fights for Existence' screamed headlines in the *St George and Sutherland Shire Leader* and the *Bankstown Torch*. But the national park became a state park in 1967 and then was demoted again to a 'state recreation area' in 1982. The government intervened further in the structure of the trust, reducing the number of local community representatives and then, in 1987, removed the local government representation altogether.

When, in 1991, the state government finally moved to reinstate the Georges River parklands as a national park, it was at the cost of winding down the trust altogether and imposing the uniform NPWS management regime onto the parks. There was to be no more local voice, however

---

40   'Shock by Government: Bill Will Strip Park of Status', *Leader*, 4 January 1967, 13; 'Georges River Parkland Fights for Existence', *Leader*, 23 August 1967, 2; 'National Park Loses Status – and Finance', *Bankstown Torch*, 23 August 1967.
41   *NPWS Table of Reserves*, generated 12 October 2005, National Parks and Wildlife Service – Georges River National Park Trust (NPWS Archive), Hurstville Library, Georges River Council Libraries.
42   'Shock by Government: Bill Will Strip Park of Status', *Leader*, 4 January 1967, 13.
43   Ibid.

flawed it may have been, in the management of these parks. The renewed designation of national park was widely welcomed as being more protective, but it meant the imposition of a very different management approach onto the Georges River parklands, much of which seemed more about raising revenue than about caring for the environment.[44] Local response was again rapid and bitter. Labor Party parliamentarians and councillors reported that they were being inundated by public complaints from across what remained a strongly working-class population.[45]

Pat Rogan, state Labor member of parliament for East Hills, summarised the complaints he was receiving:

> At the same time the park was established, the developers already had their eyes on this beautiful waterfront land. Having won the battle to keep this land in public ownership, the public is now being denied access to this scenic area by the increased charges.[46]

The shift in 1991 was depicted by opponents as a shift from a human-centred to an ecology-centred approach to park management and, in a betrayal of the people who had fought from 1950 for a park for the people who lived around it, from a more 'local' to a more distanced, state-centred orientation.

The Royal National Park survived. The tenacity of trust members like Arthur Gietzelt had kept it safe for long enough for its environmental qualities to be recognised from the 1980s and beyond. Its initial purposes, on the other hand, for recreational walks, leisurely picnics and relaxed boating have slowly been forgotten.

---

44   'Pat Rogan Critical over Recreation Area Changes', *Bankstown Torch*, 29 April 1992, 5; 'Georges River Given National Park Status', *Leader*, 29 October 1991.
45   R. Buchanan to Chris Hartcher, New South Wales minister for the environment, 26 August 1992, Correspondence Enquiries, Ministerial Representations – Georges River National Park, A/1732, NPWS Archive; Canterbury resident W. Aitken to Pat Rogan, member for East Hills, 10 December 1991, NPWS Archive; 'Pat Rogan Critical over Recreation Area Changes', Bankstown *Torch*, 29 April 1992, 5; 'Local Boaters Locked – and Priced – Out', *Bankstown Torch*, 5 August 1992, 3; 'Minister Asked for the Return of Recreation Area', *Bankstown Torch*, 31 March 1993, 9; 'Parkland Users to Offset Costs', *Leader*, 7 August 1968, 17.
46   'Pat Rogan Critical over Recreation Area Changes', *Bankstown Torch*, 29 April 1992, 5; 'Local Boaters Locked – And Priced – Out', *Bankstown Torch*, 5 August 1992, 3.

Part III: Death of the Picnic River

5

Outlooks and Oysters

The gentrification of the lower Georges River – pushed along by the changing technologies brought by the war and the expanding economy in its aftermath – exposed the rifts along class lines on the river.

Oyster production on the Georges River was booming in the early 1960s.[1] Harvests had been steadily increasing from the end of the war in the most actively farmed stretch of the river, from Lugarno downstream, past Kogarah Bay and the Woronora River, Kangaroo Point, Sylvania and Gwawley Bay and on to Towra Point. From the 1920s, oyster farmers had been troubled by oyster loss in colder months, initially called 'winter mortality' but later attributed to parasite infestation. The oyster growers had addressed this largely successfully by 're-laying' their trays of oysters to the more sheltered areas of the waterway, such as Bonnet Bay in the Woronora River, during the colder winter months. These areas are typically less saline than the former main growing areas but, importantly, the 'wintering' involved having the oysters higher in the intertidal zone so that they spent less time each day in the water. This strategy required intimate knowledge of the river as well as access to wide areas to allow movement to shelter in winter then back to spending more time in the water in warmer months.

---

1   Statistics on oyster production sourced from the Department of Primary Industry, cited in Jackson and Forbes, 'Oysters on the Georges River'; Derwent, 'Oysters: The Canaries of Our Estuary'.

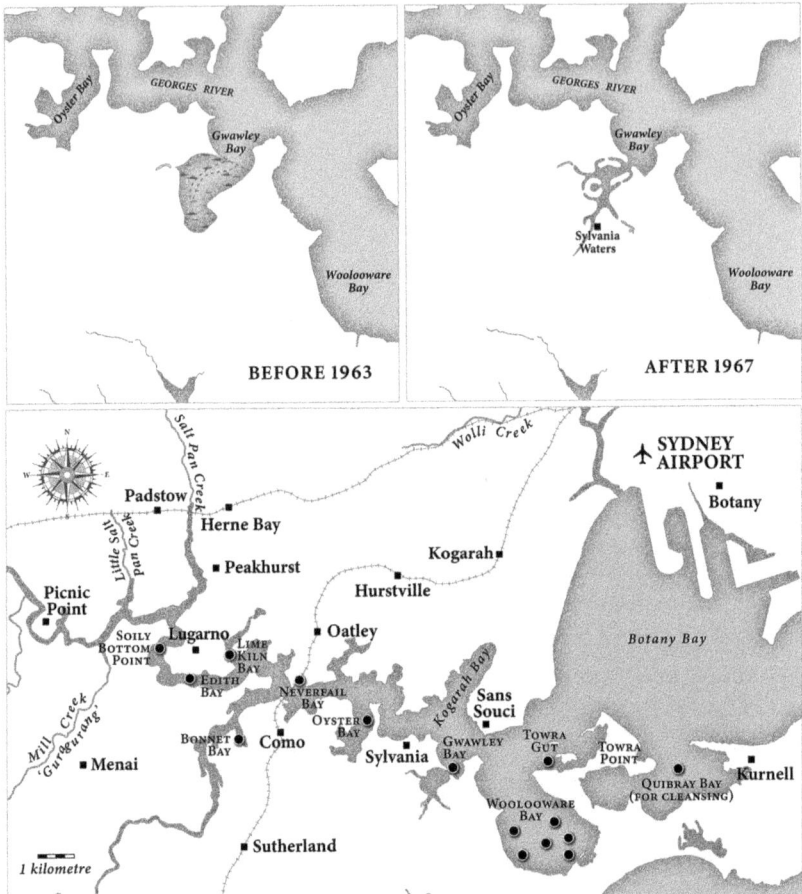

Map 5.1: Oyster farming areas in Georges River estuary, 1945–78.

Oyster farming took place in the lower estuary, at the sites indicated on this map, until the problems arising in the later 1970s, see Chapter 15. The small maps show how Gwawley Bay – previously a prolific oyster growing area – was developed by real estate agent L. J. Hooker throughout the 1960s to become Sylvania Waters. Subdivided for private sale as residential home sites, each block had a boat mooring jetty, with the first blocks going on sale in 1963. To build the estate, the developers dug out the existing mangrove and saltmarsh vegetation around the waterline of the bay and built 8 km of retaining walls to modify tidal flows. Cartography: Sharon Harrup.

Figure 5.1: Gwawley Bay oyster farming workers in 1958.

Gwawley Bay was largely transformed into Sylvania Waters in the early 1960s (see Map 5.1), with mangrove areas removed, canals created for power boat access, and jetties and other boat facilities for each waterfront block. Photograph by George Lipman, published in the *St George and Sutherland Shire Leader*, 'Flashback Friday', 6 July 2018. Courtesy of Nine Publishing.

Such knowledge had been built up over time. Many of the oyster farmers were from families like the Derwents who had lived around Oatley and other shorefront areas for at least five generations.[2] The Drake family was another that had generations farming on the river with both men and women working in the industry. Managing oyster growing and living close by, oyster farming families had a close experience of both land and water. Many children, girls as well as boys, had their own rowboats and were as comfortable rowing around family leaseholds as they were on the shores. It was a labour-intensive industry: both farm family members and local people worked in it, building racks and trays, assisting in tending the growing oysters, and sorting and shucking the oysters that were to be sold in bottles or on the half shell. Interviewed for this project, Bob Drake explained that his grandfather had taken up a lease when oyster farming first began on the Georges River. Born in 1941, Bob took up work in the oyster industry in 1954 at the age of 14, and went on to become president of the Georges River Oyster Farmers Association in 1978. The family had continued to live around Neverfail Bay, but succeeding generations, including Bob himself, farmed leases further downstream around the mouth of the Woronora River and in Woolooware Bay, on the western side of Towra Point.[3]

---

2   Many extended Derwent and Drake families lived near Neverfail Bay at Oatley. Norm Pilgrim and his extended family lived at Sans Souci on Botany Bay.
3   Drake, interview.

Figure 5.2: Oyster farmers Reg and Ken Humbley and Norm Pilgrim, Woolooware Bay, 1966.

Pilgrim was president of the Georges River Oyster Farmers Association and gave evidence at the Senate Select Committee hearings in 1969. Published in the *St George and Sutherland Shire Leader*, 'Flashback Friday', 6 July 2018. Courtesy of Nine Publishing.

The Derwent family too had farmed initially in Neverfail Bay, expanding and continuing to provide oyster farmers and workers in the industry. By the 1960s, members of the Derwent family held leaseholds in a number of Georges River areas. Laurie Derwent, also interviewed for the project, was born in 1953, spending much of his weekends and school holidays oyster farming from the age of 13, eventually taking up a lease himself and farming for some years.[4] Later he joined New South Wales Fisheries and became involved in research and administration regarding pollution and oyster purification. While oysters remained a central interest shared by many members of these and other oyster farming families, they were at the same time members of the local community, and so they took part as well in community affairs. As Bob Drake pointed out, 'the oyster farmers were members of the community as well as other people' and they joined progress associations to 'put their view forward'.[5] Another example is an aunt of Laurie Derwent, his father's sister, Evol, who married Ray Knight. Together they took leading roles in the local environmental activism aimed at stopping the reclamation of Poulton Creek (see Chapter 12).[6]

---

4   Derwent, interview.
5   Drake, interview.
6   Knight, interview. See Chapter 12, this volume.

Yet, despite the boom, Georges River oyster farmers had two related problems emerging early in the 1960s, both of which stemmed from the rapidly rising population along the river and from its complexity in terms of class. One was the rising level of human waste that was pouring into the river. The other was the increasing subdivision and development of land along the waterfront.

Human waste was a major problem for all the area's residents. Rising population, diminishing space and festering antagonism towards immigrants were only some of the many changes that the river saw in the first two decades after the war. The old mythologies that associated swamps with evil, or those that saw swamps and miasmas as the source of ill health, had been challenged in the later nineteenth century with the rise of germ theory and the recognition that waterborne contamination was a more serious threat than vapours and mists. In all cases, however, the limitations of the city's systems for disposing of human waste had reinforced the association between swamps and ill health. Little attention had been paid to the disposal of human waste in the Georges River area during the pre–World War I decades because the population had been sparse. Instead, attention had focused on the inner city and, particularly, on low-income areas like Redfern, from where human waste had been discharging into wetland on a tributary of the Cooks River at Shea's Creek, where the area drew its drinking water.[7]

The large military establishments along the Georges River, like Holsworthy and Milperra Soldier Settlement Cooperative, had never been sewered; instead, they drained human waste directly into the river. Families at Milperra had 'burial pits' where human waste was dumped but it too eventually leached into the creeks and swamps and then into the river.[8] Infrastructure to allow piped sewerage for human waste disposal had begun in the inner northern suburbs of the city and then in its central areas, but had focused on municipalities with higher income residents and more powerful municipal councils. Residents in southerly areas were either burying their waste or using septic systems that, dug into unsuitable soils in many parts of Sydney, still led to leaching of contaminants into nearby waterways.[9] Sewerage infrastructure had been intended for the more southerly suburbs but slow rates of population increase and then the Depression and World War II (WWII) halted work altogether.

7   Aird, *The Water Supply*.
8   Brooks and Burke, *The Heart of a Place*.
9   Aird, *The Water Supply*, 290–91.

With the end of WWII and the exponential rise in population on the northern banks of the Georges River, the issue of human waste became a very big problem. Sewerage infrastructure was expensive, so it was only slowly being extended to the immediate south of the city, including the Cooks River, with much of this area's human waste being directed eventually into the expanded ocean outfall system, although breakdowns and leakage continued. Yet even this imperfect infrastructure did not extend to the Georges River. In the upper estuary, from Liverpool around to Milperra, piped human waste flowed into one of several 'sewerage farms', like that at Fairfield, at which raw sewage was supposed to be treated but from which it was usually drained directly into the river. Protests from Bankstown led to the slow expansion of sewerage pipes to the eastern bank of Salt Pan Creek and then north, in an arc, around to Bankstown, reaching Bankstown Girls' High School in 1951. But human waste from all the area west of Salt Pan Creek and west of Bankstown drained sooner or later into the Georges River.[10] Downstream, on the Sutherland side of the river, there was simply no sewerage infrastructure at all, and residents relied on septic disposal that was unreliable in wet weather. Again, waste flowed into the Georges River.

As the city's numbers escalated, fresh water for drinking became the most urgent priority, and what income was at the Water Board's disposal went towards the building of Warragamba Dam to provide potable water across the city. With no governments willing to provide resources for the extension of sewerage infrastructure in the south-western areas, the situation worsened until, in 1962, the government public health analyst Ernest Samuel Ogg tested the Georges River and reported the level of *E. coli* contamination from human waste to be above safe levels, naming the Fairfield Sewage Treatment plant as one of the sources of the contamination. Ogg ordered all swimming and fishing on the Georges River to be stopped, warning that the local oyster industry would be affected if action were not taken.[11] The municipal health inspectors in

---

10 Ibid., 153; 'Twenty-Year-Long Struggle Brings Sewerage at Last to Bankstown School', *Tribune*, 24 October 1951, 4, quoting from a recent *Bankstown Torch* article on the forthcoming flush sewerage connection to Bankstown Public School.

11 Ogg's actual reports are elusive, although they are discussed widely. See Goodall, Cadzow and Byrne, 'Mangroves, Garbage and Fishing'. On Ogg's first report, see 'In NSW This Week', *Canberra Times*, 26 September 1962, 2; 'Chlorination Not Sufficient – Council Told', *Biz*, 17 October 1962, 1; 'Council Bitter on Pollution Problem', *Biz*, 24 October 1962, 3; 'Appeal May End Pollution Blame: Bid for Sewer Pipe to Sea', *Biz*, 16 January 1963, 4; 'Pollution Rise', *Biz*, 16 January 1963, 4; 'New baths for polluted river?', *St George and Sutherland Shire Leader* (hereafter *Leader*), 3 April 1963. On Ogg's first and second report, see Beder, 'From Pipe Dreams', 173, citing *Mirror*, 13 September 1962 and 19 September 1963.

Bankstown and other councils along the river acted, ordering the removal of all netted swimming enclosures in the municipality, like that at East Hills. They hoped that a public outcry might bring the funding needed for water quality improvement, but they were disappointed.[12] There was simply no outcry at all. Distaste at the worsening state of the river had already made the new Olympic pools like Bankstown Baths (opened in 1933) much more attractive than the river, and local people had abandoned the muddy brown river waters to swim in the crystal-clear pools, which, in the 1950s and 1960s, offered sociality for a new – younger – generation.[13]

***

While disposing of sewage was a major problem for everyone, not only the oyster farmers who grew their products in the river's water, the question of waterfront subdivisions involved particular class dimensions. Cars had become more affordable and more widely owned as a result of wartime engineering and a booming postwar economy. Dependence on railways and other forms of public transport had, therefore, decreased, allowing land at ever greater distances from public transport hubs to be released for subdivision. Water views were highly prized and so the value of waterfront blocks on both sides of the Georges River rose steadily. Consequently, the secluded bays where oyster farmers had held leases became increasingly visible. These subdivisions – notably those downstream, around Oatley Bay on the northern shore but particularly from Como eastwards to Kangaroo Point and Sylvania on the southern shore – were described by local aldermen and media as 'elite waterfront suburbs' and 'exclusive foreshore areas'.[14] The Sylvania Waters estate, for example, began selling blocks in 1963. It had been developed by L. J. Hooker, largely by reclaiming the estuarine mangrove area, and building retaining walls to provide each block with water frontages and boating facilities.[15] Residents across all of the riverfront suburbs were increasingly likely to own a high-powered speedboat, another outcome of wartime technological improvements in internal combustion engines. Those who did not own a powerboat themselves might still take part in, or be spectators of, the new sports associated with them – speedboat racing and water skiing.

---

12   Goodall, Cadzow and Byrne, 'Mangroves, Garbage and Fishing'. Howard, interview.
13   Bryan Brown, pers. comm.; my own memories from 1965 on.
14   'Oyster Talks Will Determine Future', *Leader*, 25 April 1966, 15; 'Controversy Likely on Oyster Lease Schemes', *Leader*, 8 June 1966, 3.
15   Pollon and Healy, *The Book of Sydney Suburbs*, 251. First blocks on sale in 1963.

From the later 1950s, councils and then progress associations began objecting to the presence of the oyster leases as 'unsightly' and insanitary, although without specific evidence of health hazards. These objections sought to have foreshores reserved for swimming, boating – often speedboating – and other recreation. Councils initially demanded that the Fisheries Branch rescind shoreside leases and force oyster farmers to move their racks into the centre of the bays and river.[16] This, however, would have meant that the oyster leases would still be visible from the newly subdivided 'elite' suburbs.

In 1964 the New South Wales Department of Public Health was reported to be developing a program of testing oysters for contamination in the Georges River but nothing eventuated.[17] At the same time, the residents of the downstream suburbs organised themselves into the Georges River Oyster Lease Protest Association (GROLPA) and demanded that the oyster leases be removed from the Georges River altogether. GROLPA members included the new landowners of the expensive waterfront blocks at Sylvania Waters, where development had destroyed the shallow mangrove area of Gwawley Bay in favour of a series of canals that serviced powerboat-accessible jetties. In the state election campaign leading up to a poll in May 1965, the conservative opposition, through Liberal Party leader Robert Askin, took up this demand, appearing to promise to remove oyster leases from the views and waterways of these 'exclusive' suburbs.[18]

Askin went on to win the election, taking power from the Australian Labor Party for the first time in 24 years. But he was slow to act on the Georges River oyster leases. GROLPA secretary Dr P. Dawson worked through local progress associations and councils to push for government action. Sutherland Shire called on the new chief secretary, Eric Willis, to hold a conference to bring all the parties together, including the oyster farmers and the protest organisation.[19] Willis agreed, circulating a set of briefing

---

16 Sutherland Council Development Committee Minutes, 16 March 1959, 7 March 1960, 16 September 1963, 1 June 1964 (complaining about the view of oyster leases from new subdivision), Sutherland Shire, 'Meetings and Minutes', accessed 3 February 2021, www.sutherlandshire.nsw.gov. au/Council/Meetings-and-Minutes; Sutherland Building, Health and Sanitation Committee Minutes, 14 October 1963 (objections from East Como and other Progress Associations to Sutherland Council), Sutherland Shire, 'Meetings and Minutes', accessed 3 February 2021, www.sutherlandshire.nsw.gov.au/ Council/Meetings-and-Minutes.
17 Commonwealth of Australia, Senate Select Committee on Water Pollution, *Minutes of Evidence*, submission from UNSW Department of Food Technology, vol. 8, 1669.
18 'Conference to Discuss Oyster Leases Sought', *Leader*, 13 April 1966, 7.
19 Ibid.; 'Oyster Talks Will Determine Future', *Leader*, 25 April 1966, 15.

papers with four options, including a map showing possible locations of offshore oyster leases.[20] None would have removed oyster leases from the river. The result was uproar!

The four riverside councils – Bankstown, Hurstville, Kogarah and Sutherland – rejected every one of Willis's proposals, as did a crowded meeting of resident protesters at Sylvania (identified in the local press as the 'elite' foreshore suburb between oyster farming areas in Oyster Bay and Gwawley Bay). The residents called for the complete removal of oyster leases by 1967. GROLPA, spearheading this opposition, argued not only that oyster leases were insanitary and unsightly but also that the locations indicated on Willis's map as possible offshore lease areas would disrupt boating routes – particularly the routes for high-powered speedboats, that, facilitated by the canals and jetties at Sylvania Waters, were increasingly owned and raced by more affluent riverside residents. Hurstville Alderman E. J. Curlisa agreed:

> The river will become strangled by these leases! … The river is a
> natural heritage of all the people and we must support them in
> demanding that the oyster famers quit.[21]

Other Hurstville Council and Sutherland Shire representatives were explicit: this was about money. The oyster lessees did not pay rates to the local government but the 'exclusive foreshore properties' did, so anything that reduced the value of those properties, like unsightly views of oyster leases, meant a financial loss to the councils.[22]

The *St George and Sutherland Shire Leader* was no less blunt. Its front page on 29 June 1966 carried a wide-angle lens photograph of Gwawley Bay (at Sylvania), with a caption that began, 'The Battle Is Joined', continuing:

> The basic incompatibility of homes and oyster leases is illustrated
> in this panoramic view of Gwawley Bay. On one side an expanse
> of leases – on the other, high-class home development.[23]

The *Leader's* picture showed expansive oyster leases but no workers anywhere; it appeared this industry employed no one. As the paper told it, both local government representatives and waterfront residents wanted

---

20 'Controversy Likely on Oyster Lease Schemes', *Leader*, 8 June 1966, 3.
21 'No Support Likely for Lease Plans', *Leader*, 22 June 1966, 12.
22 Ibid.; 'Meeting Seeks End to Leases in River', *Leader*, 29 June 1966, 3.
23 'Riverside Councils Opposed to Leases', *Leader*, 29 June 1966, 1.

the oyster farmers gone. Councillor B. Lewis from Sutherland suggested they go 'somewhere else on the coast', while GROLPA just wanted them gone – it did not matter where![24]

Yet some of the Hurstville aldermen were sympathetic to the oyster farmers, arguing, like Alderman E. J. Green, that oysters 'thrived' in the Georges River, more so than anywhere else on the New South Wales coast. Others were pessimistic about state government priorities, like A. A. Lawrance and N. W. Hobson from Hurstville who pointed out that the council could not ignore the export earnings of the oyster industry, saying: 'We would be wasting our time to try to move all the leases … The Department has made up its mind that Australia cannot afford to lose this industry.'[25] The conflict between these 'exclusive foreshore area' residents and the oyster farmers would continue over the next decade. Meanwhile, it became increasingly clear that these same 'exclusive' suburbs were also contributing to the other problem that the oyster industry had.

This second problem was bacterial pollution arising from the lack of effective sewerage infrastructure on both the northern and southern shores of the Georges River. Government analyst Ernest Ogg's first report in mid-1962 had led to the closure of swimming baths, accusations about the failures of Fairfield and other sewage treatment works and a warning for the oyster industry. Yet the treatment plants and pumping stations he identified were not the only problem. A correspondent to a local newspaper, the *Propeller*, who 'preferred to remain anonymous', argued that there was severe overflow from septic systems sited close to the waterfront in the Como area, including Sylvania Waters, and, therefore, close to many of the main oyster growing areas.[26]

Ogg's second report was even worse than his first! The *Daily Mirror* headlined the story 'Effluent Society', explaining that Ogg had made Georges River the focus of his second report because the Water Board had increased the chlorination level at its treatment works but done little else.[27] The *Propeller* led its first page with the headline 'Georges River Is POISONED!', quoting Ogg's description of the river as 'an open sewer'. It reported his finding that responsibility for water quality was so confused because there were too many bureaucracies managing waterways, including, among others, the Water

24 'Meeting Seeks End to Leases in River', *Leader*, 29 June 1966, 3.
25 'No Support Likely for Lease Plans', *Leader*, 22 June 1966, 9.
26 'Public Health Menaced', *Propeller*, 20 September 1962, 1.
27 'Effluent Society – That's Sydney Today', *Daily Mirror*, 19 September 1963, 11.

Board for sewage discharge, the Maritime Services Board for watercraft and speed controls, the Chief Secretary's Department with its Fisheries Branch, and the Department of Agriculture for commercial harvesting of aquatic species like fish and oysters.[28]

Not only did oyster farmers risk losing their Australian markets but also questions were being raised about international markets for live oysters because they had not undertaken the purification process that was widespread through the UK. Early in 1964, a number of farmers came together to form a company to install the expensive purification equipment in an attempt to sell their oysters internationally.[29] The process of constructing and installing the equipment was lengthy, however, and the plant was only just 'ready to operate' in July 1966, after requiring substantial investment.[30] Oyster farmers estimated that it would lead to a doubling of the oyster price; however, by 1973 it had not been widely installed or used.[31]

The sewage input into the river was not necessarily a problem for the oysters, for as Dr R. A. Edwards, a food technology researcher, noted, 'the oyster grows well in water which is high in nutrients'.[32] The Hurstville aldermen had observed that oysters 'thrived' in the Georges River and oyster farmers knew that it was a renowned 'fattening' area. Growers could purchase small oysters from production areas such as Port Stephens, transfer them to the Georges River racks and find they developed extremely well there, producing highly marketable harvests. They argued that, as oysters were filter feeders, they drew the nutrients from the water and expelled any damaging associated products, so they offered no risk to consumers.

Unsurprisingly, the conflict over the very presence of oyster farms in the downstream areas of the river continued. After Willis's inconclusive conference, Sutherland Council turned again to Ogg's 1962 and 1963 reports about sewage pollution. In October 1966, it asked the Government Health Department again for a formal survey of the extent of pollution

---

28 'Georges River is POISONED', *Propeller*, 26 September 1963, 1.
29 'Scheme to Crash World Markets by Local Oyster Growers', *Leader*, 16 March 1964, 3. Farmers were going to establish a company to install purification equipment 'to open up international markets'.
30 See *Australian Fisheries Newsletter* 25, no. 7 (July 1966): 23–25.
31 Commonwealth of Australia, Senate Select Committee on Water Pollution, *Minutes of Evidence*, submission of the Oyster Farmers Association, vol. 8, 1668; 'Pollution "Won't Harm an Oyster"', *Leader*, 7 February 1973, 21 (quoting from Norm Phillips, president of the NSW Oyster Farmers Association, with photograph).
32 Commonwealth of Australia, Senate Select Committee on Water Pollution, *Minutes of Evidence*, vol. 8 (13 March 1969), 1685.

in the Georges River.[33] The government seems to have done little; it failed to commit funds for any major sewerage infrastructure and yet was unwilling to lose the oyster industry. This left GROLPA frustrated but unable to pursue further action.

Figure 5.3: Cover image, *Australian Fisheries Newsletter*, July 1966.
Georges River oyster growing site with workers clearly visible, probably taken at Woolooware Bay. Courtesy of National Library of Australia.

---

33 'Infected Oysters in Georges River', *Leader*, 5 October 1966, 11.

Oyster farmers decided to take their own steps, commissioning the University of New South Wales (UNSW) to undertake a systematic study of the contaminants in live oysters at key Georges River growing sites. While awaiting the UNSW report, and given the lack of sympathy for oyster farmers in the local press, industry members took full advantage of an opportunity for substantial exposure in the state government's *Australian Fisheries Newsletter*, published in July. The issue featured the Georges River oyster production sites on its front cover (with workers!), with more photographs inside of the industry's workers, including a farmer, Ed Lewis, at Woolooware Bay, vistas of abundant cultivation and stories of scientific innovation to promote profitable – and healthy – local and international sales.

In demonstrating the expansive nature of the industry, the photographs of prolific Georges River oyster cultivation left little doubt about the source of tensions between the industry and the shoreside residents who wanted unimpeded access and open water views.

UNSW Food Technology Department researchers G. C. Wells and R. A. Edwards conducted the requested survey in 1967, reporting a bacterial contamination problem with oysters from four key oyster farming sites: Woolooware Bay, Oyster Bay, Gwawley Bay and Towra Gut (off Pelican Point).[34] The researchers explained that oysters filtered the surrounding water as food, utilised the nutrients from sewage contamination and ultimately excreted the bacteria that was harmful to themselves as well as humans. However, there was a delay in this process, so newly harvested oysters might retain some harmful contaminants during transport and storage. The researchers tested for bacteria once a week over 10 weeks in April, May and June of 1967 both in the water itself and in the flesh of freshly opened farmed oysters. The results demonstrated a problem with bacterial contamination harmful to humans at each site. Two of the sites (Woolooware and Oyster Bays) tested above internationally accepted maximum levels on three occasions of the 11 sampled and the remaining two sites (Gwawley Bay and Towra Gut) were above the level on four occasions. While the researchers identified sources of contamination as the sewage treatment plants at Liverpool and Fairfield and a pumping station near Woolooware Bay, they also blamed garbage dumping by

---

34 Commonwealth of Australia, Senate Select Committee on Water Pollution, *Minutes of Evidence*, vol. 8 (13 March 1969), 1669–74.

councils and leakage from private septic tanks all along the southern shore of the river. The levels of bacterial contamination in water and oyster flesh were significantly worse after heavy rain.

When the oyster farmers were finally heard at length, they made a number of arguments.[35] One was that they had been developing this industry over a much longer time frame than the recent arrival of the shoreside residents. This was of course true, although the Dharawal owners may have viewed this argument with amusement. More importantly, the oyster farmers pointed out that these new 'exclusive' developments had not been able to provide all they advertised for the incoming owners. The developers at Sylvania Waters, for example, had not been able to secure Water Board sewerage infrastructure, so all the blocks in this new 'elite' development were reliant on septic disposal of human waste, which flowed into the river whenever rain was heavy. Rather than the oyster farmers endangering the foreshore residents, it was actually the new developments and the resulting flow of human excreta into the river that was endangering the oysters, the industry and, indirectly, the oyster farmers themselves.

It was notable too that the oyster farmers were presenting a changed view of mangroves. Whereas in the early years of the industry, they had harvested mangroves from the Georges River and then from the Minnamurra River to use mangrove wood for catching spawn, in 1969 oyster farmers argued that mangroves needed to be protected because they offered shelter for growing oysters. Mangroves, the oyster farmers pointed out, fulfilled an essential role in defending the oyster racks by shielding them from turbulent river flow and tidal changes, not to mention the new problem of severe turbulence from speedboats.[36] Oyster farmers interviewed by the *Australian Fisheries Newsletter* in 1966 had already explained another aspect of this defensive role: mangroves sheltered oyster racks that had been moved into shallow, warmer bays during winter to protect them from the illness known as 'winter mortality'.[37]

But the most important argument the oyster farmers made was that the bacterial contamination of the water was a federal and state government responsibility. It had been government that had sited military installations along the Georges River and then failed to provide them with sewerage.

---

35 Ibid., 1667–68, 1675–91.
36 Ibid., 1680.
37 See *Australian Fisheries Newsletter* 25, no. 7 (July 1966): 23–25.

It had been government decisions that had increased industrialisation and correspondingly increased the population to provide the workforce to staff the factories. And it had been government decision-making that led to the Metropolitan Water Sewerage and Drainage Board failing to provide effective sewerage infrastructure to all these areas, as well as to the newer 'waterfront' developments on the lower estuary. Given this burden of responsibility, it was appropriate that federal and state governments should fund the remediation of the river. Further, it was clear that only the federal government had the technical and planning capacity to address a problem that was particularly acute in the Georges River but that afflicted many other urban centres as well. This was the same argument later developed by Harold C. Hunt, the chief health inspector at Bankstown Council, and it was one that the Senate inquiry members took very seriously.

In 2016 Laurie Derwent described oysters as 'the canaries in the coalmine' for the contamination of water.[38] His reference was to the use of canaries to signal dangerous gas in underground mines in the UK: if the air was dangerous, the canary would die. The oysters did indeed signal a warning about the rising contamination of the river, although the effect was the opposite of that on the canary: as the nutrient level increased in the Georges River, the oysters thrived. As discussed in later chapters, the oysters were unfairly targeted in contamination scares. The early protests against the industry arose largely from demands for unimpeded water views by waterfront property owners and from concerns by local government about threats to property values leading to reductions in rates. Nevertheless, the issues of water quality were very real and the oyster farmers were far more active in seeking data on the contamination and trying to develop remedies than were local government and landowners. The waterfront landowners like the GROLPA campaigners were still hoping they could nudge or force oyster farmers to move along.

Mangroves, another more-than-human species that appeared to be thriving in changing conditions, were not under any form of human direction except the bulldozer.

---

38   Derwent, 'Oysters: The Canaries of Our Estuary'.

6

Sewers, Sociality and Mangrove Swamps

Faecal pollution is seldom noticed. As Dr R. A. Edwards, researcher at the University of New South Wales, commented in 1969, if river water is apparently clear 'it is hard to believe it could be highly polluted'.[1]

For the Picnic Point campaigners, it was factory pollution about which they were most worried. Many of those interviewed spoke about toxic liquids dumped or spilled into the river by the increasing number of factories sited along its banks. Factories had been sited on upper Salt Pan Creek and around Bankstown from the 1920s.[2] The soldier settlement area at Milperra, having had an unstable resident body ever since its failure to support the servicemen after World War I, was being opened up as an industrial area in 1967. Confirming her brother Col's memories, Carol Jacobsen recalled him telling her about a time when George had 'come home all upset because there was a new factory going up on the river and it was going to be spewing shit into the river'.[3]

---

1   Commonwealth of Australia, Senate Select Committee on Water Pollution, *Minutes of Evidence*, vol. 8, 4683.
2   See H. C. Hunt on lead contamination in upper Salt Pan Creek, plus other factory chemical discharges, (the content of none of which were able to be recorded) in Commonwealth of Australia, Senate Select Committee on Water Pollution, *Minutes of Evidence*, vol. 20, 4633. Residual heavy metal contamination in riverbed sediments is confirmed in Birch, Evenden and Teutsch, 'Dominance of Point Source'.
3   Commonwealth of Australia, Senate Select Committee on Water Pollution, *Minutes of Evidence*, vol. 8, 4683. Carol mentioned on a number of occasions that this story was often recounted within her family, and she repeated it during the PPRA interview, 22 March 2006. During the collective Jacobsens' interview, 12 July 2006, Colin confirmed it fully. This quote is from Carol's version of it in the PPRA interview.

None of the interviewees remembered faecal pollution as a major problem in the river environment, despite their intense anxiety about the rising number of factories and the growing population of workers whom the factories demanded, leading to the feared loss of riverfront land to private development. As a number of expert witnesses at the 1969 Senate Select Committee were to explain, bacterial contamination from human waste was not detectable to smell or taste. It would, however, be human waste – faeces and urine – that led to the greatest contamination problems on the river. Concerns were being expressed as early as 1931 about the dumping of nightsoil into the Georges River and the rising contamination of its waters.[4] The effects of human waste are considered here on humans but also on what local residents regarded as the two most troublesome non-human species on the river: oysters and mangroves.

***

Despite Aird's report in 1961 and Ernest Ogg's two damning reports about bacterial contamination in the Georges River in 1962 and 1963, there had little action taken by the state's Water Sewerage and Drainage Board, responsible for the Fairfield Sewage Treatment Plant, other than heavier chlorination.[5] The federal government, responsible for the Holsworthy and other sites along the river, had taken no action at all. There had been piecemeal sewerage infrastructure laid on the northern side of the river and none on the southern side by 1969. The issue of sewage pollution had not been pressed by the Georges River National Park Trust (1961–67) in which activists like George Jacobsen were intensely worried about industrial toxic pollution.

Yet the issue of faecal pollution was not unnoticed. Public pressure had successfully gained flush toilets at Bankstown Girls' High School in 1951, leading concerned residents to form 'Operation Sewerage', demanding further infrastructure extensions, although with little positive outcome. The situation grew steadily worse until, in 1967, Bankstown Council's chief health inspector, H. C. Hunt, reported to council that Bankstown faced 'a State of Emergency'. He pointed out that the rapid population rise after the war had led to gross overloading of the council's sanitary

---

4   'Pollution in Georges River: Danger to Health', *Sun*, 11 November 1931, 11; 'Twenty-Year-Long Struggle Brings Sewerage at Last to Bankstown School', *Tribune*, 24 October 1951, 4.
5   See Hunt, in Commonwealth of Australia, Senate Select Committee on Water Pollution, *Minutes of Evidence*, vol. 20, 4631.

depot, with more than 35,000 residents and factory workers in unsewered areas relying on the 'antiquated system of nightsoil removal'. State and federal governments had both failed to fund the municipality's efforts to extend sewerage infrastructure and the nightsoil service had recently been interrupted completely for weeks because of a strike. Hunt argued that residents and factory workers were threatened by typhoid 'or some other dreaded disease' unless there was urgent change, insisting 'the problem is not one of engineering but of finance'.[6]

There was definitely rising political interest in the problem of water quality. Pressure from the waterfront's 'exclusive' landowners had led to Robert Askin's support in 1965 for the regulation and, by implication, removal of the oyster farming industry. His support, however, had been shown to be unreliable. Askin had refused to push for removal of the industry in the 1966 conference, despite being pressured by downstream progress associations and local government councils. Nevertheless, Askin's chief secretary, Eric Willis, was alert to the problems. Willis was the member for Earlwood, which lay between the Georges River and the Cooks River as they both neared Botany Bay. Willis was keenly aware of the environmental issues of the river as well as the land for which he was responsible. He had graduated with honours in history as well as geography and had worked as a geographer for some years before entering parliament. His department contained the Fisheries Branch, which was not only a frequent and energetic source of advice for local organisations on aquatic species and river environmental conditions but also took an active role in a number of the conflicts that emerged over the impacts of development on the Georges River.

Although the Australian Labor Party (ALP) had lost the New South Wales state election in 1965, the incoming ALP members were committed to the environmental policies that would flower in the federal Whitlam Labor government (1973) and the later state Wran Labor government (1976). The most notable of those newcomers in 1965 was Frank Walker, the member for Georges River. Walker's father had been a member of the Communist Party of Australia (CPA), and, although the party had not flourished along the river, individual members of the party had lived there, like Phyllis Johnson at Padstow and Bob Walshe at Jannali.[7] There had even been a well-attended CPA 'Youth Carnival for Peace and Friendship'

---

6 'Bankstown in State of Emergency', *Bankstown Torch*, 30 August 1967, 1–2.
7 Cahill, 'An Activist for All Seasons'.

at Hollywood Beach on the Georges River near Milperra in March 1952, although its location there had only come about because the Cold War atmosphere of the period led the party's preferred venue, the inner-city Harold Park Trotting Racecourse, to reject their booking.[8]

Walker had not followed his father into CPA membership, but, brought up in Papua New Guinea and in rural New South Wales, he had developed a strong awareness of racism and of landed privilege, developing a commitment in his legal education to social justice. He represented the seat of Georges River, which had been expected to return Liberal political representatives, from 1970 to 1988. Against expectations, his personal integrity and communication skills won successive elections. Walker was aligned to the left wing of the state ALP and took an active interest in environmental matters along the river.[9] He became a committed parliamentary ally for many of the campaigns we will trace in later pages.

Many Georges River residents were union or ALP members, as they often worked in industries like the railways, which had large workshops at Chullora and Everleigh. However, the Australian Railways Union, took a strongly anti-communist position, bringing a right-wing influence to the area's Labor politics. The ARU was linked to the anti-communist Industrial Groups, an alignment of conservative unions and unionists. Tony Mulvihill was one of those members of the ARU aligned with the Groupers but he also had a strong interest in environmental concerns related to water. Despite growing up at Ryde, he had worked as a railwayman and unionist, initially at the Everleigh Workshops and then at those at Chullora, as had many of the older residents along the Georges River. He became an ALP senator in the federal government from 1964 to 1983 and his concerns, as well as his constituency, drew him towards the centre of the party. He is remembered by colleagues as an advocate for migrants and a pioneer environmentalist who was a tough defender of the Colong and other national parks, and who insisted that the ALP take up the challenge of ensuring a healthier environment for all Australians.[10] One way he was to pursue his environmental commitment was in establishing a Senate Select Committee on Water Pollution, which began Australia-wide hearings in 1969 and reported in 1971. It was at this

---

8   Poynting, 'The Youth Carnival for Peace'; Deery, 'Community Carnival'.
9   Deborah Snow, 'Obituary', *Sydney Morning Herald*, 14 June 2012; 'Obituary: Francis 'Frank' John Walker', *Courier Mail*, 25 June 2012.
10   John Faulkner, pers. comm.; Clune, 'Mulvihill, James Anthony'; Taksa, 'James Anthony Mulvihill'.

federal government forum, rather than at the state level conference held in 1966, that the Georges River oyster farmers were finally able to have their say, making the points discussed in the last chapter.

Much of the evidence given to this Senate inquiry about the Georges River concerned faecal pollution. After speaking out in 1967 about Bankstown's sewerage emergency, H. C. Hunt, Bankstown's chief health inspector, was eager to bring the problem to the national stage at the Senate hearings. He became its most powerful witness.[11] He described the events since the Ogg reports of 1962 and 1963, which had resulted in heavier chlorination at Fairfield and other treatment plants as well as the continuation of sanitary pan collection across a wide area. Only piecemeal sections of piping for sewerage infrastructure had been constructed in the nine years since Aird's map of piped sewerage infrastructure had shown that most of the areas of the Georges River, northern and southern banks, were not serviced by flush toilets but instead by septic tanks or by weekly nightsoil pan collections. Such collected waste was delivered to sewage treatment plants like Fairfield.

Hunt explained in graphic terms what this meant·

> Residents were forced to sit daily on a can of faeces and urine up to seven days old. It also meant that residents were at the mercy of a militant trade union and it was often questionable whether they received a nightsoil clearance after seven days.[12]

Focusing on human waste disposal at Bankstown, Hunt pointed to the role of state and federal facilities along the river: 'There are still sewage treatment works discharging into the river at Bankstown Airport, East Hills Migrant Camp, Holsworthy Military Camp, Liverpool and Campbelltown.'[13] It was clear that Hunt was most familiar with those areas on the upper estuary, in the Bankstown Council area, from Liverpool to Salt Pan Creek. He gave no consideration to the substantial discharge from overflowing or poorly constructed septic tanks along both sides of the lower estuary, from Salt Pan Creek to Botany Bay. Nor did he consider the weekly sanitary pan collection along the northern shores of

---

11   'Bankstown in State of Emergency', *Bankstown Torch*, 30 August 1967, 1–2.
12   Hunt's evidence was taken on 5 August 1969. See Commonwealth of Australia, Senate Select Committee on Water Pollution, *Minutes of Evidence*, vol. 20, 4627–67. The committee reported in June 1970. See Commonwealth of Australia, Senate Select Committee on Water Pollution, *Report*, 4629.
13   Commonwealth of Australia, Senate Select Committee on Water Pollution, *Minutes of Evidence*, vol. 20, 4630 (see Hunt, 'Municipality of Bankstown: A Case Study', 4628–34).

the lower estuary, in the Hurstville Council area. This was dumped at what is now Gannons Park, at the top of Boggywell Creek, the western arm of Lime Kiln Bay. Nor did he mention the agricultural waste from the lower intensity land uses in the same area, like the pig farm that released effluent directly into the river.

What Hunt did point out, however, was that waste disposal was only part of the problem, because there had been no provision at all for sullage – the wastewater after all other household activities – virtually all of which flowed directly into the river. This was not just a problem for those in the inner-Bankstown area. Across the whole local government area, Hunt explained, there was a group of people:

> Equal to the combined populations of Bathurst and Orange without sewerage, and in the absence of this basic form of sanitation, the creeks and watercourses inevitably become polluted and in turn contribute to the pollution of the river.[14]

Even this was not the end of Hunt's evidence. Beyond the sewage pollution of the Georges River, by 1969, there was a significant burden of toxic industrial waste as well flowing into the river. As discussed earlier, a very high proportion of the city's expanding number of factories had been located in the Georges River area.[15] This increased the risk of contaminants being released into the water, as there was no regulation over the content of waste released into the river, only over the amount released. By 1970 there was additional concern as new industrial areas were opened up on the old abandoned soldier settlement farm blocks at Milperra.[16] As an exasperated Health Inspector Hunt pointed out in his submission to the Senate Select Committee, there was simply no means of knowing what chemicals were being dumped into the river – industries were not required to report the composition of their waste and there was no adequate testing methods for all the many thousands of chemicals that might be going into the water.

---

14   Ibid., 4630. Bathurst and Orange were both large country towns.

15   Aird, *The Water Supply*; Logan, 'Suburban Manufacturing'; Butlin, *Sydney's Environmental Amenity*; Coward, *Out of Sight*; Spearritt, *Sydney's Century*.

16   Commonwealth of Australia, Senate Select Committee on Water Pollution, *Report*. See Hunt's evidence in August 1969 and his written submission reported in *Bankstown Torch*, 4 March 1970. The New South Wales *Clean Waters Act 1970* was passed in mid-1970. The New South Wales State Pollution Control Commission was one outcome of this Select Committee, empowered by an Act passed in December 1970, although it had no regulatory power until 1974.

As Hunt gave evidence to the federal Senate inquiry, a new Bill was before the state parliament – the New South Wales Water Pollution Control Bill – which promised to mandate standard maximum discharges into the river for each chemical. This Bill had arisen because it was not only Hunt who had been concerned about the worsening damage to the Georges River among others. Many voters had become increasingly anxious, particularly in urban areas, about increasing air and water pollution. So the Bill was passed in December 1970, resulting in a new body, the State Pollution Control Commission (SPCC), although this was not given any real power until mid-1974. Yet, from its inception, the SPCC offered another body to which local government could appeal for support for waste disposal through reclamation plans. This was a strategy to which Kogarah Council was to resort in relation to Oatley Bay, discussed in Chapter 12. Hunt argued that this state legislation would be simply unworkable: not only would it take months for contaminant testing to be finalised, but also each factory might produce waste containing hundreds of chemicals. So any testing would be bogged down in the impossible task of measuring the amount dumped of each of thousands of chemicals in the water, let alone in trying to work out where they came from. Hunt had already reported this to council[17] and he also explained the problem to the Senate: the only option, in his view, was total prohibition – no toxic material at all should be released into the river.

Hunt proposed that all discharges were to be made into the sewer, which would entail a cost to the industry, with specified, particularly toxic chemicals, to be removed and treated by qualified disposal, again at the cost of the industry. He recognised that industries would try to circumvent the cost by continuing to dump illegally and so he insisted that rigorous policing and strong regulation was required to ensure that no hazardous material was dumped into the river. It was the same problem across Australia, arising from the same emerging economic and social conditions and he insisted that the federal government should take responsibility for the development and cost of a uniform waste management approach across all states and territories.

Hunt gave a chilling warning to the federal government in his submission to the Select Committee, identifying the environment of the river and its water quality as 'heritage': 'While governments are actively encouraging the

---

17   Hunt, *Garbage Disposal*; Commonwealth of Australia, Senate Select Committee on Water Pollution, *Transcript of Evidence*, vol. 8, 4632.

development of industry to improve Australia's prosperity, it is necessary to ensure that our heritage is not destroyed in the process.'[18] Despite his concerns about toxic industrial discharge, Hunt was emphatic: sewerage was the most urgent necessity in the struggle to address water quality. He was equally emphatic about the responsibility: the federal government must bear the burden.

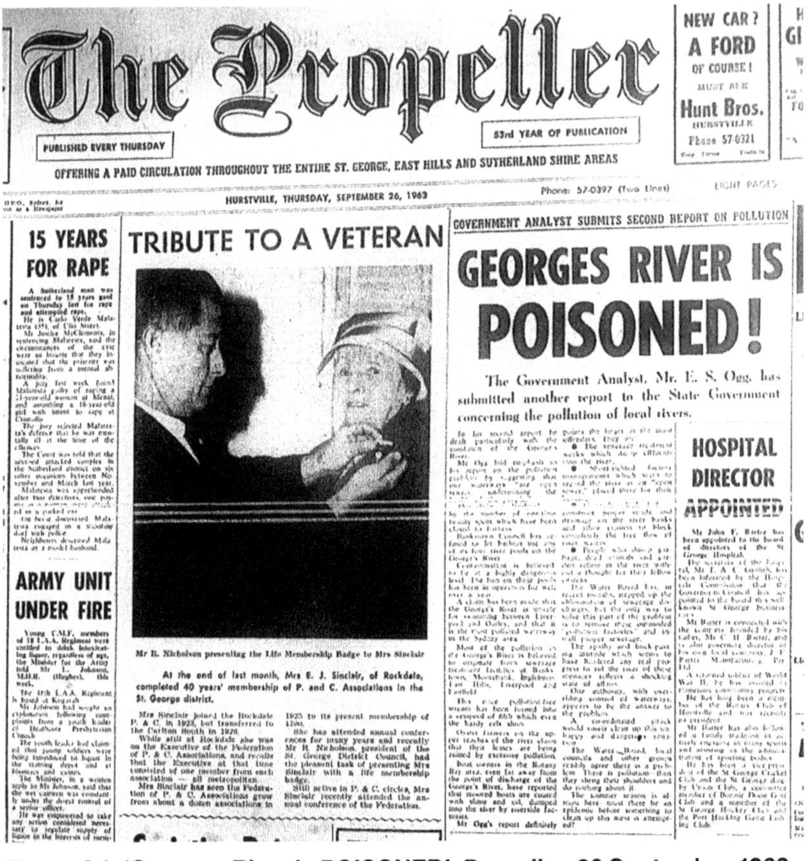
The Propeller

PUBLISHED EVERY THURSDAY

53rd YEAR OF PUBLICATION

OFFERING A PAID CIRCULATION THROUGHOUT THE ENTIRE ST. GEORGE, EAST HILLS AND SUTHERLAND SHIRE AREAS

HURSTVILLE, THURSDAY, SEPTEMBER 26, 1963

Phone: 57-0397 (Two Lines)

NEW CAR? A FORD OF COURSE! Hunt Bros. Phone 57-0321

15 YEARS FOR RAPE

ARMY UNIT UNDER FIRE

TRIBUTE TO A VETERAN

Mr R. Nicholson presenting the Life Membership Badge to Mrs Sinclair

At the end of last month, Mrs E. J. Sinclair, of Rockdale, completed 40 years' membership of P. and C. Associations in the St. George district.

Mrs Sinclair joined the Rockdale P. & C. in 1923, but transferred to the Carlton South in 1928.

While still at Rockdale she was on the Executive of the Federation of P. & C. Associations, and recalls that the Executive at that time consisted of one member from each association — all metropolitan.

Mrs Sinclair has seen the Federation of P. & C. Associations grow from about a dozen associations in 1923 to its present membership of 1700.

She has attended annual conferences for many years and recently Mr R. Nicholson, president of the St. George District Council, had the pleasant task of presenting Mrs Sinclair with a life membership badge.

Still active in P. & C. circles, Mrs Sinclair recently attended the annual conference of the Federation.

GOVERNMENT ANALYST SUBMITS SECOND REPORT ON POLLUTION

GEORGES RIVER IS POISONED!

The Government Analyst, Mr. E. S. Ogg, has submitted another report to the State Government concerning the pollution of local rivers.

HOSPITAL DIRECTOR APPOINTED

Figure 6.1: 'Georges River is POISONED', *Propeller*, 26 September 1963, front page.

The *Propeller* summarised Ogg's report, stating: 'this once pollution-free stream has been turned into a cesspool of filth which even the hardy eels shun'. The Georges River and other waterways, it said, had been turned into 'open sewers, undermining the health of the people'. Courtesy of State Library of New South Wales.

18 Commonwealth of Australia, Senate Select Committee on Water Pollution, *Minutes of Evidence*, vol. 8, 4632.

Hunt's pleas persuaded the members of the Senate Select Committee to make the Georges River into an example of Australia's urban water pollution crisis. His submission on the Georges River was drawn on repeatedly for the graphic language with which the overall report addressed water contamination in cities around Australia as well as in rural areas. The committee's final report stated that New South Wales faced the greatest water pollution problems and made the Georges River its highest profile case study illustrating urban water pollution from sewage and industrial toxicity.[19] The cover photo of the committee's report showed Salt Pan Creek, describing it as 'one of the most grossly polluted streams in the State'.[20]

Pollution, from whatever source, was one issue on which George Jacobsen and some of the council and trust officers could find strong agreement. Hunt became a member of the trust, with Kevin Howard, senior health inspector, appointed in 1975.[21] Both had been involved in the testing by Ernest Ogg that led to the closure of the river due to faecal contamination in 1962. The overall question of pollution, from whatever source, was a shared concern that allowed new alliances to be built. The pressures were intense, as George Jacobsen's sons, Kevin and Col, remembered. They recalled how furious George had become when, as a trust member, he was offered a bribe to vote in favour of a developer's plan to subdivide one of the areas zoned for parkland:

> **Kevin:** I remember him going to fight some developers that wanted to develop all along the river.
>
> **Col:** They offered him money to change sides. Developers! To throw his vote to open up this particular lot of land. And he never had any money! He was in business! Five times I think he went broke before he quit. He never had much black letters against his name in the bank and they offered him big sums of money.
>
> **Kevin:** That's what I'm talking about. It was offensive to him.
>
> **Colin:** And he *did* want to fight them too. The fact that they'd even offered him that! He was horrified.[22]

---

19 'Bankstown Evidence Used in Water Pollution Report', *Bankstown Torch*, 15 July 1970, 1.
20 Ibid.
21 Howard joined the trust as a trustee on 20 June 1975. See Application for Reappointment to Trust, 1985, Trust Appointments – Georges River SRA 1992/SR/109/32, National Parks and Wildlife Service – Georges River National Park Trust (NPWS Archive), Hurstville Library, Georges River Council Libraries.
22 Kevin and Colin Jacobsen, interview, 12 July 2006.

This may have been the reason that, despite increasing pressure from the state government to force community and local government members out of the trust, George Jacobsen persisted. He stayed on until he was 70, the last community representative left on the trust.

Sociality and its Limitations

The Picnic Point Regatta Association (PPRA) saw little role for itself after the first few years of the national park's existence. It considered dissolving itself in 1965 but rescinded the decision and instead withdrew from public activity, taking part only in occasional local fundraising.[23] Then, in 1967, the national park was downgraded to a 'state recreation reserve'. The state government had created its own National Parks and Wildlife Service (NPWS) to implement its decisions and had decided on criteria for the category of 'national park'. Its definition was related to scale and to the quality of 'wilderness', and on neither of these did the Georges River park qualify as being of 'national' significance. The trust continued but the state government exercised ever more power through its NPWS member. Local people appealed to their political representatives like Joe Kelly and Pat Rogan to protest to the state government about the reduction in their input, but the NPWS and state government view was that 'the Trust must accept the concept of a State Recreation Area as being a regional rather than a local park'.[24]

Although the first national park was short-lived and the PPRA had withdrawn from public activity even before the park was demoted, this period left a strong impression. The experience of participating in the trust had soured local activists and disabused them of any misapprehensions that their interests were going to be prioritised by local government let alone by state or federal governments. While alliances may have been built with officers like Howard and Hunt working for the councils (although Hunt's documents and Howard's interview showed little awareness of the activist groups), it was also the case that the councils were more intent on responding to the interests of local business or local organisational pressure

---

23   Correspondence with the Chief Secretary's Department, 16 October 1965, Bankstown Council, 29 August 1967, Picnic Point Regatta Association Archive, Alf Stills Collection. Davies notes that the PPRA was formally dissolved in the following year, 1968, in Davies, Mulholland and Pipe, *West of the River Road*, 39–40.

24   A. J. Chaplin, state recreation area liaison officer, to administrator state recreation areas, 13 April 1982, Trust Appointments – Georges River SRA 1992/SR/109/32, NPWS Archive.

in their planning goals as far as these offered solutions to the pressing problems of waste management that the councils faced. Disillusionment with both state and local government was only compounded during the campaigns defending local Georges River environments that began to emerge from 1967.

Yet the very quality that had contributed to the strength of the PPRA and its campaign – the tight-knit solidarities within the communities of East Hills and Picnic Point that have been so evocatively described by PPRA members and the Jacobsen family – were also the campaign's limitation. As pointed out earlier, there were parallel socialities occurring along the river at the same time as the shared community events of the Anglo-Irish families in the PPRA. There appears to have been no interaction between the PPRA campaign for a national park and the many Aboriginal families who continued to live along Prospect Creek and Salt Pan Creek, as well, no doubt, as in other areas. This was despite the frequent assertions in the Jacobsen family that Aboriginal people had understood the land better than the invading British had done. Nor was there any interaction with the Italian and German communities who were holding comparable but less public social events in the immediate area. It is ironic that a staunch environmental advocate like Senator Tony Mulvihill, in the governing party from 1973 to 1975, who was, at the same time, such a close ally of Australia's immigrant communities, was not able to achieve some communication between these two core values of a future nation. Sharing social interactions and building social solidarities were the common activities within all these groups and yet there was no interaction or collaboration – or even communication – *between* them, although there was eventually to be some common meeting ground in political parties.

The new NPWS did not address this problem at all. While wanting more women and more 'citizen members' who were sympathetic to the NPWS aims, the state government did not at any time reach out to the non-Anglo communities now entering the area. In a graphic example, in 1982, the state government expressed dissatisfaction with the community representatives on the board, asking the trust to increase its number of 'citizen representatives' to ensure more women and more environmentally active members, but it did not express any concerns around the lack of ethnic diversity on the trust.[25] In the same year, in the only (surviving)

---

25   Gleeson, private secretary on behalf of minister for planning and environment, Eric Bedford, to the director, National Parks and Wildlife Service, D. A. Johnstone, 31 May 1982, Trust Appointments – Georges River SRA 1992/SR/109/32, NPWS Archive.

trust document even to acknowledge the area's demographic change and cultural diversity, it proposed that parks offered an opportunity to erase diversity through 'assimilation':

> Ethnic family groups make up a fair proportion of our visitors. It is obvious that our park areas provide facilities for both passive and active recreation for these people, thus enabling speedy assimilation to the outdoor Australian way of life, especially the children.[26]

Then, in 1987, the director of NPWS acted to remove all local people from trusts except where necessary for local communication.[27]

The membership of the trust, particularly after the park's downgrading to a state recreation reserve in 1967, was predominantly male Anglo professionals (often involved in local government related jobs or ex-councillors) of middle age and older. Most were long-term residents of the area – especially from the Panania, Revesby and Bankstown areas – but were nevertheless members of elite groups or were council members.[28]

Resurgent Nature

During the period in which the Georges River National Park came into existence and was then undermined, and at the same time as community concern was rising over contamination of the river's water, mangroves were expanding. Their expansion is unarguably demonstrated in the aerial military photographs taken annually from 1930.[29] Many residents were becoming uncomfortably aware of this expansion and were uneasy about its impacts.[30] The conflicts over mangroves that took place among the Georges River National Park campaigners have been described above.

---

26   Mr LeClerc, Address of Welcome, GR SRA Trust, 9th Annual Conference of Trustees of SRAs, 28–29 October, Bankstown, 1982 Trustees Conference – Georges River SRA, 1992/SR/201/290, NPWS Archive.

27   Minute from Meeting 18 October, 1987, Trust Appointments – Georges River SRA 1992/SR/109/32, NPWS Archive.

28   From perusal of membership lists, held in SRA 1992/SR/109/32, NPWS Archive, undertaken by Allison Cadzow, 2006.

29   Haworth, 'Bush Tracks and Bush Blocks'; Haworth, 'Changes in Mangrove/Salt Marsh Distribution'; Saintilan, 'Relationships between Height and Girth of Mangroves'; Saintilan and Williams, 'Mangrove Transgression into Saltmarsh'; Saintilan and Williams, 'The Decline of Saltmarsh in Southeast Australia'; McLoughlin, 'Estuarine Wetlands Distribution'.

30   Williams, *The River in Sydney's Backyard*; Molloy, *A History of Padstow*; Molloy, *The History of Milperra*; Molloy, *The History of Panania*.

Some of the national park advocates, like Alf Stills, wanted the mangroves removed to create picnic grounds while others, like George Jacobsen, saw the mangroves as an integral part of the river shore value as a national park. In fact, these conflicts betrayed rising differences about how to deal with mangroves in general as well as with their expansion. The activists did not ask – at least not publicly – why this change in mangrove behaviour was occurring. The scale of the human population's expansion in Sydney and, particularly, in the Georges River area, and concomitant increase in sewage flowing into the river, offers a possible explanation. Aird, Ogg and Hunt had all warned about the continuing drainage of human waste into the river.

Faecal contamination, along with the industrial pollution that, as Hunt pointed out, was impossible to specify as there were not accurate reports of its content or volume, had increased the nutrient level, particularly of nitrogen and phosphorus, for vegetation along the river shoreline. How do mangroves and saltmarsh respond to increased nutrient levels?

Some assumed that it was inevitable that mangroves would thrive in highly populated areas, implying that the increased nutrients from human waste were beneficial.[31] However, the results of scientific studies were mixed. Some studies indicated that, in both tropical and temperate areas, mangroves accelerated their growth, particularly their underground root stock, in response to increased nutrient supply, thus obstructing some flow of tidal water to saltmarsh.[32] Other work pointed out that mangroves in the Australian environment, and particularly those in temperate areas, had adapted over long time periods to low nutrient environments, and so were perhaps disadvantaged by increased nutrient levels. The most comprehensive study argued that, while in general mangroves in Australia had survived on low nutrient environments, their adaptations have offered them an increased plasticity in their responses – that is, while they could survive well in low nutrient environments, mangroves were still also able to respond to, and benefit from, increases in nutrient level.[33] So local conditions could still shape the overall outcomes in the expansion of mangroves. In this case, mangroves in the Georges River area are likely to have increased their growth rates as a result of increased nutrients in the water, although it is still unclear whether this offered mangroves

---

31 Tyrrell, *River Dreams*, 230.
32 Alongi, 'Impact of Global Change'.
33 Reef, Feller and Lovelock, 'Nutrition of Mangroves'.

a competitive advantage over saltmarsh. Just as important, however, is how such increased nutrients may have affected underwater vegetation such as Zostera.

While diversity in growth rates may have been shaped by local variations in nutrient levels as well as, for example, changing salinity due to higher rates of freshwater draining from paved surfaces, there have been wider changes over this period that are significant in mangrove expansion. Neil Saintilan and Kerrylee Rogers have argued that rising temperatures have influenced the expansion of both coastal temperate mangroves in estuaries and inland 'woody weed' (immature, coppicing eucalypts), which emerged in the same period across grasslands like that in western New South Wales.[34] This is an extremely important observation. Because mangroves appeared to be increasing close to dense urban populations that were releasing high levels of waste (and nutrients) into the water ways, it was easy to assume that the increased nutrient levels associated with dense urban populations had caused the mangrove increase. Yet the 'woody weeds' were becoming more abundant in marginal and arid areas, like the wide plains around Cobar, far away from any dense human or animal populations. So, it could not be simply 'urban conditions' or higher nutrient levels thar were causing the expansion.

More recently, Saintilan's work with Rogers and others has suggested that rising sea levels, associated with climate change–induced temperature rises, have led to a global expansion of mangroves into areas previously dominated by saltmarsh, which has been disadvantaged by longer immersion. They reviewed studies over long periods of time – investigating the archaeology of swamps in the Holocene – as well as a global range of sites that have demonstrated mangrove encroachment onto saltmarsh. Such sites are in the US, Central America, South America, Australia, South Africa and China. Their 2019 article concludes:

> The changing distribution of mangrove and saltmarsh may serve as an important indicator of climate change impacts, a sentinel of change for the broad range of ecosystem services dependent on these habitats … Environmental variability can therefore profoundly influence the competitive interactions between mangrove and saltmarsh … In South East Australia and New

---

34 Saintilan and Rogers, 'Woody Plant Encroachment of Grasslands'. Woody weed grows in remote areas, far removed from large urban populations, undermining any easy assumptions that expansions were somehow due to proximity to dense human settlements.

Zealand, the growth of the mangrove *A. marina* will be aided not only by increased temperatures toward its southern limit of distribution but also by higher sea levels.[35]

Overall, Saintilan and others point to the expansion of mangroves and their encroachment onto saltmarsh as early signs of climate change.[36] This was not something that activists or councils were aware of in the 1960s. All they saw were mangroves expanding. It became very clear, as the following accounts show, that council arguments were framed within many of the older mythologies about mangroves but were also shaped by recent wartime experiences in tropical war zones. On the activist side, the rising influence of ecology (and selective use of metaphors drawn from biological sciences) was mobilised in conflicts over what should, or could, be done about mangroves. Mangroves were increasingly seen as offering safe spaces and nutrients for immature fish and crustaceans – as essential elements for river health through filtering and slowing its flow as they nurtured the life of the river.

***

The oyster farming industry was the only one on the Georges River that may have gained any benefit from increased numbers of mangroves, as it began its resurgence in the 1950s. It had, after all, used mangrove wood in its early development to catch oyster spat as oysters spawned upstream. But the industry had exhausted the supply of Georges River mangroves in the early twentieth century. Older oyster farmers interviewed for this study, beginning their farming career in the 1940s, had early memories of travelling to the Minnamurra River, 150 kilometres south, to gather red mangroves for the oyster spat. Just a few years later, in the 1950s, oyster farmers were no longer catching spawn at all in the Georges River. Instead, they bought young oysters from Port Stephens to the north and brought them back to mature and 'fatten' on hardwood racks in the rich waters of the Georges River.

---

35   Saintilan, Rogers and McKee, 'The Shifting Saltmarsh-Mangrove Ecotone'.
36   There may, however, be a limit to any relative advantage that climate change has offered to mangroves. Recent modelling, led again by Neil Saintilan, shows that, for worst-case outcomes with intensifying climate change on tropical coastlines, sea levels would rise so rapidly that mangroves would not be able to grow quickly enough to survive. Saintilan et al., 'Thresholds of Mangrove Survival'; Saintilan, Rogers, Kelleway, Ens and Sloane, 'Climate Change Impacts'; Woodroffe, Rogers, McKee, Lovelock, Mendelssohn and Saintilan, 'Mangrove Sedimentation'.

7

Garbage: 'Reclamations' and Casualties

Don't it always seem to go
That you don't know what you've got
Till it's gone.[1]

Problems around the disposal of human waste have been present for human societies for millennia. Nearby, the Cooks River had suffered continuing pollution, both from human waste and the organic waste from noxious industries, throughout the nineteenth century. The problem was being worsened in the mid-twentieth century through the rapidly increasing area and density of industrial cities, and the Georges River was also facing an intense and rapid population rise.

An unprecedented garbage crisis added to this growing problem. Never in history had there been so much household and industrial garbage as began to accumulate after World War II (WWII) in all cities in capitalist economies – and Sydney was no exception. The garbage crisis that the Georges River – and all of Sydney – faced arose from a new economic model based on growth and consumption, producing new disposable materials and exponentially increasing scales of accumulation. Yet there was so little preparedness in any Western political structures that there was virtually no data for civil authorities to use to build a solution. This chapter will look in more detail at the origins and impact of the garbage emergency on the Georges River, the solutions proposed and the casualties these solutions created.

---

1 Joni Mitchell, 'Big Yellow Taxi', 1970.

Another significant change in the postwar world also began to shape the way people and environments interacted at this time. This was a new source of information on which Georges River resident groups, along with many others, could draw: the emerging science of ecology. It was beginning to circulate through the science community, and particularly among members of the Fisheries Branch, established during the 1950s within the New South Wales Chief Secretary's Department. However, the public role of these Fisheries biologists began slowly. They had little impact, for example, in the 1950s campaign for a Georges River national park. While George Jacobsen was one who came to glimpse ecological interactions, there had been no talks or visits from the Fisheries Branch or other biologists to the Picnic Point Regatta Association (PPRA) or even the National Park Trust.[2] Such interactions would become more common during the 1960s through organisations like the Oatley Flora and Fauna Society on the lower estuary, which invited speakers from a range of departments and universities to give educational talks about the local environment. The outcome, as will be discussed in later chapters, was that the resulting popular ecology grew to be a significant influence in the environmental campaigning of the late 1960s and 1970s.

The root cause of the garbage crisis was the major change in the economy of the developed capitalist world, which had drawn on new technologies and materials developed during the war to shift into what is now called a 'consumer' model. Rising wages and 'modernising' electrification encouraged increased spending on household appliances, clothing and other goods. In parallel, the packaging industry expanded to meet the needs of moving all these consumer goods in ever-wider trade circuits around the globe. The postwar decades saw an escalation in household waste, rising to alarming proportions in the later 1960s. We will consider this origin of the postwar garbage crisis before returning to the environmental casualties of the solutions implemented for it.

Harold Hunt, the chief health inspector at Bankstown Council, was just as disturbed by the garbage problem as he was by the sewage problems that had led him, in 1962, to endorse the closure of the Georges River to swimming and fishing. He made a lengthy submission directly to Bankstown Council about its garbage problem in 1968. The postwar

---

2   There are no references in Alf Stills's Collection, including in the minutes of the PPRA meetings; nor are there in references in the archives of the Georges River National Park (later State Parklands) Trust (NPWS Archive).

conditions, as well as rapidly changing both the demography and water quality of the Georges River area, had rapidly changed the economy. Postwar employment had enabled a greater degree of disposable income than had previously been the case, and the culture of the economy had changed to foster disposability of packaging and products. Over time, this packaging material became less biodegradable, as plastics and polystyrenes replaced paper and cardboard. Hunt wrote that, from 1958 to 1968:

> A noticeable increase in the volume of refuse has occurred which has aptly been described as an 'explosion': – articles are purposely manufactured to have a short life, packaging has become a big business resulting in huge amounts of waste, the public has become more conscious of the need for clean air and, as a result, there is less incineration, twice-weekly garbage services have become more common, industries have been developed and their wastes, both liquid and solid, now provide our most difficult problem.

> The undisputed fact is that the amount of garbage per person has increased – but we are confronted with the problem of lack of data – no Council in Sydney has consistently weighted its refuse and no authoritative statement can be made regarding the amount of refuse being generated in Sydney nor the rate of annual increase.[3]

According to Hunt, all councils were experiencing dilemmas in trying to deal with this unprecedented torrent of both packaging and putrescible waste. The problem was not limited to Sydney or even to Australia; Hunt had compared solutions being devised in a number of comparable countries, including the US and the UK.[4] Here he was commenting on a report on the garbage problem from the Local Government Association of New South Wales that proposed that each council could choose from a number of options to address this problem. Arising from his assessment of the US and UK situations, Hunt argued strongly that councils could not address this problem on their own but rather that state and federal governments needed to accept responsibility and provide coordination – and funds – to address this problem overall.[5]

---

3   Hunt, *Garbage Disposal,* 6.
4   Ibid., 9–12. There has since been significant research published on conditions in the US, notably by Melosi, *Garbage in the Cities.* There were differences in US and Australian conditions regarding the responsibility for waste removal and disposal in this period (corporate in US, municipal in Australia).
5   Hunt, *Garbage Disposal.* The W. D. Scott consultancy report was Appendix B to Hunt's submission to council.

Figure 7.1: An unidentified Sydney municipal rubbish tip.
This is similar to tips around Padstow operated by Bankstown Council, which I remember seeing as a child. There were piles of rubbish in the open and fire was used to reduce the volume. Government Printing Office 2 – 15100. Original negative held by State Library of New South Wales.

A particular dimension of the questions around garbage, water quality and the expansion of factories along the Georges River was the issue of class. The changing demographics of the area were based on the rapidly increasing numbers of factory workers. Spearritt argues that 'the most spectacular growth in manufacturing jobs' in the postwar years was in the municipalities of Bankstown and Parramatta. The number of people employed in factories in Bankstown in 1944–45 had been 3,346 but by 1953–54 there were 11,442 and in 1960–61 there were 25,159 factory employees. Liverpool, just a little upstream on the Georges River, similarly attracted new and relocated industrial plants, and David Jones moved its knitwear production from Surry Hills to Hargrave Park – a Housing Commission hostel area – because 'that's where the labour was'.[6]

6   Spearritt, *Sydney's Century,* 114–16.

In addition to the 'assembly line' or 'process' workers who lived in the area, there were many others whose work related closely to this form of factory production, including the many managers needed to organise workers and marketing and the 'time and motion study' analysts who arranged these workers around the machinery. All these people brought families and, in these baby boom years, there were many young children and increasingly teenagers in areas associated with factories.

The County of Cumberland Plan (CCP) had envisaged neighbourhoods growing around centres of amenities and services that offered places for sociality and support as well as for products and consumption. As the CCP had fallen apart in so many ways, it is not surprising that these hubs of community life did not eventuate in most areas. Municipal councils may have attempted to fill the gaps, and certainly libraries and baby health centres did emerge, but, as Allport has pointed out, the structure that came to fulfil most of the functions the CCP had envisaged was the shopping centre.[7]

A related concern with environmental implications was anxiety about working-class youth, particularly young male teenagers and men who called themselves 'bodgies', 'widgies', 'sharpies' or 'rockers'. It was feared these young people would become 'vandals' who would damage public amenities, challenge sexual morality and undermine social values.[8] The solutions suggested by all, including the New South Wales Child Welfare Department in 1952, involved imposing 'discipline' – either through military service or through ensuring that 'new areas' had many playing fields and sports grounds to enable competitive sport.[9] The expectation that organised sport would be a remedy for 'juvenile delinquency' was made explicit in 1963 when Rockdale Council agreed to sponsor sporting and after-school group activities in its parks – a plan it hoped would 'combat juvenile delinquency in its area'.[10]

---

7   Allport, 'The Unrealized Promise', on the County of Cumberland Plan.
8   'Bodgies, Widgees Defend New Cult', *Truth*, 18 February 1951, 3; 'Dean's Views on "Bodgies"', *Sun*, 21 May 1951, 3; 'Criminal Influence of Bodgies', *Daily Telegraph*, 21 November 1952, 13; 'The Bodgie-Widgie Cult: Its Bad Influence is Spreading', *Mail*, 15 December 1961, 7. See also Moore, 'Bodgies, Widgies and Moral Panic'.
9   'Criminal Influence of Bodgies', *Daily Telegraph*, 21 November 1952, 13.
10 'Park Plan for Youth', *Propeller*, 9 January 1963, 1. The *Propeller* was taken over by the *St George and Sutherland Shire Leader* (hereafter *Leader*) in December 1969.

This fear of juvenile delinquents had certainly been present among the PPRA campaigners who worried that their 'improvements' to parks would be damaged by vandals. But these working-class activists were also worried about their own children, and were seeking ways to protect them from 'bad influences' by offering activities such as organised sports and recreation.[11] Many, however, yearned for the activities they had found so satisfying in earlier years, in particular, the picnics and informal outdoor sociality that had been so widespread throughout the early twentieth century.[12]

***

Escalating Reclamations

Although the Georges River National Park was downgraded in 1967, the goals and strategies of the trust had left a deep impression. Both Bankstown and Hurstville councils had been involved in the trust along with Sutherland, and the aldermen saw themselves as carrying on the goals of the trust, but there were earlier foundations. Many of these projects had first been planned in the 1920s but had been obstructed by the Depression and the war. Within the context of the challenges posed by the broader changes along the river – the increasing working-class population, the garbage 'explosion' and the expanding mangroves – these precedents added to the legacy of the Georges River National Park Trust. The earlier plans seemed to offer solutions to these challenges, leading to an escalation of the practice of reclaiming swamplands along the Georges River from Little Salt Pan Creek downstream to Botany Bay.

'Reclaiming' swamps by dumping garbage into them has a long history. It was common in Britain and Europe and, since the colonial occupation of the Georges River, had been pursued (although relatively slowly) by local communities in the building of picnic grounds and golf courses and by municipal councils. Chris Cunneen has pointed out that most parklands in Sydney were built on reclaimed swamps, including Centennial Park in the nineteenth century. On the Georges River, Bankstown Council had slowly dumped garbage in Kelso Swamp during the Depression and

---

11   The concerns of PPRA campaigners, both about 'vandals' and their own children, were evident in their collective interview, 22 March 2006. Powell, *Out West*.
12   Staples, interview, 27 May 2005.

before.[13] Initially, local communities had welcomed such 'reclamation' of swamps, as it offered relief from insects like mosquitoes and from deeper subconscious fears about swamps as unnatural places that bred not only miasmas and illness but also more malevolent forces.

Figure 7.2: The impact of 'reclamation', seen here at Homebush Bay on the Parramatta River, c. 1950s.
'Reclamation consolidation of spoil among mangroves'. Government Printing Office 1 – 07935. Original negative held by State Archives and Records Authority of New South Wales.

Figure 7.3: Duck Creek, Granville, 1939, 'reclamation' to turn creek into playing field.
Original negative held by State Archives and Records Authority of New South Wales.

With the massive increase in household waste that the postwar economy produced, the pace of reclamation increased exponentially. More significantly, it increased in the working-class areas of the Georges River because there was more apparently 'vacant' land into which garbage could be dumped. There was also more motivation by state and local governments to build sports fields to ensure that working-class youth were properly supervised and disciplined through competitive and organised sports. Surveys into the amount and use of 'open space' in various local government areas began in 1947 and was repeated with changing criteria and definitions in 1962, 1972 and 1982. These surveys were compared and analysed in 1985 by the New South Wales Department of Environment and Planning. The results suggested that councils with significant proportions of low socio-economic status populations tended to have substantial numbers of playing fields, although this varied according to population density and availability of potential locations. As Cunneen has pointed out, marshy, low-lying land had commonly been targeted for reclamation in order to build parks, and this process escalated

---

13   Cunneen, 'Hands Off the Parks!'.

after WWII as garbage disposal became more problematic.[14] Harold Hunt had identified the processes in the Bankstown area and had argued that this was a problem right along the river. He had demanded a unified federal policy rather than stop-gap solutions devised council by council or even state by state.

As mangroves were expanding, the goal of uprooting them and replacing the 'mangrove swamps' with parks and sporting fields was a common solution, particularly on the Georges River where they were increasingly evident (and unwelcome). 'Swamps' had become less visible than 'mangroves' or were frequently referred to as 'mangrove swamps' – as if the mangroves were the primary and causative factor. Memories of tropical swamps and mangroves in WWII battlegrounds in South-East Asia still circulated, confirming popular mythologies about mangroves as threatening, uncomfortable and unnatural.[15]

Councils expected they would have little opposition. In 1964, for example, Vincent Durick, Australian Labor Party state member for Lakemba, proposed that the removal of mangroves and the building of sports grounds would be an enhancement to the troubled Housing Commission hostel at Herne Bay:

> In my own area at the present time there is a section of wasteland which consists for the most part of mangrove swamps. It forms the upper section of Salt Pan Creek … It is estimated that by controlled tipping of household refuse 1,250,000 cubic yards of rubbish will be disposed of. If this plan comes to fruition … it will have a three-fold result. First it will overcome the problems of some metropolitan councils with regard to garbage disposal, which have become urgent … Second, it will result in the reclamation of an area which is at present wasteland and an eyesore … Third it will result in the provision of spacious playing fields.[16]

14   News South Wales Department of Environment and Planning, 'Open Space in the Sydney Region', 66–86.
15   See editor's response to letter, re: 'witnessing first-hand the damage mangroves can do in Papua New Guinea and Queensland', *Leader*, 21 August 1974, 21. Engineer A. H. Brewer, quoted below, had served in Borneo and his wartime memories may have coloured his advice to Hurstville Council.
16   V. P. Durick, ALP, MLA Lakemba, 21 October 1964, in New South Wales Legislative Council, *Votes and Proceedings*, vol. 54, 1522.

Figure 7.4: Goal posts erected after swamp 'clearance'.
This Public Works photograph, titled 'sewerage clearance', shows a large, unidentified Sydney area where 'clearance' had occurred. Goal posts on the right are a lonely indication of the intended playing field. Original negative held by State Archives and Records Authority of New South Wales.

By 1968, many council officials along the river were aware of the recent expansion of mangroves and saw 'mangrove swamps' as offering the spaces needed for the sports grounds that would solve social problems, although this was not only in areas with higher working-class populations. All councils were suffering from the masses of expanding garbage. Hurstville Council Engineer Albert Brewer, for example, reported in 1968 that, at Lime Kiln Bay, 'the mangroves ... are quite a new development'.[17] Brewer, however, had served in WWII in Borneo, and so had fought in tropical mangrove forests.[18] His lingering wartime trauma may have influenced his hostility to the expanding mangroves on the Georges River. In the following year, Brewer reported again on the 'tremendous increase' in Hurstville of mangroves, which he described as 'a noxious weed and a cancerous growth':

---

17   Dunstan, 'Some Early Environmental Problems', 3, citing Municipal Engineer A. H. Brewer in 'Hurstville Municipal Council [HMC] Minutes, 5 September 1968', Local Studies Archive, Hurstville Library, Georges River Council Libraries. Dunstan was the New South Wales state fisheries officer, Division of Fisheries and Oceanography, CSIRO, Cronulla. Note that Brewer had been in WWII battles in tropical Borneo and may have brought wartime memories of fear and pain among tropical mangroves to his depiction of temperate wetlands as 'foul mangrove swamps'.
18   John MacRitchie, Georges River librarian, pers. comm.

It is tragic to see the waterways silting to this extent and anything
that can rid the river of these unsightly mudflats and foul mangrove
swamps should be applauded by everyone.[19]

While others in the municipal councils were more troubled by the
removal of mangroves, they were even more alarmed by the expansion
of the garbage problem. Kevin Howard, one of the health inspectors at
Bankstown Council, explained the decision in the early 1970s to bury
rubbish at the head of Little Salt Pan Creek and later to build playing fields:

The Little Salt Pan tip arose out of a thought that we were running
out of tipping space … One of my colleagues at the Council was
looking after tips and his idea was to cut down the mangroves at
the back of Padstow and do the filling job down there. They had
playing fields they wanted to put in … See it wasn't just a matter
of 'let's get rid of a few more mangroves', it was: 'what are we going
to do with the rubbish? We've got nowhere else to go with it!'[20]

Through their expansion, particularly across the saltmarsh, the mangroves
themselves had become the focus of municipal councils' reclamation plans,
which, as Howard had observed, had arisen largely because of the need
to dispose of an increased amount of household waste. The mangroves,
however, had gained political as well as environmental dominance, and
were mentioned far more often in council statements than the 'swamps'
that had, for so long, been the major source of fear and dread.[21]

Meanings for Mangroves: Pleasures and Fears

For young people – and particularly for young boys with bikes – the
riverbanks and mangroves were an important resource. This was
a gendered experience in the postwar period, and it varied from area
to area and between communities. In the Padstow area in the 1960s, boys
rather than girls tended to explore the riverbanks, although there were

---

19   Dunstan, 'Some Early Environmental Problems', 1, citing HSC Minutes, 6 March 1969.
20   Howard, interview. These places were uniformly referred to as 'the tip' and trips to 'the tip' with
parents and family formed a large part of childhood leisure in the 1960s. (Aside: I loved going to
the tip with dad in the 1970s in suburban Melbourne. It was an adventure!) They may also now be
known as a 'dump'.
21   See Goodall, 'Frankenstein, Triffids and Mangroves', for old fears regarding swamps and miasmas.

girls who knew the banks too.[22] Oral histories offer glimpses of the many ways in which boys knew the riverbanks and the expanding mangroves. One from the east of Salt Pan Creek, around Lime Kiln Bay, was Robert Haworth, who recalled experiences of the 1940s. For him, the mangroves offered retreat and sanctuary – once the terrors of the snakes had been braved – where he could read undisturbed by gangs of his young comrades from Mortdale.[23]

Another set of stories comes from friends who were boys in the 1960s. Glenn Goodacre and my brothers, Craig and Mark Goodall – with the wonderful mobility and independence that bikes afforded them – could show off, speeding down the steep hills like Dilke to reach the shelter of the mangroves. There they could do all sorts of forbidden things: feast on a bag of broken biscuits bought cheap from Woolies; play around, or in, the big pipes along the banks; scale the heights of the railway bridge that crossed the creek; marvel at the amazing orb spiders (*Nephila*) that favoured mangroves to spin their glistening webs; or wonder at the many other insects that inhabited the rich, muddy environments of the mangroves.[24] Girls like me and my friends did not think it cool to hang out in the mud (even if we could ride bikes) and were perhaps more fearful about venturing into the wild riverbanks. Our attitudes reflected the effectiveness of a broader tendency to discourage girls from being alone in dense bush, suggested to us as a place where 'bad things' happened to women, leading us – rightly or wrongly – to see ourselves as more vulnerable than our brothers.

Some people remember being taught explicitly that the overgrown riverbanks were frightening places. Young boys, for example, were warned against riverside scrub as beats where men might meet others for illicit sex.[25] In a period when homophobia was common and ignorance widespread, it was difficult, if not impossible, to express same-sex attractions openly, and

---

22 Sharyn Cullis's memories were of Prospect Creek, 'my patch'. Her home backed onto the creek, and she kayaked. Her father, Fred Cullis, recalled fishing, swimming and collecting bird eggs at Sandy and Rocky points, Swingy Bridge and Horseshoe Bend in the areas around Milperra. He said pollution became noticeable about 1955, with froth on the water, especially on weekends, as toxic wastes were released from surrounding factories ('they thought no one would notice then'). He phoned an Alderman who asked him to keep an eye on the river there. See Sharyn Cullis, interview notes, 10 May 2007; Fred Cullis, interview. See also Knight, interview, for the experiences of girls in oyster farming families on the Georges River in the 1960s and 1970s.
23 Haworth, interview.
24 Goodacre, interview; Craig and Mark Goodall, interview.
25 Goodacre, interview; Craig and Mark Goodall, interview.

choices were few. There were either secluded beats or there was silence. Some of this anxiety on all sides – among men and women – was overcome through the excesses of technology. 'Chucking wheelies' on pushbikes – or more noisily on motorbikes – over the drier areas of salt-scalded land behind the mangroves might damage the fragile vegetation, but it helped the riders to feel stronger against the wild, dark banks. The perils and the joys of secluded places – even once they had been 'disciplined' – is a theme to which we return in the final chapter.[26]

The experiences of girls in oyster farming families could be very different. One oyster farming daughter, Maxine Drake, grew up at Gunyah Bay (or Gungah Bay) and has written a vivid and informative book for children about the industry. Recalling the pleasures of her 1970s childhood, playing on boats and exploring the mudflats, Maxine wrote: 'The only tree that can grow in salt water, mangrove forests make safe breeding places for fish and crabs. They are magical places that keep the river healthy'.[27] Alexandra Knight has explained that, like her, all the children of the extended Derwent families, including the girls, were comfortable exploring the waters of the Georges River.[28] The oyster farming sheds, equipment and boats in Neverfail Bay all belonged to their family members or to close friends.[29] Alex remembers frequently walking through the mangroves at the end of Wyong Street and jumping onto one of the punts heading off up or down the river to the oyster racks. Each of these boats was, after all, owned by one or other of her uncles or close relations. She would be able to roam around, on or near the oyster leases for as long as she liked and then, when she was ready to come home, there was always a relation to catch a lift with. This sense of comfort and safety on the river allowed her to come to know the river far better than those of us who had been firmly confined to dry land or the tangled mangroves or the old swimming enclosures.

---

26   Kelleway, interview; Kelleway, 'Ecological Impacts of Recreational Vehicle Use'. See also Byrne, 'Time on the Waterline'.
27   Drake, *Georges River Tale*, 5. Maxine Drake's father, Bob Drake, was interviewed for this project, see Chapter 5, this volume.
28   This draws on the memories of Alex Knight. See Knight, interview.
29   See Drake, *Georges River Tale,* 15, for a wonderful hand-drawn sketch of the Derwent and Drake homes and oyster sheds and gear at Neverfail Bay.

Early Solutions and Their Casualties

'Reclamations' – which made 'real' dry land by dumping various types of filling onto saline swamps along the Georges River – had begun at least as early as the 1920s, as discussed earlier, but it had been done at a relatively slow pace. Even in the 1940s, as Harold Hunt had pointed out, amounts of household garbage had been relatively low because backyard incinerators had been used to burn moderate amounts of waste. So garbage disposal was done 'on the cheap'.[30] But, with the noticeable increase in garbage occurring over the 1950s, the 'reclaiming' of swampland began to accelerate.

The first casualties were the mangroves and saltmarsh that were uprooted and covered with dumped garbage. These areas were the habitat of many species of birds that became the second and, perhaps, more serious casualties, as this bigger impact was harder to notice until it was too late. Kel Connell and Kevin Jacobsen have both remembered the importance of Kelso Swamp and other wet places along the river as the source of ducks and other birds that were shot for sport and also for food for hungry families during the Depression.[31] Recalling more peaceful memories of the profusion of birdlife and flowers, Zina Laundess, who lived on Bransgrove Road, remembered that, in the 1930s, Kelso was:

> A beautiful tidal stream that came in and made a swamp the size of a racetrack. It was very pretty with she-oaks all around and wild birds who came to roost in the night times. On the other side off towards East Hills there were numerous wild flowers – Boronias, Five Corners and many more. At springtime, I used to love to wander through it.[32]

Sue Rosen has recorded the extensive work Canterbury Council undertook in 1964 to 'reclaim' 70 acres on upper Salt Pan Creek, including 50 acres of 'swampland'.[33] Meanwhile, Bankstown Council, in collaboration with the Georges River National Park Trust, was busy 'reclaiming' 100 acres

---

30 Hunt, *Garbage Disposal*, 5.
31 Kevin, Colin and Carol Jacobsen, interview, 12 July 2006; Connell and Seitch, interview, 5 May 2006.
32 Zina Laundess, quoted in Molloy, *The History of Panania*, 244.
33 Rosen, *Bankstown*, 148, citing Bankstown City Council (BCC): PF 122-1 (Reclamations); 'Georges River Polluted with Sewerage Outfall', *Bankstown Torch*, 16 April 1953, 1; 'Pollution of Georges River Protest', *Bankstown Torch*, 30 April 1953, 1; 'Swamp Land May be Mecca Soon for Tourists', *Bankstown Torch*, 28 October 1964, 1; 'Garbage Plan for Swamp in Creek', *Bankstown Torch*, 28 October 1964, 1.

of saltmarsh at Picnic Point, with the freshwater Yeramba Lagoon to be constructed by 'bulldozing thousands of mangroves and the construction of a weir to keep out salt-water from the Georges River'.[34] Kelso Swamp too had been damaged by 1964, when W. H. Dane, the Bankstown Council administrator, described the outcome of the bulldozing and dumping there, the same place where Zina Laundess had remembered the 'wild birds who came to roost in the night times'.

Figure 7.5: Aerial photograph of Kelso Swamp, 1 May 1951, showing extent of the wetlands in that year.

There had been higher than average rainfall in 1950, but the limits of building in the area demonstrates the usual broad extent of swamp and low-lying land. Courtesy of Spatial Services, NSW Lands. Sheetname: Sydney, Film: CCC466, Run R17, Frame 57. Creative Commons.

---

34   Ibid., citing Bankstown Municipal Council Files. PF 122-1 (Dredging).

Figure 7.6: Aerial photograph of remains of Kelso Swamp, 1 January 1970.

Most had been lost by 1964 as reported by Bankstown Council administrator W. H. Dane, but this 1970 aerial photograph shows the carving up of the swamp for playing fields. Courtesy of Spatial Services, NSW Lands. Sheetname: Penrith, Film: 1908, Run R21, Frame 5130. Creative Commons.

Dane reported:

> We have found that the Kelso Swamp abounds with bird life, but this area – which apparently had been a home for thousands of birds for years – is disappearing quickly. The Kelso Swamp is being filled with rubbish and eventually fifteen playing fields will be formed on this former swampland.[35]

'Reclamations' that damaged the habitat of birdlife along the river were not the only challenges bird species were facing. The memories quoted earlier pointed to the hunting of ducks and other water species for food during the Depression, and no doubt this continued with increasing pressure as the population grew so rapidly. Based on my own memories of growing up in Padstow, the gendered recreations of young boys in the bush in the 1950s and 1960s included hunting for birds. Little boys,

---

35 'Swamp Land May be Mecca Soon for Tourists', *Bankstown Torch,* 28 October 1964, 1; 'Garbage Plan for Swamp in Creek', *Bankstown Torch,* 28 October 1964, 1.

especially, hunted them with shanghais (slingshots or catapults) and, later, with air rifles, and sought out birds' nests to plunder for eggs to add to collections. While such recreations meant those young boys learnt a great deal about bird habitats and habits, they were rightly seen as threats to birdlife. The New South Wales chapter of the Gould League of Bird Lovers was founded in 1910 in Wellington after successful activity in Victoria. The league was taken up strongly in the New South Wales Public Schools Curriculum, with teachers encouraging students to join and pledge to protect birds. It was hoped that these pledges and the league's education about Australian birdlife, as well as competitions to identify birds and imitate their calls, would help to conserve local bird species. The league initially had a strong hold in the public school system in New South Wales, reinforcing the interest in nature study that the new 1905 curriculum endorsed.[36] This interest persisted in some areas, as Robert Haworth recalled about the Mortdale area in the 1940s. He claimed that girls at Mortdale Public School were particularly likely to take part because of an affinity with the moral dimension of the league's call to protect bird species. Of greater interest at Mortdale, however, were the bird call competitions. Mortdale Public were the champions, with boys as well as girls excelling year after year during the 1940s in the Sydney-wide competitions.[37]

By the 1960s, however, the loss of habitat because of the expanding 'reclamations' had significantly reduced the readily sighted birdlife, eroding support for the Gould League. While the league continued to be known in the public schools I went to in the late 1950s and early 1960s in Padstow and Kogarah, few children joined. People going to school in the East Hills to Salt Pan Creek stretch of the river in the 1980s had simply never heard of the Gould League.[38] There may have been more habitat remaining on the southern side or further downstream, but the rising

---

36   Gould League, [Home Page], accessed 14 January 2021, www.gould.org.au/; Roberts and Tribe, *The Gould League*. See Kass, *Educational Reform*, 146, quoting an optimistic 1913 acting chief inspector who attributed to the Gould League such intervention that: the destruction of bird life has dwindled nearly to vanishing point'.
37   Robert Haworth, pers. comm., 8 July 2020.
38   Andrew Molloy, pers. comm.; Kass, *Educational Reform*, 174. John Huxley suggests the peak of membership was in the 1950s. Huxley, 'Down Binoculars'.

population and the expanding 'reclamations' were taking a toll by then. The New South Wales chapter was disbanded in 2011, but Gould League Australia groups continue to exist today in some rural areas.[39]

These early experiences of environmental interest on the Georges River while some habitat persisted shaped the later careers of many of the children attending public schools in the 1940s and 1950s, encouraging them to take up careers in ecology across a number of disciplines and professions.[40] As the Georges River became even more damaged during the 1960s, it was sometimes these young people or their families who became active in campaigning against a new wave of 'reclamation', addressed in the following chapters, that suddenly burst into view in the late 1960s.

---

39   See, for example, those on the far South Coast of New South Wales at Eden and Bournda (near Tathra). Houston, 'Former Bird Calling Champions'.

40   Kass, *Educational Reform*, 159; Haworth, interview. After his early training as a plumber, Bob Haworth took an active role in the Terania Creek protests against rainforest logging in 1979, completed doctoral research in geography, taught at the University of New England and has written since, among other studies, analyses of mid-twentieth-century habitat change on the Georges River. See, for example, Haworth, 'Changes in Mangrove/Salt Marsh Distribution'.

Part IV:
The 'Mangrovites' Fight Back

8

Change and the Picnic River

By 1970 the Georges River could no longer be seen as a picnic river. The rapid postwar rise in population of the area, the increasing number of factories along its banks and the multiplying rubbish tips dumped on its swamps had led to metropolitan and local headlines like 'River Ruined by Pollution' in 1962, 'Georges River Poisoned' in 1963 and 'Georges River Could Become Sewage Waterway' in 1973.[1] The main source of contamination was human and garbage waste, but residents feared industrial contamination in the waterways. There certainly was discharge from factories: Bankstown's chief health inspector H. C. Hunt had pointed in 1969 to the high lead levels being discharged into Salt Pan Creek from the battery factory in its upstream reaches.[2] Hunt had warned too that the damage being caused by the 'garbage explosion' was leading to more and more land being turned into council dumps, scarring the landscape and leaching into the river.[3] Overall, however, as Kevin Howard, the Bankstown Council health inspector pointed out in March 1973, it was not industrial chemicals that were causing the problems but rather bacterial pollution from human and organic rubbish waste that was so damaging to the Georges River water and, consequently, to the

---

1   *Daily Mirror,* 13 September 1962, 7; *Propeller,* 26 September 1963, 1; *Bankstown Torch,* 3 January 1973, 1.
2   Commonwealth of Australia, Senate Select Committee on Water Pollution, *Minutes of Evidence,* vol. 20, 4631, 4664.
3   Hunt, *Garbage Disposal,* 5.

land on which it was dumped.[4] New South Wales Fisheries biologist W. B. Malcolm promised in 1969 that there would be thorough pollution testing of the Georges and Cooks rivers and Botany Bay. Malcolm's grim warning about the lessons from the Cooks River were not lost on Georges River residents when his words were reported in the *Bankstown Torch*:

> Mangrove swamps, river mud flats and sea grasses were essential to nurture young fish. Deepening of rivers through dredging and reclamation of swamps was therefore depriving fish of feeding grounds … Many swamplands and river flats had been taken over as garbage dumps and playing fields, and waterfront home owners had encroached onto the shallow areas with river pools and jetties. Cooks River was a perfect example of an estuary completely despoiled with playing fields in places where swamps and river flats used to be.[5]

Many mangrove and saltmarsh areas had already been 'reclaimed' on the Georges River by 1965, with playing fields planned or already built over the dumped mud and garbage, so a sense of the vulnerability of the remaining low-lying areas must have been widespread among the Georges River estuary communities.

Earlier chapters have traced the first tensions in the 1960s under the impact of postwar pressure. The Picnic Point Regatta Association (PPRA) campaign for the Georges River National Park (mid-1950s to 1961) had tried, and largely failed, to save people's access to river bushland from privatised new home blocks. Then, downstream, the very types of riverbank subdivisions feared by the East Hills campaigners had led to the conflicts after 1962 between the Georges River Oyster Lease Protest Association (GROLPA) – the 'exclusive' waterfront landowners from Como to Sylvania – and the oyster farmers, who were long-established members of the riverside communities round Oatley. The escalating pace of reclamation plans – dumping dredged river mud and rubbish on swamps and mangroves to build playing fields – was spreading alarm along the river.

---

4   Interchange between CSIRO scientist, G. A. Major, who reassured readers that trace metal content was not a problem in oysters, which he said 'gave a good indication' of the content in river water, and Kevin Howard, Bankstown Council health inspector, who pointed out that the 'real threat' to oysters and the river was bacterial pollution. 'No River Pollution if Proper Care Taken', *St George and Sutherland Shire Leader* (hereafter *Leader*), 21 February 1973, 7; 'Oysters' Future "Not So Bright"', *Leader*, 14 March 1973, 29.
5   'River Test for Pollution', *Bankstown Torch*, 20 August 1969, 3, reporting on Malcolm's talk to the Cooks River Valley Association.

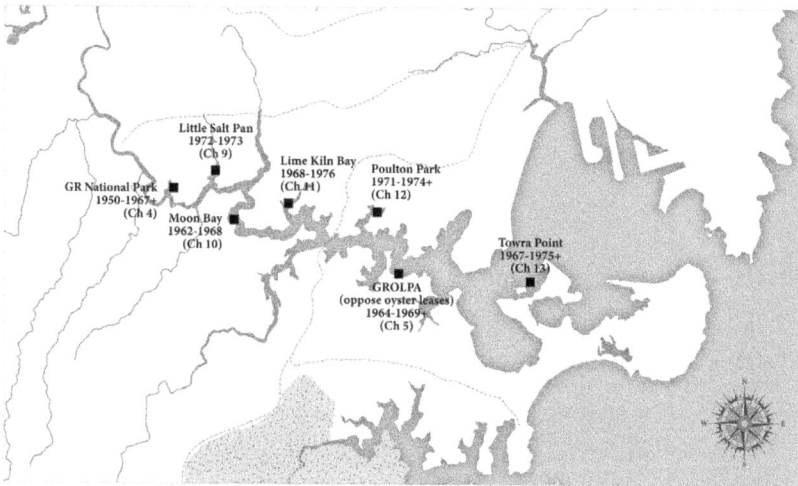

1 kilometre

Map 8.1: Locations of the five resident environmental campaigns discussed in the following chapters.
Cartography: Sharon Harrup.

The following chapters consider the five local resident environmental campaigns that flared up on the lower estuary from the mid-1960s to the mid-1970s.

Each of the following chapters will discuss one dispute in detail and the chapters proceed roughly downstream – from Little Salt Pan Creek to Great Moon Bay, Lime Kiln Bay and Oatley Bay and on to Towra Point at the entrance of the Georges River into Botany Bay. Two of these campaigns focused initially on dredging and fishing: those about Great Moon Bay and the airport extensions to Towra Point. The remaining three, Little Salt Pan Creek, Lime Kiln Bay and Poulton Creek at Oatley Bay, were focused largely on the destruction of low-lying land caused by 'reclamation'. Although their emphases varied, each of the campaigns opposed both dredging and the dumping of mud and rubbish onto swamps, mangroves and saltmarsh.

These campaigns are considered separately in the following chapters because each highlights a distinctive strategy or concern. Yet, in fact, all these disputes were occurring at roughly the same time (mid-1960s to mid-1970s) and only a short distance away from each other. They shared information and observed each other's tactics and victories, as well as defeats. The reasons behind their distinctive emphases will be considered in the concluding section.

As distinctive as each campaign was, and, indeed, as the whole Georges River in itself was, there were developments in the wider national and international scene that shaped the ways these campaigns were conducted and how successful each was able to be.

* * *

Interest in remote areas had been high in the interwar period, with the Sydney Bush Walkers Club a noted example. Led by Myles Dunphy, Marie Byles and others, this group had nurtured plans for a Greater Blue Mountains National Park.[6] Dunphy (who had moved from Melbourne to Oatley on the Georges River) and others had felt they had succeeded in gaining protection for many of the areas they walked through by interacting with establishment figures and government bureaucracies.[7]

However, these interwar gains had come under threat with postwar changes in technology and economy. Mining for sand threatened coastal areas like Myall Lakes and then oil mining threatened the Great Barrier Reef. Aggressive development and the expansion of farming threatened inland areas like the Little Desert, and the demands of newly electrified homes and industries threatened and eventually destroyed Lake Pedder.[8] New organisations had developed in response, such as the Nature Conservation Council (NCC) in 1955, but its strategies continued to take the same approaches as the Sydney Bush Walkers: that of negotiating unobtrusively with governments. These threatened places were, in general, remote from cities and were seen as embodying iconic and often pristine examples of Australian natural environments. None of the campaigns aimed to protect damaged and compromised environments – and this was certainly what the Georges River had become! Consequently, the campaigns considered in the following chapters against dredging and reclamations on the Georges

---

6   Mulligan and Hill, *Ecological Pioneers*; McLeod, *The Summit of Her Ambition*.
7   Mulligan and Hill, *Ecological Pioneers*, 138–53; Hutton and Connors, *A History of the Australian Environment Movement*, 114–18.
8   Hutton and Connors, *A History of the Australian Environment Movement*, 92–124.

River did not initially gain the support of the established environmental organisations like the NCC or its successors, including the Australian Conservation Foundation.

Yet, the desire to protect – and conserve – the unique and the pristine was also felt on the Georges River, and was most clearly expressed by the Oatley Flora and Fauna Society (OFF), also founded in 1955, on the lower estuary.[9] This society was not involved in either of the resident environmental organisations considered earlier – neither the upstream and working-class PPRA (or the Georges River National Park Trust) in the 1950s and 1960s nor GROLPA, the Como and Sylvania waterfront landowners fighting the oyster farmers during the 1960s. Members of OFF concentrated on educating themselves about issues of conservation on the lower estuary with invited speakers and study visits to scenic and informative conserved landscapes. Some members took more active roles, writing to politicians or to the press, but many were most involved in this self-education process.

At the same time, however, as postwar changes were increasingly threatening iconic landscapes, the decade of the 1960s was one of dramatic national and international social and political change. Rising opposition to the Vietnam War dominated this decade with growing protests against the American intervention in Vietnam and Australia's role in sending conscripts to fight there. This was especially relevant to the Georges River suburban campaigns because it affected many young Georges River men – and their friends and families – in this area where so many children had been settled and grown up since the population increases of the 1950s. Historians of the political campaigns of the late 1960s have often focused on university students (in that period, still necessarily middle class) and the inner-city areas of Sydney or Melbourne.[10] Yet suburbs like Bankstown had far more young men of conscription age than the inner cities. And the Georges River continued to play host to military spaces like Holsworthy to which conscripts were taken.

---

9   Fairley, *Being Green*.
10   See Murphy, *Harvest of Fear*; King, *Australia's Vietnam*. In the late 1960s and early 1970s, no Australian government offered financial support for university enrolment. Only after the federal Labor government came to power in 1972 was tertiary education made financially possible for working-class families.

Figure 8.1: Bill White, Vietnam War conscientious objector.

Bill White, a primary school teacher, refused to comply with notices to report for national service because, first, he refused to kill another human being, and, second, because he objected to the US war in Vietnam. This photograph, originally published in the *Sun Herald*, shows him being dragged from his Gladesville home in late 1966 by police. The photograph was included in K. J. Mason's text for Year 10 history, *Experience of Nationhood*. Courtesy of Nine Publishing.

Unsurprisingly, then, these 'suburban' areas also had activist movements and protests around the Vietnam War. Bill White, the first conscientious objector against the Vietnam War, was a primary school teacher living in Gladesville, an older area closer to the city, but just as suburban as Bankstown. In July 1966 he refused to cooperate with conscription for Vietnam and was dragged from his home by burly policemen, the scene photographed and published widely in the Sydney press.[11] The Reverend Ron Page from the Methodist Church in Bankstown was an outspoken critic of Australia's role in the Vietnam War and preached regularly through the later 1960s from his Bankstown pulpit against the conscription

---

11 'Objector Asked by Army to Consider Position', *Sydney Morning Herald,* 22 November 1966, 5; 'William White New Charges', *Sydney Morning Herald,* 28 November 1966, 1; 'Out of Army, White Sets His Wedding Day', *Sydney Morning Herald,* 24 December 1966, 1; 'Young Teacher's Anti-War Stand Wins Wide Support', *Tribune,* 27 July 1966, 1; 'Persecuting a Brave Man', *Tribune,* 10 August 1966, 2; King, *Australia's Vietnam,* 110; Mason, *Experience of Nationhood*; ABC Education, 'Fighting Conscription', 6 May 1990, accessed 15 January 2021, education.abc.net.au/home#!/media/1245268/fighting-conscription-1966.

of young men to fight there.[12] Environmental issues were raised in relation to the weapons used to prosecute the war, not only the defoliants dropped across farming lands but also the new weapons of warfare like napalm and the massive amounts of unexploded ordinances that remained to make farming dangerous for years after. Many small church fellowship groups, such as the St John's Anglican Fellowship I attended at Padstow, took up Page's questions and offered gathering places where young people could discuss the controversies of the war and conscription as well as environmental issues – often without the knowledge or consent of older congregants and ministers.[13]

Concern about the war was widespread among young people around Liverpool at the time, and was discussed widely among students at Liverpool Girls High, who supported their teachers when they struck on 8 May 1970 in the first Sydney Moratorium against the war.[14] At least some young people growing up in the area went on to university or teachers' college, despite the continuing economic difficulties faced by working-class families in funding tertiary education. Once there, they contributed to the anti-war activism on the early 1970s.[15] In one widely publicised example, on 14 February 1972, the draft resister Robert Wood was ordered to report for his national service medical examination at Bankstown District Hospital. He arrived accompanied by nine fellow members of the newly formed Draft Resisters Union, carrying a stuffed dummy of a soldier with a sign around its neck reading: 'I won't go'. Twenty-five other young local men, who all shared the same randomly selected birthday as Wood, had also been ordered to report to the hospital that day. One of them completed his medical but refused to be drafted. Bob Wood burnt his medical notice in front of the group of young men and the surrounding medical staff. The police were called, and Wood and his companions were thrown out and the hospital doors were locked. Although not arrested then, Wood was jailed later in the year for refusing to comply with the draft.[16] As will be seen in the following chapters, opposition to the war in Vietnam had a very direct impact on one of the campaigns against 'reclamation' along the river.

---

12   'Provocative Discussion', *Bankstown Torch*, 9 July 1969, 1.
13   Ray Jarrett, pers. comm.; my own personal observation, Padstow, 1960–70.
14   Dr Meredith Burgmann, a teacher at Liverpool in 1970, pers. comm., 1 Nov 2020.
15   From my own experience and that of others interviewed, Robert Haworth from Peakhurst.
16   'Mucking Up the Medicals', *Tribune*, 22 Feb 1972, 11; 'Robert Wood: A Man Committed to Peace', *Canberra Times*, 12 November 1987, 19; Mansell, 'Taking to the Streets'.

As suggested by Ron Page's work, as well as by the often-whispered conversations about Vietnam that I remember in the Padstow Anglican Fellowship, churches along the Georges River were subject to the wider tensions in social debates at this time, despite continuing to have a role as community gathering places. Some churches played valuable roles in circulating information about the environmental campaigns in this area, but others expressed opposition, alienating long-time parishioners.

Further platforms for agitation around environments were the progress associations. These were secular bodies, but their records were just as diverse and tension ridden as the churches. Progress associations could offer a basis for local racism, as when the PPRA complained about 'unsightly' Aboriginal settlements as well as other 'unauthorised' dwellings on Salt Pan Creek in the 1930s. At times they could call for reclamations, offering strong support for council action as they did for dumping in the upper reaches of Salt Pan Creek in 1941 and 1943. But because they reflected collective, secular expressions of local interests, at times they also demanded action on water quality, as the Padstow Progress Association did when it campaigned against river pollution in 1953.[17]

These progress associations reflected the political orientations of the population. Although the lower Georges River communities were gentrifying in areas like Como and Sylvania, they still – in general – contained significant numbers of working people and unionists. Areas like Peakhurst and Lime Kiln Bay were close to the old factories around Mortdale as well as the newly located ones on the upstream reaches and were also close to the railway workshops at Chullora. Many people remained in these areas who were active members of the Communist Party of Australia (CPA), like Mick Staples, a printer who lived at Lime Kiln Bay and had continued to be an activist even after he left his printing job to take up work at Fisher Library. He published his fictionalised life story, *Paddo*, in 1964.[18] Some people with a CPA background, like Frank Walker, discussed earlier, had moved to an Australian Labor Party affiliation, while there were others whose sympathies lay on the Liberal side of state politics. All of these networks, across left and right, were

---

17 Molloy, *A History of Padstow*, 243–44, citing Padstow Progress Association requests to Bankstown Municipal Council; Rosen, *Bankstown: A Sense of Identity*, 117, 148, citing Padstow Progress Association protests about pollution in Salt Pan Creek, 1953.
18 Staples, *Paddo*.

accessible to local residents through the progress associations, and each of the activists and parliamentarians introduced here and in earlier chapters will reappear as the local conflicts are traced in detail.

The rising pressures on iconic landscapes forced the elderly Myles Dunphy to take up the fight again to save the Colong Caves from mining. At the age of 78, he gave lengthy evidence to the federal Senate Select Committee on Water Pollution in August 1969 as he tried to defend the idea of the pristine Blue Mountains National Park.[19]

But there was a very different style of environmental defence emerging involving direct and often innovative confrontations with major corporations seen to be damaging the environment. The most dramatic example was the first green ban, arising from an unlikely alliance in 1971 between middle-class Hunters Hill matrons and the New South Wales Builders Labourers' Federation (BLF). The Hunters Hill group, calling themselves the Battlers of Kelly's Bush, were trying to stop building developer A. V. Jennings, which had the support of local government, from clearing 4.9 hectares of land (Kelly's Bush) to build 24 'luxury houses'. The battlers called on the BLF for support in mid 1971, and the union responded by refusing to work on the development project. They had used this tactic in their union work before, usually to protect their members' safety or conditions, but increasingly they had been called on to support inner-city residents as they attempted to stop the demolition of their longstanding homes as the city's building boom accelerated. The BLF had previously followed union practice by calling this denial of work on particular sites a 'black ban', but their deepening affiliation with the Aboriginal movement led them to invent a new term due to the implied racism in the term 'black ban'. So, the Kelly's Bush campaign became the world's first 'green ban'.[20]

---

19 Commonwealth of Australia, Senate Select Committee on Water Pollution, *Minutes of Evidence*, vol. 19, 4503–38.
20 Burgmann and Burgmann, *Green Bans, Red Union*, 8–9.

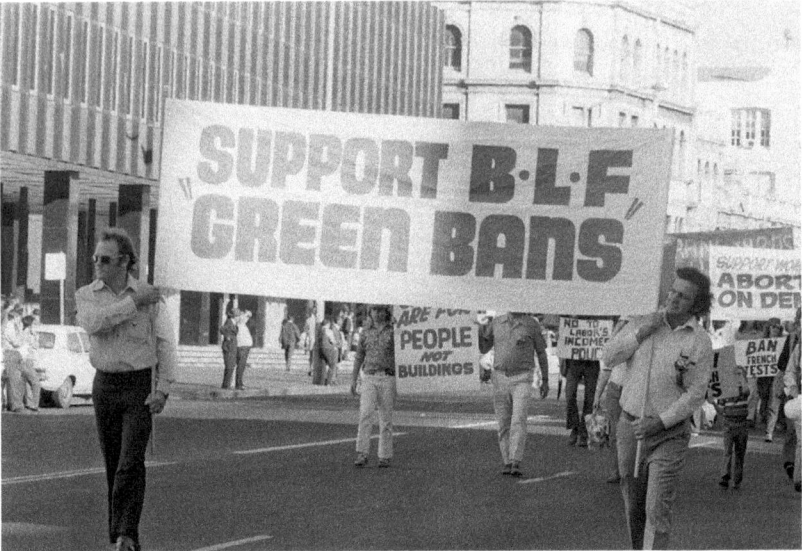

Figure 8.2: Green bans banner, carried by Builders Labourers' Federation activists, Bob Pringle (left) and Jack Mundey (right) in the 1973 May Day March.

The placard just behind is also carried by BLF members and reads: 'Parks are for People, Not Buildings'. Courtesy of Search Foundation, Creative Commons.

The green bans and related resident action of the early 1970s were notable because of the diversity of social and class interests. Alliances forged by the BLF with university students and other 'trendies' from 'enlightened middle-class' groups were aimed at stopping the 'power of the developers' dollar'. Jack Mundey, well-known communist and BLF spokesperson, argued that Kelly's Bush brought together people he called 'Upper Middle-Class Morning Tea Matrons' with those he identified as 'the other end of the social ladder'. Many BLF campaigns defended working-class and Aboriginal housing, and some actions that began as interventions in demolitions diversified into social issues, such as 'low cost social housing, tenants' rights, public transport and prison issues'.[21] Although the Kelly's Bush dispute did defend a remnant of endemic vegetation, most green bans were mounted to defend the built environment by intervening in urban planning and blunting the 'power of the developers' dollar'.

---

21 Ibid., 56–58, citing interviews with Jack Mundey, Joe Owens, Kevin Cook and others along with analyses by Mundey (1973), Wendy Bacon (1974) and Andrew Jakubowicz (1984).

Much of the rising attention in the early 1970s on urban issues focused on big battles with developers and transnational corporations in defence of vulnerable or low-income groups. This came to include the living environment, as the Kelly's Bush green ban demonstrated; however, the battles became more directly related to environmental disturbance with the founding in 1972 of the Total Environment Centre (TEC) by Milo Dunphy, elder son of Myles Dunphy, with Bob Walshe, a teacher from the Sutherland Shire, and others. The TEC rapidly became involved in highly publicised environmental justice conflicts involving major industrial polluters like the oil refineries in Botany Bay.[22] Although Milo Dunphy had grown up on the Georges River, and retained close friendships in the area, the TEC did not take an active role in any of the Georges River disputes. It did, however, become involved with the Cooks River after a major fish kill when the Sunbeam Corporation Plating factory at Campsie allowed potassium cyanide to be released into the river.[23] Jeff Nichols, through TEC, investigated environmental conditions on the river and his 1976 report focused on the importance of conserving river environments for informal recreation – like picnics – exactly as the residents had stressed in the Georges River National Park campaign.[24] In general, however, the TEC concentrated on challenging major corporations and big businesses that were damaging the environment.

There had been some state government attention to the growing popular disquiet about urban environmental amenity. Robert Askin had made promises to GROLPA (which he failed to honour) in the campaign for the 1965 election, and his subsequent government had enacted a number of laws in 1970 aimed at establishing standards for noise and pollution control and for waste disposal, building on the first steps already taken in 1961 with the *Clean Air Act*. Yet, as the Bankstown health inspector, H. C. Hunt, explained to the federal Senate Select Committee in 1969, the Clean Waters Bill before the New South Wales Parliament, which set maximum allowable discharge volumes for separate chemicals, was simply unworkable on rivers where industries utilised many different chemicals. The Bill would, Hunt maintained, only create a 'licence to

22   Meredith, *Myles and Milo*; Gowers, 'Dunphy, Myles Joseph (1891–1985)'; Orlovich, 'Dunphy, Milo Kanangra (1929–1996)'. Dexter Dunphy, the younger son of Myles and Margaret Dunphy, is Emeritus Professor in Business at the University of Technology Sydney and has contributed significantly to literature in business on sustainability.
23   '15 Tons of Fish Die in Poisoned Waters', *Canberra Times*, 29 December 1973, 3; 'Pollution "To Have Long Term Affect"', *Canberra Times*, 3 January 1974, 7; Tyrrell, *River Dreams*, 171–74.
24   Tyrrell, *River Dreams*, 188–93; Nicholls, *Cooks River Environmental Survey.*

pollute'. Nevertheless, based on its new legislation, the state proceeded to set up the State Pollution Control Commission, although it had no regulatory power until mid-1974. This was the body to which the residents campaigning for Georges River environments would appeal for support in the coming years.

Disputes multiplied in the early 1970s, with the Kelly's Bush campaign just one of a growing number of residents' groups in the inner city who were threatened by the galloping pace of development in Sydney. In 1971 a network developed between them known as the Coalition of Resident Action Groups (CRAG). Just two years later, in August 1973, it had over 80 groups affiliated to it. CRAG was dominated, however, by inner-city groups who were campaigning to stop demolitions of low-income and working-class housing. Among all members, those that CRAG identified as 'parks and conservation' groups were only a small minority and, according to *Tharunka*, they felt marginalised and out of place. Even then, this small minority were opposing large corporate developments that threatened long-established inner-urban parks like Centennial Park – itself established in 1888 by 'reclaiming' a swamp. There were, in 1973, no apparent links in CRAG with the south-western suburbs of the city and few calls to conserve native bushland, other than the Kelly's Bush campaign at Hunters Hill.[25]

Conflicts with big corporations and major developers over pollution and demolitions would today be readily recognised as 'environmental', whether the issues are about living environments like Kelly's Bush or built environments like derelict housing at The Rocks or Millers Point. Yet recognition of the issues *as* environmental, even the language used to identify environmental problems, was not a given but instead emerged over time, shaped by local and international processes. The central concerns of all of the campaigns in the following chapters exemplify this process of change, because they are about places that, in the 1960s and 1970s, the campaigners called 'mangrove swamps'.

Over these same decades, a new body of ideas was emerging about such places, which became known as 'wetlands', although the language in which they were named took a long time to evolve. The initiating event was the 1971 international intergovernmental agreement known as the *Ramsar*

---

25 Roddewig, *Green Bans*, 22–28; 'CRAG', *Tharunka*, 2 August 1973, 16, article reviewing CRAG membership and directions.

Convention on Wetlands of International Importance Especially as Waterfowl Habitat. The convention listed all the places it identified as 'wetlands', including inland marshes and estuarine or coastal swamps. Australia was one of the first signatories of the convention and soon after pursued international diplomacy possibilities by negotiating a treaty with Japan to protect the resting and feeding places needed by migrating birds. Yet the term 'wetlands' was unfamiliar in Australia, as was the Ramsar Convention's focus on birdlife.[26] Migrating birds were only one way to understand the ecology and behaviour of the places protected by the Ramsar Convention. Such places have many roles in relation to a wide variety of wildlife – aquatic, earthbound and avian. The Georges River campaigns traced over the following chapters offer insight into the diverse and changing ways that places later understood as 'wetlands' were identified and valued in the 1960s and 1970s, before that terminology and body of ideas became dominant. At the same time, the changes in language about the places that the Georges River residents were so concerned about suggests one reason these campaigns have not been recognised as part of the emerging environmental movement of the times.

While the spectacular conflicts over green bans or the TEC campaigns against oil refineries in Botany Bay are today readily recognised as 'environmental' or 'environmental justice' campaigns, the problems faced by Georges River campaigners were seldom over private development. They were much more frequently about the actions of local government in the context of waste disposal and recreational land management, as the following chapters discuss. The campaigners consistently argued that it was state and federal governments that should be bearing the financial, technical and policy responsibility, but it was invariably local governments at the frontline of these conflicts. Since the private developers who tended to be involved in inner-city conflicts were absent, the unions on whom the campaigners could call for support were also very different in membership and political affiliation, as the following chapters show.

The Georges River National Park Trust had initially involved both residents and officials from three local government councils: Bankstown and Hurstville on the northern side and Sutherland on the southern side. The interests of councils and local residents often seemed to diverge over

---

26   This recognition of the historical process of change in popular understanding of 'watery places' and in the language used to represent them is discussed extensively by O'Gorman, *Wetlands in a Dry Land.*

the life of the trust, as the local government bodies focused on shoring up votes and employee jobs, rather than on the interests of resident groups like the PPRA. The state government eventually preferred its own employees, like those in its National Parks and Wildlife Service (NPWS) and, as discussed earlier, in 1987 it ended all local resident or council involvement with park management.

Yet, by the late 1960s, even though clumsy, it was local government councils and their staff who were most directly grappling with the impacts of economic, social and environmental change. This was why these local councils became the frontline. In each of the environmental conflicts along the more industrialised and heavily populated northern side of the river, resident groups became pitted against councils who were supposed to be representing them: Bankstown, Hurstville and, on the lower reaches, Kogarah.

There were differences between the councils that showed the continuing effects of earlier conflicts over the national park, as the case of Little Salt Pan Creek demonstrates. Distrust of formal environmental management bodies had lingered after the marginalisation of local representatives on the Georges River National Park Trust and, most of all, after the dismissal by the state government of the Georges River lands *as* a national park in 1967. So, when the pace of 'reclamations' began to gather from 1968 onwards, there were ready audiences for dissatisfaction with councils and state government agencies like NPWS.

Bankstown appeared to have learnt some lessons from its earlier encounters as well as from the changing views of local residents about 'reclamations'. As we consider in the following chapters, the council at Hurstville – along with Kogarah with whom it shared similar concerns and policies – did not draw this lesson at all. These two councils seemed determined to escalate the old strategies of dredging, dumping and 'reclaiming' to make controlled and disciplined spaces. On the southern side, Sutherland Council had jurisdiction over the whole bank of the Georges River estuary, and it retained more local resident support. Unlike Hurstville and Kogarah, it contained some councillors who were sympathetic to the new ecological concerns but, as we shall see, Sutherland also faced very different issues to those on the northern shore.

9

View from the Heights: Little Salt Pan Creek

The first Georges River National Park had seen conflicts about mangroves. Some people, like George Jacobsen, wanted to keep them, but others, like Alf Stills, thought they needed to be chopped out to make way for parklands. For Alf and others in this early resident action group, mangroves did not count as 'bushland' or as 'river views'. In the early 1960s, another group of residents, those with 'exclusive waterfront blocks' on the southern shore between Como and Sylvania who formed the Georges River Oyster Lease Protest Association, had been very clear that oyster farms did not constitute 'natural' river views and they did not like mangroves much either. The oyster farmers, on the other hand, were pointing out by 1966 that mangroves slowed the flow of the river and protected their growing oysters. For kids who had grown up around the mangrove flats, like my brothers at Padstow and Alex Knight at Neverfail Bay, the smell of mangrove mud signalled freedom and adventure. For all of them, mangroves formed an essential component of a healthy river. So, it was not only George Jacobsen who was unhappy about the loss of mangroves as bushland.

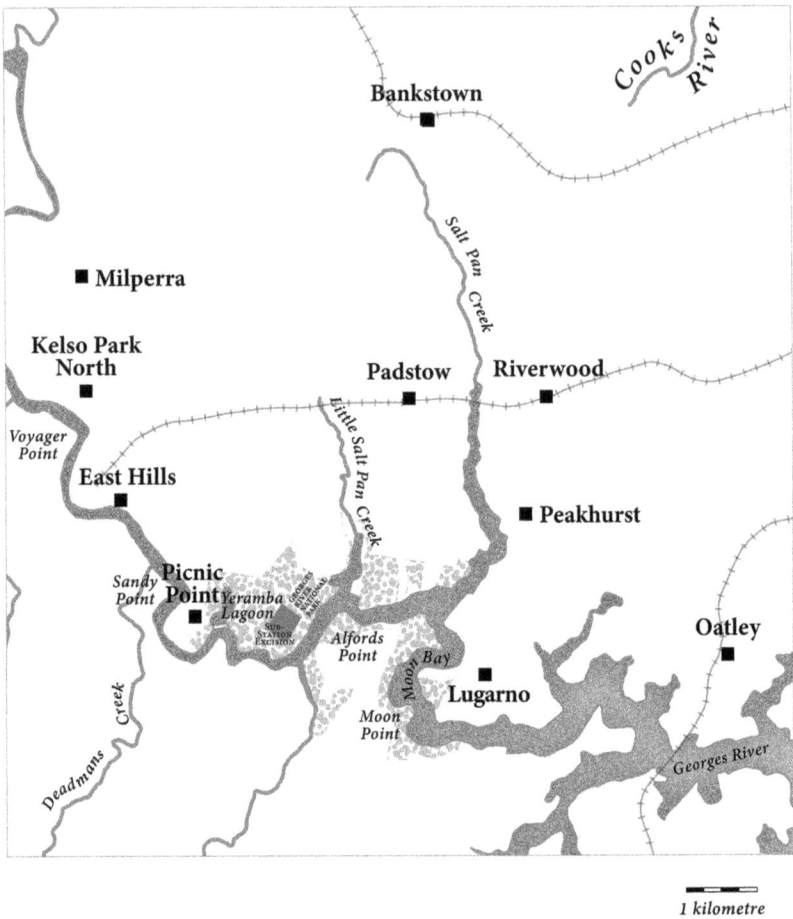

Map 9.1: Little Salt Pan Creek.

Cartography: Sharon Harrup.

Yet there were many people who, like Alf, saw that the mangroves were expanding. Andrew Molloy has trawled through memoirs and found many uneasy references to the loss of earlier, clearer banks because of mangrove expansion rather than from garbage dumping or reclamation. Such memories came not only from the recreational fishers using boats launched from the jetties along the waterways, but also from swimmers and picnickers. The expanding mangroves were making the water more difficult for them to access, which added to their unease about losing 'safe' spaces to higher density development.[1] One was Betty Goodger, who

---

1   'More Object to Town Plan', *Bankstown Torch*, 20 August 1969, 3.

wrote in the *Bankstown Historical Society Newsletter* in 1992 that 'people reminiscing about their childhoods around the turn of the century all commented on how clear the water was, and how few mangroves there were'.[2] Allan Smith, one of Andrew Molloy's interviewees, was another who remembered that the mangroves came to the banks at Padstow much later than his 1920s childhood.[3] Defence Department aerial photographs confirm the absence of mangroves even as late as 1949.[4]

Nevertheless, the greatest fear, which was held by the majority of the population, was about rising densities of housing – a fear fuelled by the County of Cumberland Plan and by the rapid increase in population in the Bankstown area, which had taken up so much of what had been earlier open space, whether market garden or 'wasteland', now subdivided and built on.[5] In June 1969, complying with Sydney-wide planning requirements, Bankstown Council announced its town plan, which endorsed the possibility of some areas moving from single block, freestanding homes to medium- or high-density housing. At first there were few objections but protests soon rose to a crescendo over the possibility of higher density development. As Mayor D. B. Carruthers recognised, many Bankstown residents feared that their town would become like the adjacent Canterbury Council area along the Cooks River, where many two-, three- or four-storey 'walk-up' blocks of flats had been built over the previous decades, as local owners of large house blocks had sold to developers.[6] The protests persisted and indeed escalated as high-rise and villa home developments began to appear. By late 1972, many more had been approved, leading to a *Bankstown Torch* editorial in December voicing widespread community fears about 'the rash of two-storey blocks of soulless units' that had occurred in Canterbury when 'high density [was] allowed to run riot'.[7] I remember this anxiety about rising densities and loss of open spaces to have been widely troubling and commonly expressed.

2   Goodger, 'History Notes'.

3   Molloy, *A History of Padstow*, 120, 242.

4   Haworth, 'Changes in Mangrove/Salt Marsh Distribution'. Australian Defence Force photographs taken in 1930 and 1949.

5   Spearritt, *Sydney's Century*, 116.

6   'Third of Population Will Live in Flats', *Bankstown Torch*, 20 August 1969, 3; 'More Object to Town Plan', *Bankstown Torch*, 20 August 1969, 3.

7   Editorial, *Bankstown Torch*, 27 December 1972, 2. This concurs with my memories of the discussion around my home in Padstow from 1969 in relation to the town plan.

The debates over the city plan were being reported on the same pages of the local paper as accounts of evidence being given at the hearings of the Senate Select Committee on Water Pollution that was taking place at the same time. So local readers could see the continued debates over rising population and higher density housing framed by accounts of the massive pollution of the Georges River by sewage and industrial pollution – with both processes leading to the loss of riverbank open spaces. Just one example was 20 August 1969, when the third page was divided evenly (apart from a photograph of footballers and a supermarket advertisement) between an account of rising objections to higher density housing and the evidence of Dr W. B. Malcolm, senior biologist with the Fisheries Branch, that:

> The majority of fish caught by both commercial and professional fishermen in NSW spent all or most of their lives in the estuaries … These fish depended on mangrove swamps, river mud flats and shallow areas with marine grasses both for food and shelter, while marshlands adjacent to rivers were rich in organic and insect life on which fish fed after flooding and high tides. Rapid development of the metropolitan area so far as homes and recreation areas are concerned had despoiled many of the mangrove swamps and marshlands over the years, and were depleting these important feeding grounds … Many swamp lands and river flats had been taken over as garbage dumps and playing fields, and waterfront home-owners had encroached onto the shallow areas with swimming pools and jetties.[8]

Long-term factory-working residents of the Bankstown area, like those, for example, in Ryan Road, were protesting most loudly about the possibilities of flats in their street, using the channels of the local newspaper to ventilate their anxieties and anger.[9]

But the area was changing rapidly as the population numbers suggested. The swimming pools closed by Hunt and Howard in 1962 had been community and council-built pools, while the jetties had usually been built with local people's voluntary labour. By the early 1970s, there were patches of the area that were gentrifying. As incomes rose, the presence of private motor vehicles increased and dependence on public transport was reduced, making housing land along the river's sandstone escarpments

---

8   'Exhaustive Pollution Tests Soon', *Bankstown Torch*, 20 August 1969, 3. See also page 1 ('River Test for Pollution') and editorial for continuing comment on both issues.
9   'Exhaustive Pollution Tests Soon', *Bankstown Torch*, 20 August 1969, 3.

more accessible and, with its water views over river and creeks, more desirable – and, therefore, more expensive. The residents of the newly settled (and named) Padstow Heights had been able to afford not only cars but also the larger blocks of land available in this recently subdivided and sold area. They were the ones who were to become the most effective campaigners to save Little Salt Pan Creek.

Bankstown Council, desperate to solve its escalating 'explosion' of garbage, decided in November 1972 to put a garbage tip on the upper stretches of Little Salt Pan Creek.[10] This creek did have mangroves along its water's edge in 1935 when a bushwalk along its waters was described, giving insight into how few houses were present and how little developed the area had been before the postwar population increase.[11] However, these mangroves were expanding and at least some early commentators saw no problem with getting rid of them. In December 1972, Sally Faulkner, a columnist for the *Bankstown Torch*, was enthusiastic about the council's plans to get rid of the mangroves, both in Little Salt Pan and at Kelso Reserve, because she believed the area needed more accessible open space, but she complained that there were already enough playing fields:

> Most people would agree that Bankstown is well endowed with sporting facilities and children's playgrounds, but when it comes to getting away from it all for a family picnic in a natural setting, the choice is limited.[12]

Faulkner wanted an artificial freshwater wetland on the model of Bankstown Council's work with the Georges River Trust, already completed at Yeramba and underway at Georges Hall. Her vision was for freshwater wetlands because these 'natural settings' would 'attract wildlife back into the area and provide a haven of quiet'.[13] Her argument, then, was that the mangroves and the salt water had damaged the environment and what was needed was for council work to 'reclaim' the area to freshwater and 'nature'.

---

10   Howard, interview, discussed in Goodall, Cadzow and Byrne, 'Mangroves, Garbage and Fishing'.
11   E. Caines Phillips, 'Where to Hike during the Week-End: Little Salt Pan', *Daily Telegraph*, 30 November 1935, 7.
12   '160 Acre Nature Reserve Planned', *Bankstown Torch*, 19 December 1972, 5.
13   Ibid.

Figure 9.1: Padstow Heights residents, Mrs J. Pethyridge and daughter, 1973, showing mangrove views.

Originally captioned: 'View of Little Salt Pan Creek from Seeland Place, Padstow Heights. Mrs. J. Pethybridge and her daughter Kylie Ann (9½ mths) and their pet dog Cleo enjoy the view from their home (No 21) Seeland Place Padstow Heights'. The photograph accompanied an article by Jon Powis entitled 'Ecology Action by the Text Book: How to Save Little Salt Pan Creek'. The mangroves are the low-lying vegetation in the central middle distance. Bankstown Council proposed to dig up the mangroves and replace them with a garbage dump, which would eventually be turned into playing fields. Courtesy of Nine Publishing.

A high-profile – and successful – protest movement soon emerged, however, in opposition to the council plan for the tip and reclamation. This campaign drew on the newest group of incoming residents. These were very different from the first arrivals in the 1950s when the population had expanded suddenly because the New South Wales Housing Commission had located its hostels and then housing developments in the area, bringing, as Col Jacobsen had put it, 'new people'. These 'new people' had been similar to the other source of postwar population expansion – working-class and lower middle-class, owner-builder families who had been living with parents and relations in townships like Bankstown in the 1940s and had finally been able to buy a small block of their own, close to the railway lines.

But the blocks closest to the creeks and rivers, like Padstow Heights overlooking Little Salt Pan, had not been taken up until long after the initial Housing Commission hostel residents and the owner-builders of the 1950s had moved in. Only in the mid-1960s did Padstow Heights, previously regarded as 'out the back' and isolated, become attractive. The growing ownership of cars meant that these incoming homeowners were no longer dependent on living close to railway stations.[14] For them, it was the view and the surrounding environment that was attractive. Their land purchases had included a distant view of the river, so the expanding mangroves allowed a pleasing, dense, green *bush* expanse over which to glimpse the water's edge. These new residents seldom had close encounters with the muddy, smelly, snake- and spider-inhabited wilderness that the boys on bikes were enjoying around the same time.[15]

Mr C. Austwick, spokesperson for the protesting residents, pointed to the valuable iconic role of mangroves as *bush* when he said in December 1972:

> Apart from residents' natural reluctance to have a garbage tip over their back fences, the group was also concerned that one of the few remaining areas of natural bushland should be destroyed. It is a marvellous place, an adventure ground for hundreds of children, and a haven for numerous wild animals and birds ... All this would disappear and in return we would have a garbage tip for years, and eventually, playing fields. No one could possibly think a flat playing field is an improvement on the glorious water views we now have.[16]

---

14   Molloy, *A History of Padstow*, 157–63 and 122, with photograph of undated page from the *Sun*, c. 1978, reporting local real estate agents identifying 'top streets' in the area as being in 'Padstow Hights [sic] developed only since the mid-sixties'.
15   Powis, 'Ecology Action'.
16   'Residents Set to Force Council into Court', *Bankstown Torch*, 27 December 1972, 1.

The residents of this Padstow Heights group were not acting alone. Kevin Howard, the health inspector at Bankstown Council who was troubled by the garbage dumping plans, was also contacting local media and politicians to alert them. Yet he did not remember being in touch with the Padstow Heights activist group nor was he aware of the East Hills and Picnic Point residents who had been so active in campaigning for the national park in the 1950s, despite sharing membership with George Jacobsen on the park trust in the 1960s.[17] The communication between, and the memory of, these local movements did not circulate for long.

The Little Salt Pan Creek campaign against the garbage tip was successful because it drew on the cultural capital of the recent, more affluent, wave of residents, whose efficiency was suggested by this headline in *Nation Review*: 'Ecology Action by the Text Book: How to Save Little Salt Pan Creek'. The campaign counted among its ranks executives with management training, four medical doctors, a pharmacist, a pathologist, accountants and a company secretary.[18] This was a very different employment and class profile than those who had been living in the areas close to the river in the 1940s and 1950s and certainly very different from those from East Hills involved in the 1950s campaign for a national park. This 1970s campaign to save Little Salt Pan Creek was organised with precision and efficiency, using the media to apply strong pressure to Bankstown Council, which capitulated within months. The continuing opposition from George Jacobsen and others over the years had made Bankstown Council sensitive to criticism about its environmental policies and this campaign added momentum to its later decisions to adopt more careful policies on conservation.

There had also, of course, been persistent voices within the senior staff of Bankstown Council itself. As has been discussed in previous chapters, Harold Hunt, the council's chief health surveyor, had made extensive and powerful submissions in 1969 on the extent of sewage and industrial pollution of the Georges River to the Senate Select Committee on Water Pollution. Hunt's response to state government plans for solid waste disposal made to council in 1968 had been just as scathing. He had argued, on the basis not only of his experience in Bankstown but also his research internationally, that the federal government needed to develop

17   Howard, interview, discussed in Goodall, Cadzow and Byrne, 'Mangroves, Garbage and Fishing'.
18   Powis, 'Ecology Action'.

a coordinated national plan for waste disposal so that local government bodies were not left to manage an insoluble problem with scattered facilities and few resources.

Kevin Howard, mentioned earlier, had supported Hunt, his senior officer, at the Select Committee hearings and had endorsed his attempts to mitigate the problems of uncontrolled waste dumping and toxic pollutant release into the river. Whereas Hunt had drawn on international studies and statistics, Howard drew on his formal training as a health inspector and his own long experience as a Georges River fisherman as well as the observations of other experienced fishers. He had put all these resources to good use in contacting media and passing on information in support of the Little Salt Pan campaign, including his refutation of CSIRO (Commonwealth Scientific and Industrial Research Organisation) researcher G. A. Mills who asserted that neither oysters nor the river itself carried industrial pollutants.[19] These experiences convinced Howard to take up further study and he enrolled in a diploma of environmental studies at Macquarie University in Sydney. Late in 1973 he wrote an investigative report on the state of the Georges River, presenting it as his final essay and then submitting it to Bankstown Council. His work extended the reports Hunt had submitted in the later 1960s, reviewing the issues facing the river in 1973. Howard's assessments offer valuable insights into the state of the river five years after Hunt's impassioned pleas for its defence to the Senate Select Committee. Building on his knowledge as a fisherman, Howard pointed out that all the recoverable sand for building had been dredged from the freshwater sections of the Georges River by the mid-1940s, after which sand mining had begun in the estuarine sections of the river between Liverpool and Padstow on Salt Pan Creek. He argued that the sand mining was 'reducing the area of gently sloping intertidal zones', leading to a reduction in 'the shallows' with an inevitable damaging effect on immature fish and crustaceans.[20]

Howard stressed mangrove loss in three of his five key conclusions. He pointed out that 'mangrove removal has been popular for the past 30 or 40 years' but that now the Fisheries Branch and at least some local government bodies had a better appreciation of the damage caused by doing so. In Howard's assessment, the greatest impact had been on the abundance of all fish and crustacean species. As he explained, there had

---

19 'Oysters' Future "Not So Bright"', *St George and Sutherland Shire Leader,* 14 March 1973, 29.
20 Howard, 'An Essay on Contemporary Change', 3.

been no systematic collection of figures, so his sources had to be the observations of experienced fishers. This led him to believe that numbers among all species had decreased significantly and he saw the removal of mangroves as habitat for immature fish and crustaceans as a critical factor in this decline.

His second point was that the loss of both mangroves and saltmarsh in reclamation projects had led to a severe reduction in the numbers of birds along the river, and his third point was that sewage pollution continued to be severe along the river. He estimated that 45 million litres of sewage was being released into the river from all sources each day in 1973. In his view, this release had led directly to the loss of a 1.2-kilometre (0.75-mile) stretch of mature mangrove trees at East Hills. While a fourth key point reiterated the health problems associated with sewage pollution, Howard's final key conclusion was that, in spite of all his earlier arguments about mangrove removal, there were some areas in which mangroves were expanding. He argued this was due to rising silt deposition into creek beds, leading to the expansion of mangrove stands into what had previously been deep water. His example was Salt Pan Creek, where the expansion of mangroves was confirmed in Defence Department aerial photography from 1930 onwards.[21] His report demonstrated that, even with determined advocates like Hunt and Howard on the council staff, action by one local government authority alone was not enough to save the river.[22]

---

21   Discussed in Haworth, 'Bush Tracks and Bush Blocks'; Goodall, Cadzow and Byrne, 'Mangroves, Garbage and Fishing'.
22   Howard, 'An Essay on Contemporary Change'.

10

Fishers, Boats and Dredges: Great Moon Bay

The dispute over Great Moon Bay had brought the issue of dredging into the foreground. And, in comparison with Bankstown Council later at Little Salt Pan, Hurstville Council pushed far harder to dredge the river and 'reclaim' low-lying land. While the issues of mangroves and saltmarsh were just one of the points of conflict in the dispute with Bankstown Council over Little Salt Pan Creek, this was not the case in the series of disputes with Hurstville and, later, with Kogarah Council, where mangroves became the centre of attention. The first of these disputes – the campaign, beginning in 1962, to stop the dredging of the Great Moon Bay – also made visible the wider ecology of mangroves, showing the threatened areas to be not only the visible saltmarsh and mangroves but also the underwater seagrass beds.

The Great Moon Bay conflict showed the divergence of the interests of the longer-established residents with the newer or more affluent residents. The longer-established residents who lived on the more industrialised upper estuary from Liverpool down to Peakhurst, were predominantly working class or lower income and, most importantly, they fished for food as well as for recreation. They might fish from the bank or from rowboats or small 'tinnies' with low-powered engines. At least some of those residents who lived on the downstream reaches, from Oatley, Como and Sylvania in newer blocks, tended to be more affluent and middle class, often professionals and usually more securely employed. The residents who had formed themselves into the Georges River Oyster Lease Protest Association had unashamedly advertised themselves as owning 'exclusive' waterfrontage blocks. They not only owned more expensive land but also more often owned the new technology of private cars and powerboats, which they raced along with water skiers.

'Reclamation' – the 'rescuing' of low-lying land to make it into 'real' dry land – was an old idea, but it could not happen on its own. The material to fill in the low-lying land had to come from somewhere. The Little Salt Pan Creek dispute was focused on the land that was to be 'reclaimed' or filled in. It was not uncommon for this infill to be formed by dumping garbage into the area to be 'reclaimed' and this was certainly the case in areas like Little Salt Pan.

Map 10.1: Lugarno and the Moon bays.
Cartography: Sharon Harrup.

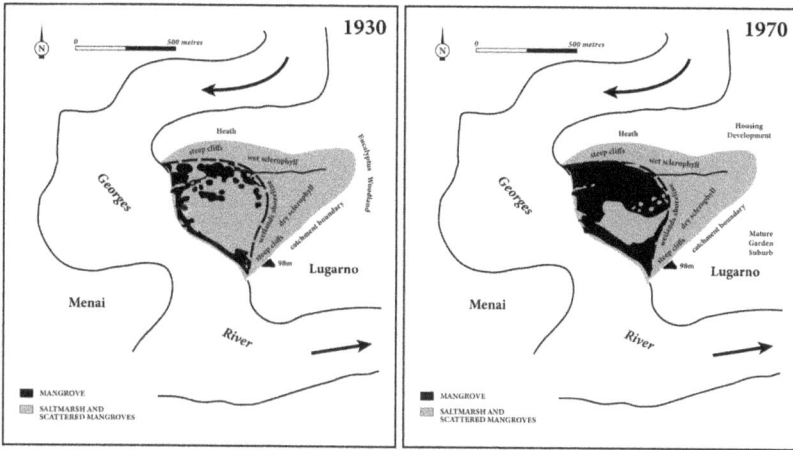

Map 10.2: Mangrove expansion at Half Moon Bay.
Maps redrawn for this volume with permission from Haworth (2003).
Cartography: Sharon Harrup.

The other way to gain landfill – and often the preferred way in the years before the garbage explosion – was to dredge the bed of the river. The geological shift that had depressed the Cumberland Plain relative to the Blue Mountains to the west and the Woronora Plateau to the east had diverted the Georges River from its original northward path to be eventually captured by a stream that channelled the waters eastward to what became Botany Bay. Extensive quantities of sediment were deposited where the highland river met the lowlands of the Cumberland Plain around Chipping Norton and Milperra. Dredging the bed of the middle of the estuary therefore offered excellent clean sand for building. The councils along the river held the rights to extract royalties from commercial dredging companies that tendered to dredge. The three councils in the Georges River National Park Trust – Sutherland on the southern shore and Bankstown and Hurstville on the north – passed this royalty fee over to the National Park Trust, which used it – with additional contributions from the councils – to fund the improvements they made to the national park like toilets, picnic areas and reclamations.

But dredging the edges of the river and dumping the silt onto surrounding land to 'reclaim' it brought acid sulphate soils to the surface. The contamination arose not only from whatever had leached down into the waters from the area's factories, like the Union Carbide battery makers on Salt Pan Creek, but also from the chemical interactions of the bacteria on aquatic vegetation. Seagrass and mangrove roots interacted with the saline waters of the creeks as sea levels rose and fell over millennia, forming and trapping toxic acidic chemicals in sediments that, when disturbed, released them, often with deadly effects on the environment.[1] Although this was not well understood in 1966, there were other problems with the dredging that quickly emerged.

Just like reclamations, dredging had not been considered a problematic issue in the period prior to World War II (WWII). But rising population and industrialisation after WWII seemed to threaten riverside access. This was what had led troubled residents like Alf and Eileen Stills (whose brothers were commercial fishermen on the Georges River) and George Jacobsen to campaign for the Georges River National Park in the 1950s and, even though the trust was dependent on dredging royalties, there were members of the campaign group who, as fishing people, found dredging the riverbed to be a problem as well.

The Georges River National Park Trust had focused most of its 'improvements' on the areas of the national park within the Bankstown Council span of the river, from East Hills to Picnic Point and, notably, the Yeramba Lake artificial wetland, created by sealing the inlet off from the main river and 'improving' it by allowing freshwater run-off to fill the inlet and turn it into what, the trust congratulated itself, was a far better and more 'natural' freshwater wetland. The next proposal was the dredging of the Moon bays – a series of bends in the river just south of the mouth of Salt Pan Creek, between Illawong on the west and Lugarno on the east. The river bends were named as two bays – Great Moon Bay and Little Moon Bay – and were separated on the Illawong side by Moon Point (see Map 10.1) The trust had, since 1962, nurtured a plan to use the dredged material to fill low-lying areas at Mickey's Point and Alfords Point to create further flat grassed picnic and recreation areas as part of the national park.[2]

One of the local government bodies on the trust, Hurstville Council, thought it was a particularly good idea, because it would also enable it to fill the large mangrove and saltmarsh area on the Lugarno side, which was not in the national park. Both Great Moon Bay and Little Moon Bay were shallow, with the sandy bed clearly visible in aerial photographs, and were opposite swampland called Half Moon Bay, a mangrove and saltmarsh complex on the western side of the Lugarno peninsula.

---

1   Haworth, Baker and Flood, 'Predicted and Observed Holocene Sea-Levels'; Haworth, Baker and Flood, 'A 6000-Year-Old Fossil Dugong'; Baker, Haworth and Flood, 'An Oscillating Holocene Sea-Level'.
2   Hurstville Council Minutes, 1 March 1962, items 264, 265, 266 and 304, Local Studies Archive, Hurstville Library, Georges River Council Libraries.

But, by 1967, another motive for Hurstville Council was apparent. As ownership of cars increased, more higher-cost subdivisions had been opened with river frontages, such as those at Padstow Heights overlooking Little Salt Pan Creek, which brought in higher rates to the council. Ownership of – or the aspirations to own – powerboats or ocean-going yachts was similarly increasing. The more affluent residents in the Hurstville area, from downstream bays like Oatley, were eager to increase their access to deeper quiet waters for mooring boats or to deeper channels with lower speed limits so their powerboats could take part in the new sport of water skiing. Both added to the motivations of Hurstville Council to dredge the Moon bays in order to deepen the channel, which lay on the western, or Illawong, side of the river, allowing greater access – and speed – for the powerboats owned by the residents downstream.

Figure 10.1: Speedboats on the Georges River.
The demand for dredging arose because of the pressure of rising numbers of powerboats on the lower Georges River. Photographer: Heather Goodall.

This raised the legal problem of the management of the waterways. The land beside the river – whether in public or private hands – was managed by local government and in the care of the state Department of Lands. Waterways, however, were technically under the control of the Maritime Services Board, particularly waters that were navigable and used by any types of shipping. Yet councils managed development on land all along the river, and they, as well as bodies like the National Park Trust, benefited from the profits from dredging royalties. As we have also seen, the New South Wales Department of Agriculture, through its Fisheries Branch, was the lessee for oyster leases. This legal complexity ensured that the National Park Trust and Hurstville Council needed the approval of the chief secretary to proceed with the dredging plan.

In December 1966 Sutherland Shire Council took the independent step of calling for an investigation into the conditions of the river. A member of the Georges River National Park Trust, Sutherland Shire was back under Labor Party control after a period of conservative dominance and had environmentally sympathetic councillors in key positions. One was Arthur Gietzelt, now shire president and a tenacious defender of the Royal National Park, although he was dismissive of the Georges River bushland. Kevin Skinner[3] was chair of the Sutherland Shire Parks and Playgrounds Committee, which had also demonstrated its support for the Royal National Park as well as increasing the number of playing fields in the shire. The shire asked the Fisheries Branch to conduct a survey into the Georges River waterways to inform the projects of the three trust councils regarding the effects of dredging in the Georges and Woronora rivers and at Port Hacking. In announcing the survey, Kevin Skinner took the extraordinary step of breaking ranks with the other two Georges River National Park Trust councils, Bankstown and Hurstville, who were at that same time eagerly proposing major reclamation projects:

> The Council has a responsibility in administering the waters of the Sutherland Shire … The survey would guide the Council in any future applications for waterfront development or reclamation.

> Because of conflicting views on dredging it was essential that a policy be formed.

> The survey is necessary for the development of the river.[4]

---

3   Cr Kevin Skinner (ALP) (councillor 1962–87), a plumber by trade, was, for many years, chairman of the Parks and Playgrounds Committee, during which time more than 60 ovals and recreation areas were developed.
4   'Survey Planned for Waterways', *St George and Sutherland Shire Leader* (hereafter *Leader*), 14 December 1966, 11.

Just like Kevin Howard, the Bankstown health inspector involved in the Little Salt Pan dispute, Skinner drew on the new principles of ecology as the Fisheries Branch biologists and others had been suggesting.

As the Sutherland Shire invitation demonstrated, the Fisheries Branch had become very active in outreach over the 1960s, carrying the new science of ecology to local resident groups. Skinner, Howard and local fishers were increasingly referring to emerging approaches that considered not individual species but, rather, the interactions between living creatures, including plants, insects and animals, in ways that facilitated both change and stability. This information was penetrating widely through the community in this period and it is as evident in Skinner's announcement in December 1966 as it was in Howard's memories of the period across the whole decade.[5] There was much complex information in this new input, but there was one strand in particular that offered a new way to represent mangroves, a new metaphor – as protective and nurturing spaces for young fish.

The Fisheries Branch had been established in 1962 within the New South Wales Chief Secretary's Department. Heading it was Don Francois, a Canadian who had come to Australia first in 1958 to undertake research then, after completing his doctorate, had returned to take up the role of senior Fisheries biologist in the newly established Fisheries Branch. Francois was not a 'nativist' in that he did not believe that only native species should be protected. His interest was instead in fishing people. Although he strongly encouraged research into native species and the restocking of rivers with natives, he also introduced Atlantic salmon, eventually used in Tasmania as a resource for sport fishing as well as table fish.[6] One of the Fisheries' senior biologists, W. B. Malcolm, who gave evidence before the Senate Select Committee, addressed many local groups as well as lead a major inquiry into the state of the Cooks and Georges rivers in 1969.[7] Even earlier, in the mid-1960s, Francois was encouraging his staff to give talks to local groups like the Oatley Flora and Fauna Society (OFF).

---

5   Howard, interview.
6   James Halliday, 'Quietly Flows the Don', *Australian*, 14 March 2011; Australian Society of Fish Biology, 'Don Francois', accessed 4 February 2021, www.asfb.org.au/don-francois.
7   'Exhaustive Pollution Tests Soon', continued 'River Test for Pollution', *Bankstown Torch*, 20 August 1969, 1, 3; Editorial, *Bankstown Torch*, 20 August 1969, 2. Fairley, *Being Green*, 31.

Figure 10.2: Dr Don Francois, first director of New South Wales Fisheries.

Don Francois was a fearless defender of aquatic habitats. He gave tireless support to Georges River fishing people, community activists and environmental campaigners. This photograph, taken in the mid-1970s, was one he liked, framed and gave to his daughters. Courtesy of Rachel Francois.

This Oatley group, introduced in the previous chapter, was composed of interested local people who focused on self-education about the native bush of the area. They invited expert speakers to their regular meetings, hearing from Francois, Malcolm and others.[8] Although their polite advocacy had achieved little by the later 1960s, their regular meetings had brought about fruitful contacts with experts and concerned citizens who were to play increasing roles in the disputes of the coming years.

Francois himself became personally involved in the dispute over the dredging of the Moons, explaining to the trust and to the chief secretary that the two Moon bays were important precisely because the shallow bed of the river grew extensive beds of Zostera seagrass. The Zostera offered crucial habitat for whiting, one of the preferred catches for fishers along the river, and it was this invaluable resource that was being put at risk.

Francois's role could not have been effective had there not been a large proportion of the population who enjoyed fishing, were therefore knowledgeable about the bed of the river and were interested in protecting fish habitats. Recreational fishing had been an important source of knowledge and motivation for Kevin Howard in his support for the government analyst, Ernest Ogg's recommendation to close the river to both swimming and fishing in 1962, for the Little Salt Pan Creek campaign and then in his decision to undertaken further tertiary study

---

8   See Fairley, *Being Green*, a history of OFF, published online by OFF.

in ecology.[9] Local fishing people were responsive to the information that Don Francois and W. B. Malcolm conveyed as they built up a case to protect the fish in the riverine environment in ways that were less apparent in relation to other creatures like birds in this area.

Migratory birds were the focus of the Ramsar agreement, discussed in the previous chapter, and birds were the focus of the Australian treaty with Japan soon after.[10] The extensive Kelso Swamp on the Georges River near Milperra is remembered to have hosted vivid birdlife up to the 1950s, and there was some input into river environment protection campaigns further downstream about birdlife from nature study schoolteachers. In Mortdale, for example, in the 1940s, Robert Haworth has remembered that Mortdale Boys Public won the 'hotly contested' Gould League bird whistling competition year after year:

> We went out with or without teachers to a promising bit of bush, and waited quietly for birds to appear and sing, the rarer the better – [these were] big tough boys who also played rugby league.[11]

Yet by the 1960s, when the Moon bays in the river and Half Moon Bay, the swamp on Lugarno, were all threatened, much habitat had already been lost as the population had grown and subdivision had expanded so rapidly.[12] Rather than birds, the sustained concern among Georges River residents further upstream about water quality was around fish and fishing, although hunting ducks and other birdlife had figured strongly in memories of growing up along the river, around Kelso Swamp and other swamplands, like Half Moon Bay. So the language of the campaign against the dredging of the Moon bays and the destruction of the Half Moon Bay swamp was around fish and aquatic life, not about birds.

Despite such concerns from local people and his own Fisheries Branch, Chief Secretary Eric Willis agreed early in 1967 to the application from the Georges River National Park Trust through Hurstville Council for the dredging of Great Moon Bay and the stretch of the river where Zostera was

---

9   Goodall, Cadzow and Byrne, 'Mangroves, Garbage and Fishing'.
10   Bino, Jenkins and Kingsford, 'Adaptive Management of Ramsar Wetlands'; Kingsford, 'Ecological Impacts of Dams', Kingsford, 'Conservation Management of Rivers'.
11   Robert Haworth, pers. comm., June 2020; Kass, *Educational Reform*, 170–74; Roberts and Tribe, *The Gould League*.
12   Molloy, *The History of Milperra*, 86. See Fairley, *Being Green*, for OFF talks by fisheries as well as by schoolteachers re birds. See single letter in the *Leader*, 25 September 1968, 42, regarding mangroves as habitat for birds. See Kass *Educational Reform* regarding nature study in schools and its significance in development of environmental awareness.

most vulnerable. The trust's confidence that this proposal was underway added to its shock when, in July, the premier announced that the Georges River parklands would be stripped of their national park status and be demoted to a 'state recreation park', later a 'regional park'. The trust was alarmed not only by the loss of status and the denigration of their community resource as unworthy of the status of 'the nation', but also by the loss of funds to undertake more work. Nevertheless, it was sure that the Moons dredging would go ahead, gloating to the local press about winning the 'long fight with the Fisheries Department'.[13] The trust had not counted, however, on the tenacity of Francois and the fishers of the Georges River.

Don Francois redoubled his efforts to persuade Eric Willis against dredging. Local fishing people were deeply concerned and Francois conveyed their angry protests as well.[14] This time Francois had more success. Although Willis was a senior minister in the conservative Askin government, he was also a thoughtful and serious environmentalist, having worked as a geographer before standing for parliament.[15] Over the next year, Willis considered carefully the arguments put to him by fishermen and the Fisheries Branch, supported by letters from local groups like OFF.[16] Then, in November 1968, Willis withdrew his consent for the dredging.

In announcing his decision, Willis explained that he had been persuaded by the Fisheries Branch that the Zostera beds were indeed important for fish and he instructed the trust and Francois to investigate alternative sources of landfill material.[17] Willis had not acted explicitly to protect the mangroves and saltmarsh, but had instead focused on the riverbed and the seagrasses – and the whiting and recreational fishers. Willis explained that he was responding to the science as well as to widespread community concerns about the swamp and the fishing.[18]

---

13 'Shock by Government: Bill Will Strip Park of Status', *Leader*, 4 January 1967, 13; 'Georges River Parkland Fights for Existence', *Leader*, 23 August 1967, 2; 'National Park Loses Status – and Finance', *Bankstown Torch*, 23 August 1967.
14 Denise Walsh, Georges River fishing family member, pers. comm., October 2019.
15 Elizabeth Willis (Eric Willis's daughter), interview. Eric held a double honours BA in history as well as geography.
16 'Oatley Park – Limekiln Bay', *OFF News,* January 1969, 3.
17 'Willis Opposes Dredging in Bay', *Leader*, 4 November 1968, 27.
18 'Oatley Park – Limekiln Bay', *OFF News,* January 1969, 3.

Figure 10.3: Aerial photograph of the Moon bays and Lugarno, 1 January 1970.

Illawong is on the Sutherland side of the river, lower left; the Moon bays and Half Moon Bay (mangroves and saltmarsh) are on the Lugarno peninsula, lower centre. This aerial photograph shows swamps also at Mickey's Point (centre left) and on both sides of where the road bridge was being constructed across Little Salt Pan Creek (upper left; see Chapter 4 for discussion of George Jacobsen's protest). Courtesy of Spatial Services, New South Wales Lands. Sheetname: Penrith, Film: 1908, Run R22, Frame 5093. Creative Commons.

In his letter to Hurstville Council, Willis stated:

> The sands in the bay were renowned as a popular area for whiting. Dredging would have an adverse influence on the natural food for fish and be highly detrimental to amateur fishing.[19]

---

19 'Willis Opposes Dredging in Bay', *Leader*, 4 November 1968, 27.

Hurstville Council aldermen were furious, setting up the conflict as one between people and the environment and demanding that Willis fund the additional costs:

> Ald A.A. Lawrance (ALP) said he did not think it was the concern of Hurstville Council to provide spawning grounds for fish. 'But we do have to provide parks for the municipality.' Ald Lawrance said he wondered what excuse would be used next to stop the dredging ... 'When the council had discussed previously a commercial venture involving dredging in the area, Mr Willis' department had not been concerned about the effect on fish. We would be quite prepared to fill from somewhere else if Mr Willis is prepared to make up the financial difference. If he is so interested in the spawning of fish, he won't mind paying out the money.'[20]

Figure 10.4: Recent aerial photograph, looking from Illawong in the lower foreground towards Botany Bay and the coast.

Salt Pan Creek is on the left, then Mickey's Point and Alfords Point, then the peninsula of Lugarno. The protected shallow riverbed of both Great Moon Bay and Little Moon Bay are clearly visible, as is Half Moon Bay, the mangrove and saltmarsh area on the western point of Lugarno peninsula. The bridge over the river at Alfords Point (on the A6) is on the left of the photograph, the Como rail bridge is in the middle distance and then, going downstream, Tom Ugly's Bridge (on the A1) and finally Tarren Point Bridge cross the river before it becomes Botany Bay just before Towra Point. Courtesy of AirviewOnline Pty Ltd.

---

20   Ibid.

11

Politics, Picnics and Playing Fields: Lime Kiln Bay

The campaigns around the bays along the Georges River from Lime Kiln Bay to Gungah Bay in Oatley West were different from the fishing community orientation of the Great Moon Bay dispute. The Lime Kiln Bay resident campaigners did call on expert advice in their conflict with Hurstville Council, just like others. Overall, however, they used two main strategies. First, they undertook energetic outreach through word of mouth and community groups of all sorts, including church groups, to build up persuasive demonstrations of community support with which to force Hurstville Council to concede. Second, they mobilised political networks very early by calling on state and federal Australian Labor Party (ALP) politicians and later by intervening in local government elections.

The campaigners were people from many different occupations, including teachers, but much of their cohesion arose from the wide support for the secular local West Oatley Progress Association and a background of working-class solidarity exemplified by the working and community activist life of Mick Staples, even though he had passed away before the main campaign began. Just as important as Mick, however, was his wife, Ruth, from the Haworth family. Ruth had grown up in Seaforth Avenue, which, in her childhood in the 1930s, was little more than a dirt track. But it had a view of the Dairy Creek, which ran through swampland before reaching Lime Kiln Bay. When Ruth married Mick, they bought a house on Dame Mary Gilmore Road, just 500 metres further downstream and closer to Lime Kiln Bay. Between Ruth's two homes – and even closer to the creek and swamp – Don McMinn lived most of his life. All three of them knew each other well – and they knew that waterway, its plants and its wildlife, just as well as they knew each other.

Don talked about it in 2002 to a neighbour, David Waterhouse, remembering that there had been few mangroves on Lime Kiln Bay swampland at all until the end of World War II, when he believed that clearing for subdivisions upstream had increased the siltation and allowed the mangroves to expand. Don recalled many animals and plants along the river, and spoke particularly about the birds, which he knew from the swamp and creek as well as his family aviary. Waterhouse recorded Don telling him that:

> Wild ducks, ibis and spoonbills did not occur then as now, but Red-eyed Tree Frogs bred after rain and Stubble Quail called from the grass and could be heard on still evenings. Yellow-tufted and New Holland Honeyeaters nested in the shrubs. Peewees by the hundred flocked to roost. Whipbirds, Double-barred Finches and Rufous Whistlers were common and Wood-swallows and Jacky Winters nested each year in the few tall trees. None of these birds occur locally today.[1]

The campaigners who tried to save Dairy Creek and the bushland around it were people like Mick and Ruth and Don, as well as their newer neighbours, like Dave and Tricia Koffel. Eventually, when their petitions and meetings failed to move the council, the activists took up campaigning in the local government elections in 1974. Their motivations, exemplified by those of Ruth Staples, stressed the value of natural bushland, including the mangroves, to allow informal 'passive' recreation rather than the intrusive competitive discipline of organised sports. Yet there was interest too, as Dave Koffel's memories show, in the ecological networks of the area, and widespread commitment to protecting local people's access to this rich local resource. But we can start the story from earlier on.

Lime Kiln Bay

Lime Kiln Bay lies to the east of Salt Pan Creek, with three tributaries running into it. On the western side, Boggywell Creek had had riverbed sand and mud dumped on it several times in the 1930s to 'reclaim' it as

---

1   Waterhouse, 'Lime Kiln Bay', 1.

Gannons Park. There had been a further 1930s plan to utilise relief workers to fill in more of the remaining reaches, over the central one of which a golf course had been partially built while Dairy Creek continued to flow in from the east. But such plans had been overtaken by war and had not been considered until, in 1964, residents began to hear that council hoped to reactivate the proposed tip in the west (north) arm. A vocal opponent of such plans had been the West Oatley Progress Association – in which Mick Staples and Don McMinn were involved.

Mick Staples was a printer and an outspoken unionist who took a strongly activist role in community protest over damage to the river. As technological change had reorganised the printing trade, Staples had taken work at Fisher Library but had also begun writing. He published *Paddo* in 1964.[2] His long commitment to the local environment had many repercussions, even though he died suddenly in 1970. He had become close friends with Don McMinn, who knew the river and its wildlife so well.[3] McMinn recalled that the Progress Association had been active in pushing for the damage to the river to be addressed, remembering:

> My neighbour, Mick Staples, agreed that the place was going to blazes and more needed to be done. He had heard of the conservation meeting at Rafe and Moyia Kowron's place and he suggested we go along. We were in anything but a bath in those days! The feeling was that we would do anything to save Oatley.[4]

Staples's nephew, Robert Haworth, has recalled that, in the 1940s:

> The wetlands offered the natural 'adventure playground' that real bush and swamp give, or even exotic weeds like lantana, as opposed to the truck tyre 'adventure playgrounds' that some councils spend a fortune on today. The big attraction of the Lime Kiln Bay swamp for kids over generations was not just the mangroves, but the huge reed swamps of canegrass, looking like the scenery in the 'African Queen' adventure movie of the 1950s.[5]

---

2   Using his given name, Arthur Staples, published by Ure Smith.
3   David Waterhouse interviewed Don in 2002, and reported Don's rich environmental memories in Waterhouse, 'Lime Kiln Bay', 1.
4   Fairley, *Being Green*, Ch. 2.
5   Robert Haworth, pers. comm., June 2020. Lantana is an exotic and invasive plant, understood as a weed. Swamp canegrass, *Eragrostis australasica*, is a native, saline-tolerant tussock grass.

Council applied to the state government for permission to reclaim the two remaining upper reaches of Lime Kiln Bay in February 1967, proposing to build a causeway to cut across from Oatley Park to Lorraine Street, Peakhurst, cutting off both the north and easterly arms of the bay so they could be 'reclaimed' by rooting out the existing mangroves, swamp and bush, levelling it and filling the space with rubbish.[6] This was to take some years of active dumping but eventually would extend the existing golf course and allow for the building of a new playing field.

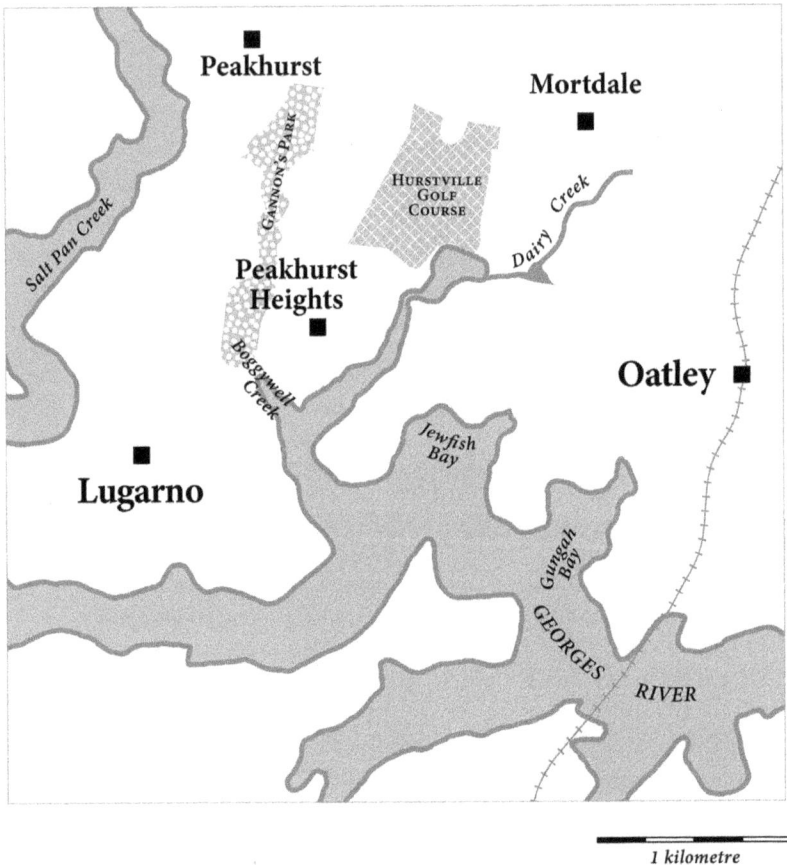

Map 11.1: Lime Kiln Bay and neighbouring waterways.

Cartography: Sharon Harrup.

6   For the impact of such levelling, see Figures 7.2 and 7.4, this volume.

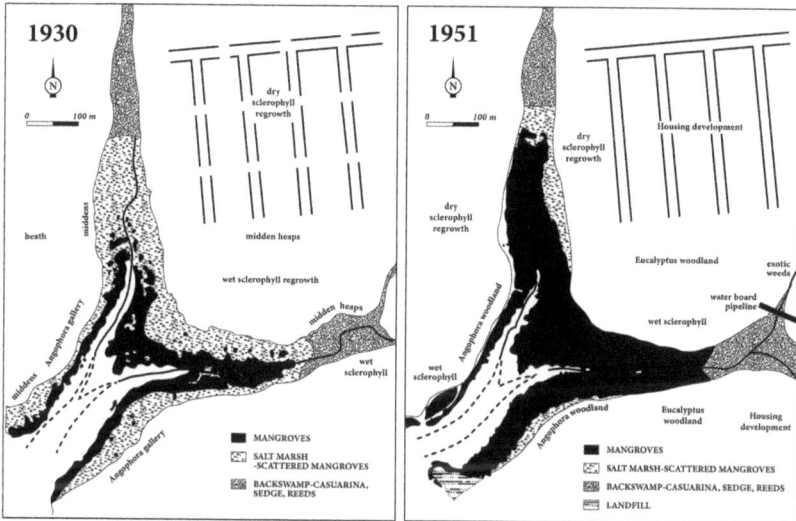

Map 11.2: Mangrove expansion at Lime Kiln Bay.

These drawings were derived from Defence Force aerial photographs taken in 1930 and 1951, drawn initially by geographer Robert Haworth, for his 2003 paper 'Changes in Mangrove/Salt Marsh Distribution'. As Haworth showed, the aerial photos confirm Don McMinn's memories that mangrove expansion had occurred after 1930. Maps redrawn for this volume with permission by Sharon Harrup, cartographer.

The Oatley Flora and Fauna Society (OFF) had been formed further downstream as a self-education body, but a number of people living around Lime Kiln Bay had become members by the mid-1960s. Rumours had begun to circulate by early 1968 that Hurstville Council was planning to undertake 'reclamation' by dumping rubbish for landfill. Some members of OFF wrote to the local press in September 1968 expressing fears that this would lead to a loss of 'mangrove swamp at Lime Kiln Bay', which was habitat for native fauna and provided an educational resource.[7] These concerned local residents wrote as well to the Department of Education and the chief secretary to propose using the site as a special study area for schools and for the conservation of fish stock in the Georges River.[8] By December 1968, barely a month after his earlier intervention over Great Moon Bay, Chief Secretary Eric Willis acted again, writing to inform OFF that he would not be approving the reclamation application because:

---

7 See letter to *St George and Sutherland Shire Leader* (hereafter *Leader*), 25 September 1968, 2.
8 'Oatley Park', *OFF News*, October 1968, 2.

> [As] the area is a nursery for fish, disruption of the mangroves
> would accelerate siltation which would affect the tidal storage of
> the river, and increased turbidity would endanger the adjacent
> oyster leases.[9]

OFF agreed that it was important to preserve the saline swamp in its
natural state as a feeding ground for birds and fish and as study area
for school children, and so it invited Allen Strom to become involved.
A former teacher, Strom was a bushwalker and environmental activist who
had grown up around Belmore and spent much of his adolescence in Mill
Creek, a tributary of the Georges River running in from the south, nearly
opposite Salt Pan Creek. From as early as 1958, Strom had been speaking
at OFF meetings.[10] Previously an officer in the National Parks and Wildlife
Service, he had recently become the environmental education officer to
the Department of Education. Strom was a lifelong advocate of 'citizen-
based nature conservation movements' and he strongly supported local
'citizen fighters for conservation' like the members of OFF. He advised
them to stress to the council that mangroves were crucially important
to the river's ecology.[11] Then, through the Department of Education,
Strom wrote to Hurstville Council requesting that it keep Lime Kiln Bay
as a 'special study area for schools', but the council rejected the request
in March 1969.[12] Nevertheless, OFF continued to ask questions and
referred the matter to Senator Tony Mulvihill, to be followed up in the
Senate Select Committee on Water Pollution in which he was taking
a vocal role.[13]

By July 1969, a petition had been organised by one of the concerned local
residents, Arnold Bryden, to protest against:

> The reclamation of the Lime Kiln Bay swamp area in Oatley West
> with the dumping of rubbish and filling. We understand from
> information supplied by the NSW Department of Fisheries that
> this area supplies food and protection to a very large number of
> fish during part of their life cycle. The loss of this habitat will only
> result in a considerable decrease in the fish population. Also that

---

9 'Oatley Park – Limekiln Bay', *OFF News,* January 1969, 3.
10 Fairley, *Being Green*; Fox, *Chief Guardian*, Ch. 2.
11 Fox, *Chief Guardian*, Ch. 2.
12 'Oatley Park', *OFF News*, April 1969, 4.
13 Ibid.; Fox, *Chief Guardian*, Ch. 11.

the swamp helps to prevent silting of the Georges River. A large number of native birds make use of the area and it provides a study area for local schools.[14]

Council agreed to a meeting with Mrs Ida Carder (then secretary of OFF) and officers of New South Wales Fisheries and Health departments. The compromise apparently reached was that council would reduce the original area it had planned to fill to only the upper part of the north (western) arm of the bay. Fisheries had imposed stringent conditions on the project, approving filling only to the high-water mark even on that arm, and eventually OFF had agreed – unhappily – to the compromise.[15] There the matter rested uneasily. The council began filling the upper reaches of the north arm, but the eastern arm, Dairy Creek, appeared to be untouched.

Then, unexpectedly, in later 1973, Hurstville Council reactivated its intention to dump rubbish in the eastern arm of the bay and moved swiftly to begin work. In October, Lewis Staples (Mick Staples's son) discovered survey pegs staked out across the upper bay. Mick had already passed away, but his commitment to community activism was shared by his family, in particular, by his widow, Ruth, who had grown up loving the area and valuing the possibilities the bush offered for picnics and social gatherings in natural settings.

It was extremely rare for women to take public roles in these Georges River campaigns. At Hunters Hill, the 'Battlers for Kelly's Bush' who approached the Builders Labourers' Federation (BLF) were all women, but on the Georges River this was not the case. This was not because women were not involved. From the earliest campaign in the 1950s for the national park, women took many supporting roles. Minnie Jacobsen, Eileen Stills, Esme Clisby and Eileen Birch, along with many other women, all took part in the fundraising, the networking and the meetings. Yet none of them ever spoke in public to represent it.[16] Again, downstream

---

14 Content of petition and sketch of proposed reclamation held by David Koffel, secretary, in Lime Kiln Bay Preservation Committee Archive, David Koffel Collection (hereafter LKBPC Archive), and partly reproduced in Fairley, *Being Green*. Fairley notes that Arnold Bryden organised this 1969 petition. Koffel remembered that it was Phyl and Arnold Bryden, with their deep knowledge of the local environment, who were crucial to his rapid education in ecology when he became involved in the next wave of activism to save Lime Kiln Bay in 1973. Mick Curlisa, then mayor of Hurstville Council, had been source of information for sketch.

15 David Koffel notes, 2005, LKBPC Archive; Fairley, *Being Green*.

16 Alf and Eileen Stills and Carol Jacobsen, interview; PPRA, interview; Carol, Colin and Kevin Jacobsen, interview, 12 July 2006.

in the campaigning to save Poulton Creek and surrounding bush, women were important in the initiation of activities as well as in building and maintaining connections between disparate participants.[17] Yet it was only in this Lime Kiln Bay campaign that a woman became visible. Ruth's decision to become a public spokesperson demonstrates the level of her concern but also suggests her courage and conviction.

Figure 11.1: Ruth Staples at Thredbo, 1966.
Photograph by Mick Staples, Ruth's husband, while on a family holiday. Courtesy of the Haworth family collection.

17 See Chapter 12, this volume.

Ruth and her teenage son, Lewis, raised this sudden council activity with their new neighbours, Dave and Tricia Koffel, both schoolteachers, who had recently moved from Bankstown. David, a secondary teacher, was an active member of the ALP.[18] At university and teachers' college, Dave had taken part in the opposition to the Vietnam War, meeting Bill White, the unassuming primary teacher who, in 1966, had become Australia's first conscientious objector (see Chapter 8). Since moving to Lime Kiln Bay, Dave had taught at Hurstville High School, where Lewis and other young local people studied. While they all objected to the threat of further rubbish on their doorstep, both the Staples and Koffel families valued the bushland they lived near and were angered that it was going to be eroded even further. Together they formed a new organisation, the Lime Kiln Bay Preservation Committee (LKBPC), with Dave as secretary, and began to collect supporters. They called on the State Pollution Control Commission for support – with little response – and went to the press for coverage, with both Lewis Staples and his sister Caroline speaking to television reporters.[19] By 9 January 1974, the LKBPC had Frank Walker and Pat Rogan inspecting the 'filthy mess' of the river and, barely a month later, on 6 February, the Opposition leader Neville Wran had announced that the pollution of the Georges River would set the Labor Party agenda for the next New South Wales election.[20]

The council's reaction to them was vitriolic. Dave has recalled that key councillors believed that anyone who was progressive must be a communist and so they had no hesitation in declaring to the local press 'that we were communists defending a mosquito-ridden swamp'. Dave admitted: 'It's very nasty when you read that sort of stuff in the papers! But at no stage did I anticipate how personally unpleasant it would become'. He reflected ruefully about the small group of campaigners who 'began this tilt at a windmill'.[21]

And yet, despite their small numbers, they found rapid support among fellow residents. Dave learnt much from Phyl and Arnold Bryden, who insisted that commitment was not enough without knowledge of the natural environment being defended. The Brydens were both interested in birdlife, just like Mick Staples's old friend, Don McMinn, but Dave

18   Mitchell, *Teachers, Education, and Politics*.
19   Staples, interview, 27 May 2005. No archival TV footage has been located.
20   'River's a "Filthy Mess"', *St George Pictorial*, 9 January, 1974, 1; 'River Vote Angle' and 'River Sets Labor's Strategy: Pollution is a Vote Clincher', *St George Pictorial*, 6 February 1974, 1, 3.
21   Koffel, interview.

does not recall that interest in birds to have dominated over concern for other parts of the environment. The Brydens talked to Dave about the important role of mangroves in river ecology and gave him an armful of reading about estuarine environments.

The mangroves were the most identified form of vegetation in the LKBPC documents and press coverage of the debates, the terms 'mangroves' and 'mangrove swamp' being used to refer to the whole wetland complex – the mangrove species and the saltmarsh, all regularly inundated and waterlogged. In its very first press release in December 1973, for example, the committee referred in general terms to the vegetation and fauna that would be destroyed by a tip but referred by name only to mangroves.[22] The committee cited the recent Australian Conservation Foundation (ACF) statement that mangroves were of 'national importance' because of their high productivity and as key elements in the long-term maintenance of the coastal environment. The LKBPC built on this ACF statement to argue: 'We just cannot go on forever tipping into our rivers and estuaries. No mangrove area is safe anymore'.[23] In its third press release it stated:

> Lime Kiln Bay Preservation Committee has attacked the plan [for the tip] which would mean the destruction of hundreds of square yards of mangroves, and the destruction of natural bushland. Natural bushland would be destroyed at a time when such areas are rapidly disappearing from Sydney.[24]

This pattern was repeated throughout all the LKBPC's letters and press releases for 1974, with mangroves being the only vegetation specified among the more generalised references to 'bushland' and 'natural vegetation'. Their letters often referred to the support they had received from state and federal parliamentarians, like the ALP member for Barton and former teacher, Len Reynolds.[25] The people actually involved in these campaigns, however, were local residents in the Lime Kiln Bay and the nearby Oatley West areas. Most of the Lime Kiln Bay activists and supporters were not involved with OFF or other conservation groups and were probably more diverse than OFF papers suggest. Some in the Lime Kiln Bay organisation were tradespeople, union activists and housewives while others were teachers. In this area, the Progress Association was seen

---

22   LKBPC to HMC, 10 January 1974, Press Release 2, 14 January 1974, LKBPC Archive.
23   LKBPC, Press Release 1, December 1973, LKBPC Archive.
24   LKBPC Press Release 3, undated, LKBPC Archive.
25   LKBPC Press Release 4, undated, LKBPC Archive.

as an activist and radical body. Ruth Staples was retraining as a teacher, but the area continued in 1974 to be home to a significant proportion of workers. Ruth's father had been a waterside worker and a member of the Communist Party of Australia. Many other men around the Bankstown and Peakhurst area were railway workers, just as Senator Tony Mulvihill had been, employed at the Chullora railway workshops – and with a corresponding orientation to working-class politics. Dave Koffel was a university-trained secondary teacher but had grown up in Bankstown where his mother told him about her childhood in Broken Hill as the daughter of a miner and strong union activist. Dave himself was an active ALP member and was able to draw in continuing support from local ALP state and federal representatives throughout this campaign.

Ruth's and Dave's motives for involvement suggest the range of concerns in suburban environmental activism. In remembering the main issues, neither activist raised sewage or industrial pollution, but the LKBPC most definitely saw this as a problem. It had been of concern in the Lime Kiln Bay dispute but the LKBPC also took a stand on the Poulton Park conflict in relation to Oatley Bay, where it argued strongly that Hurstville and Kogarah councils' plans would exacerbate the problems of sewage flow into the bay by obstructing tidal flows, thus limiting the capacity of the estuary to clean itself.[26] But, as Ruth and Dave recorded in their interviews, it was the issue of garbage and the impact its disposal would have on the destruction of swamps and natural bush that primarily concerned them both. They were each certainly worried about the aesthetic and health implications of a rubbish tip so close to their homes on the edge of the Creek Reserve, which would make this a simple 'NIMBY' (not in my backyard) issue, but their memories of their motives for involvement went much further.

For the rest of her life, although Ruth remained deeply interested in the vegetation and ecology of the creek, she was just as concerned that opportunities for informal social interactions – picnics and leisure time – spent in natural surroundings would be lost if the bush was converted to playing fields or golf course fairways.[27] Whatever the touted benefits of competitive sports, Ruth did not believe they offered either relaxation or restoration; nor did they provide opportunities for socialising with friends or relations, which she saw as central to community life. She was deeply

---

26   LKBPC to town clerk, Hurstville, 10 August 1974, LKBPC Archive.
27   Ruth passed away in 2020.

suspicious of the coercive nature of organised sports – suspicious precisely about the discipline that authorities hoped would be beneficially imposed on working-class youth.

In his interviews, Dave focused instead on the intricacies of creek ecology. He had embraced the biological knowledge he gained from Phyl and Arnold Bryden and had begun exploring the interdependencies between species that ecological science opened for him. As a higher degree student in later years, he became an avid birdwatcher, a pursuit that now leads him around the world watching, identifying and writing about birds.[28]

While these were individual motivations, they reflect the themes presented by many activists in the area. Women were also prominent in the advocacy of informal social activities on the Cooks River, as Tyrrell has noted, suggesting that such gatherings may have been particularly important for women, indicating a gendered relationship to the riverbanks.[29] The LKBPC reflected all of these motives in its press statements and letters to council, as did the OFF newsletters of the time. Significantly, throughout their correspondence, the LKBPC used quotation marks to enclose the terms 'reclamation' and 'reclaim', pointing to their argument that this was not a legitimate concept. Rather, they argued that local and state governments should be acting to *conserve* all forms of natural vegetation, not artificially seeking to 'restore' to dry land something that had always been an area of interaction between land and water. This would allow, the campaigners argued, a more varied experience of recreation and learning for children and young people, rather than the uniformity and discipline of competitive sports. OFF echoed this view, which was the one Ruth Staples has remembered as one of her driving motivations. OFF argued:

> Council proposes to use the final filled area in this case as a 'much needed recreation area.' No-one would deny that recreation areas are a must in any large centre of population. But must all recreation be formalised? City children today have very little opportunity to experience that affinity with natural things that is everyone's birthright and as the city grows, this opportunity shrinks … It would be cheaper and more rewarding to care for the little natural bush we have left than to try to create a future substitute.[30]

---

28 The details of remembered motives are drawn from the interviews recorded with each: with Ruth on 27 May and 27 October 2005, and with David on 16 October 2019.
29 In the 1950s, Coleen Mary Webster, secretary of the Cooks River Valley Association, spoke up against plans for soccer stadiums for men in favour of quieter, 'passive' recreation places for families and women. Women were also notable in the campaigning against the development of Nanny Goat Hill near Wolli Creek and the extension of the airport at Botany Bay. Tyrrell, *River Dreams*, 163–64.
30 Editorial, *OFF News*, August 1974, 1–2, LKBPC Archive.

It is notable, however, that of the many complex and often competitive interrelationships that ecology revealed in saline estuaries, it was the most anthropomorphic qualities of mangroves that were stressed. Mangroves were presented as nurturing the immature stages of species like fish, prawns and crabs as well as protecting saltmarsh and open spaces against increased siltation. From the wide range of ecological advice, it was this maternal role – as protective nurturers – that activists chose to present most commonly in their campaigns, as it was the characterisation most likely to attract public empathy and support. This is analogous to the choices of charismatic species (e.g. koalas, dolphins, whales and penguins) as emblems in environmental campaigns because such animals evoke emotional responses in human audiences, fostering approval for protective measures that affect a far wider ecosystem than the focal species. This selective approach, taking the most sympathetic from a far wider range of attributes, can be seen as an attempt to counter the long-established, deep-seated prejudices against mangroves that continued to be used to support reclamation.

LIME Kiln Bay Preservation Committee officials, Ruth Staples, David Koffel and Tricia Koffel, study the petition before handing it in at Hurstville Council offices.

Figure 11.2: Lime Kiln Bay Preservation Committee founding activists Ruth Staples and Dave and Tricia Koffel.

St George Pictorial, 8 May 1974. Courtesy of Dave Koffel, LKBPC Archive.

Beyond their fears and interests, as well as their media strategies, the LKBPC, early in 1974, proposed alternatives to Hurstville Council, again taking their campaign beyond any NIMBY desire simply to move the problem somewhere else. They, like the OFF activists in the 1969 negotiations, recognised the difficulties councils were facing with the escalating volumes of solid waste being collected from homes and industries. From its first letter to Hurstville Council in December 1973, LKBPC called on the council to increase processing of the garbage it collected, not only through further technology but also, as a long-term solution, to initiate recycling – the separation and reprocessing of materials within the collected waste – no matter how expensive it might appear at first.[31] Recycling was not an accepted practice in Australia at that time[32] but the Lime Kiln Bay group persisted in spreading the idea both locally and more broadly among environmental activists.

Further, although sewage pollution was not their priority campaign focus, the group developed a plan for ongoing future management of the local sullage flows into these suburban waterways. First, from their very earliest meetings, they proposed that there be a pooling system created in the as yet 'un-reclaimed' eastern (Dairy Creek) arm of Lime Kiln Bay that would filter the run-off from the surrounding built-up areas before it flowed into the creek. Then they addressed – and organised – a system of rotating voluntary 'bush regenerators', another innovative approach developed only recently among nearby resident action groups in areas where bushland was at stake. This method of bank regeneration, one of minimal disturbance, became known as the 'Bradley method'. It involved painstaking, labour-intensive removal of invasive species (i.e. 'weeds') by hand, in small patches around healthy native plants in order to allow those native species to regenerate and regain their earlier distributions. The committee met with council in February 1975 to argue for both the bank regeneration proposal and the engineering strategy suggested by committee member Norm Tonkin for the tidal pooling system to filter run-off.[33]

Despite the hostile reaction they had received, the LKBPC sustained pressure on Hurstville Council, urging it to adopt the conciliatory approach that Bankstown had taken on the Little Salt Pan dispute, in which the council had not only abandoned its dumping plans but also had set up a consultative committee to give local residents a voice in future environmental planning. Strategically, however, drawing on the political experience of Koffel and others in the group, the Lime Kiln Bay group communicated with the state Labor Party, then in opposition but taking an active stand on environmental issues. While questions of land were legally in the hands of state governments, the federal Senate Select Committee had condemned the New South Wales Government's handling of its waterways in its pollution report and, after November

---

31   LKBPC to HMC, December 1973, included in Press Release 1, LKBPC Archive.
32   Waste Not, 'History of Waste', accessed 21 January 2021, www.wastenot.org.au. This is a Total Environment Centre project.
33   David Koffel, notes of the meeting, 28 February 1975, LKBPC Archive.

1972, Labor was in power federally for the first time in decades. Labor had a reforming agenda – for Environment, under Minister Moss Cass, and for Urban Affairs, under Tom Uren. The Lime Kiln Bay group had strong support from the local member in state parliament, Frank Walker – a powerful activist on the left of the party as well as a highly respected local member – and he drew support from Pat Rogan, an ALP member from upstream who had supported the activists in the East Hills and Picnic Point areas. Even in opposition, Walker was able to bring the state Labor shadow minister Bob Carr out to the Georges River, highlighting the problems under the conservative Askin government but, even more importantly, to set the state ALP agenda on environmental reform as it campaigned for the next election.[34]

On 6 March 1974, the LKBPC wrote to the Municipal and Shire Council Employees' Union (MSCEU) to ask for their support in stopping the council's plans to dump rubbish and reclaim the wetlands of Lime Kiln Bay. Their letter listed their concerns about both loss of amenity and recreation facilities for all citizens of the area and the city, as well as the destruction threatened for the swamp and mangrove area. They explained further that they had major support from community members, with petitions signed, positive responses on door knocking, support from many local groups (e.g. the parents and citizen's organisations), endorsement from the federal member, Len Reynolds (ALP, member of the House of Representatives), as well as state members Frank Walker and others. Finally, they appealed for MSCEU support, saying:

> If your members objected to the proposal of the Council, our committee believes that it would be extremely difficult for the Council to pursue its plans and that a unique area of the South Western Suburbs could be saved.

Dave Koffel signed the letter as committee secretary: 'Yours fraternally.'[35] The union never wrote back.

---

34 'NSW Pollution Laws No Deterrent to Big Business', *National Times*, 21–26 January 1974, 47–48; 'River Sets Labor's Strategy: Pollution Is Vote Clincher', *St George Pictorial*, 6 February 1974, 3; 'Pollution in Georges River "Alarming" – Wran: Mangroves Go', *Leader*, 20 February 1974, 11; 'Pollution … Mangroves Go', *Leader*, 20 February 1974, 15.
35 LKBPC to MSCEU, 6 March 1974, LKBPC Archive.

The Lime Kiln Bay campaigners also contacted the New South Wales BLF through its president, Jack Mundey, writing:

> So far we have tried just about everything to stop the Council: publicity (within our local area); petitions; calls for an Environmental Impact Study (which has been ignored); and calls for the Council to reconsider the project (which it has promised to do, and 'deferred' at its last two meetings, etc, etc.

> We have also asked the Municipal and Shire Council Employees' Union to object to the proposal, so making it extremely difficult for the Council to pursue its plans. However, although the Union did not even bother to reply to our requests (made 3 months ago) we know that our request was rejected unanimously by the union's executive.

> Mr Mundey, can you advise of us anyone in that union to contact?[36]

Jack Mundey wrote back supportively on 15 July 1974, suggesting they write to BLF Secretary Joe Owens, asking him to bring the matter before the union executive, where Mundey would support it. He offered to come to the preservation committee's proposed 'clean up' of the area to demonstrate his support and explained that he had made enquiries about the MSCEU, learning that 'this Union hasn't been active at all on conservation issues'. He suggested a formal letter to the New South Wales Branch and federal secretary of the MSCEU to see if that elicited any response; it did not. With no support forthcoming, the Lime Kiln Bay activists focused instead on the local government elections and did not make any further attempts to gain union support.[37]

Hurstville Council eventually, and grudgingly, produced the environmental impact assessment for which the Lime Kiln Bay committee had been asking.[38] The joint report of the council engineer, E. Anderson, and the health surveyor, D. A. Webster, on the proposed reclamation was tabled before council in June. The report made it clear that the need for space for additional garbage disposal was the council's priority and had been planned for some years. Having reviewed the alternatives, including a shredder or incineration, the engineer and the health surveyor advised

---

36   LKBPC to NSW BLF, 15 June 1974, LKBPC Archive.
37   Jack Mundey for NSW BLF to LKBPC, 15 July 1974, LKBPC Archive.
38   'The Municipal Engineer and the Municipal Health Surveyor's Special Report, Incorporating a Study of the Reclamation of Lime Kiln Bay', 20 June 1974, LKBPC Archive.

council that the reclamation of Lime Kiln Bay was the cheapest option. In addition, it would also enhance property values for neighbours by the expansion of the golf course.

Engineer Anderson drew on military aerial photographs from 1937, just as the earlier municipal engineer, Albert Brewer, had done in 1969. Brewer, however, had used emotive language, arguing that the expanding and 'foul mangrove swamp' was a 'noxious weed' and a 'cancerous growth' and so must be stopped.[39] Anderson was more restrained, relying on scientific language and the evidence of figures from the quantified aerial photos to argue that from 1937 to 1974, mangrove area had expanded from 4.5 acres to 24.5 acres. The phrase 'natural reclamation' was repeated several times, indicating the engineer's belief that siltation from upstream clearing was the cause of the mangrove expansion and would eventually lead to the mangroves' decline as they were starved of tidal flow. The council was just hastening the process by a few years. It planned to completely 'eliminate' the 'wetlands', which were 'undesirable because of their attraction to mosquitoes, snakes and rodents' and produced 'offensive odours'. The council's reclamation, the report continued, would also reduce the prevalence of spiders and other insects (as they were mangrove dwellers). The goal of this special report was clear from the title of Section 4, which was 'Advantages of Reclamation over other systems of Garbage Disposal'. This section then argued that the reclamation would be of:

> Inestimatable [sic] value to the Community for the creation of sporting fields ... which are a necessity of paramount importance and, with the ever increasing requirements of the growing Community, difficulty is experienced in satisfying the needs.[40]

The report confirmed the worst fears of the Lime Kiln Bay campaigners. After attending some acrimonious meetings with councillors, which just compounded the rejection they had met from the Municipal Employees' Union, the LKBPC threw itself into campaigning for the local government elections in September. Their flyers portrayed the area as 'bush', evoking all the complex symbolism of the 'bush' as the core of Australian identity in their call not to betray the nation: 'Don't Rubbish Our Bush' (see Figure 11.3).

---

39   F. N. Brewer, Hurstville Council Minutes, 6 March 1969, item 274, Hurstville Local Studies Archive, Georges River Council Libraries.
40   Ibid., 4.

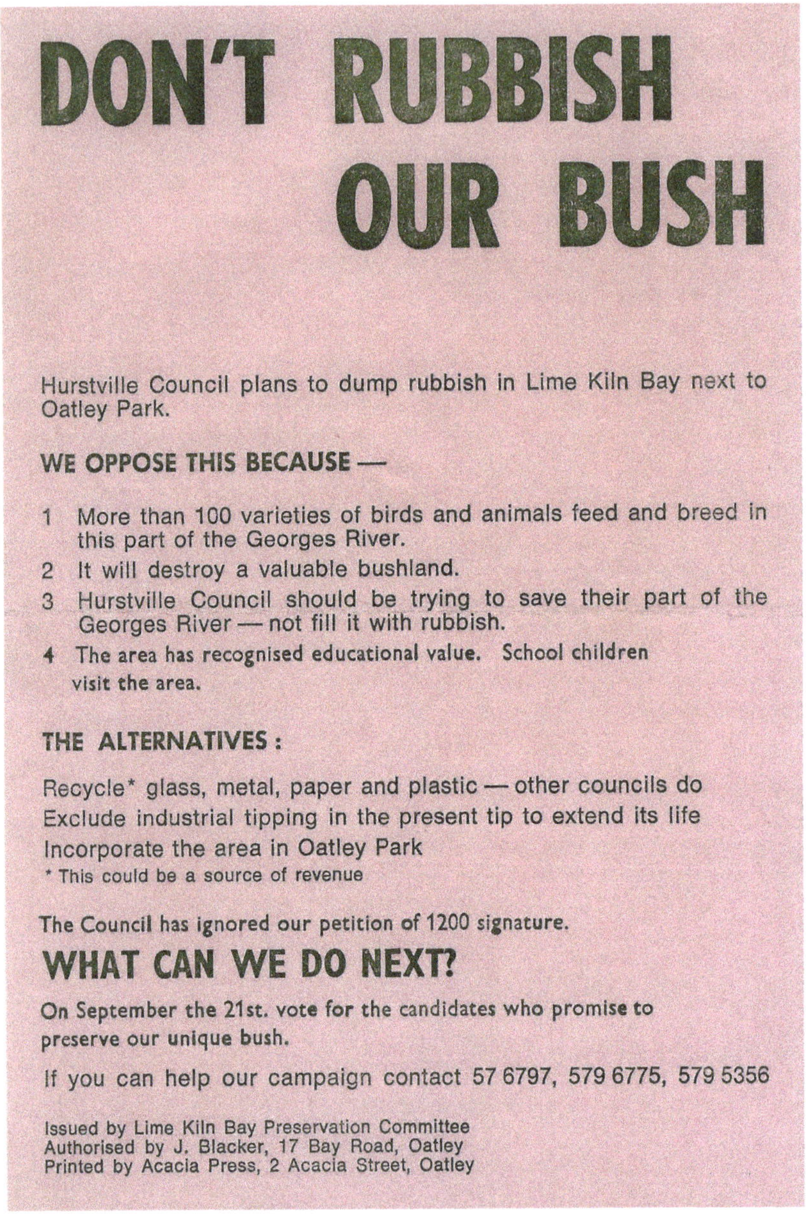

DON'T RUBBISH
OUR BUSH

Hurstville Council plans to dump rubbish in Lime Kiln Bay next to Oatley Park.

WE OPPOSE THIS BECAUSE —

1   More than 100 varieties of birds and animals feed and breed in this part of the Georges River.
2   It will destroy a valuable bushland.
3   Hurstville Council should be trying to save their part of the Georges River — not fill it with rubbish.
4   The area has recognised educational value. School children visit the area.

THE ALTERNATIVES :

Recycle* glass, metal, paper and plastic — other councils do
Exclude industrial tipping in the present tip to extend its life
Incorporate the area in Oatley Park
* This could be a source of revenue

The Council has ignored our petition of 1200 signature.

WHAT CAN WE DO NEXT?

On September the 21st. vote for the candidates who promise to preserve our unique bush.

If you can help our campaign contact 57 6797, 579 6775, 579 5356

Issued by Lime Kiln Bay Preservation Committee
Authorised by J. Blacker, 17 Bay Road, Oatley
Printed by Acacia Press, 2 Acacia Street, Oatley

Figure 11.3: LKBPC election flyer: 'Don't Rubbish Our Bush', September 1974.

LKBPC election flyer encouraging voters in the local election to 'vote for the candidates who promise to preserve our unique bush'. Courtesy of Dave Koffel, LKBPC Archive.

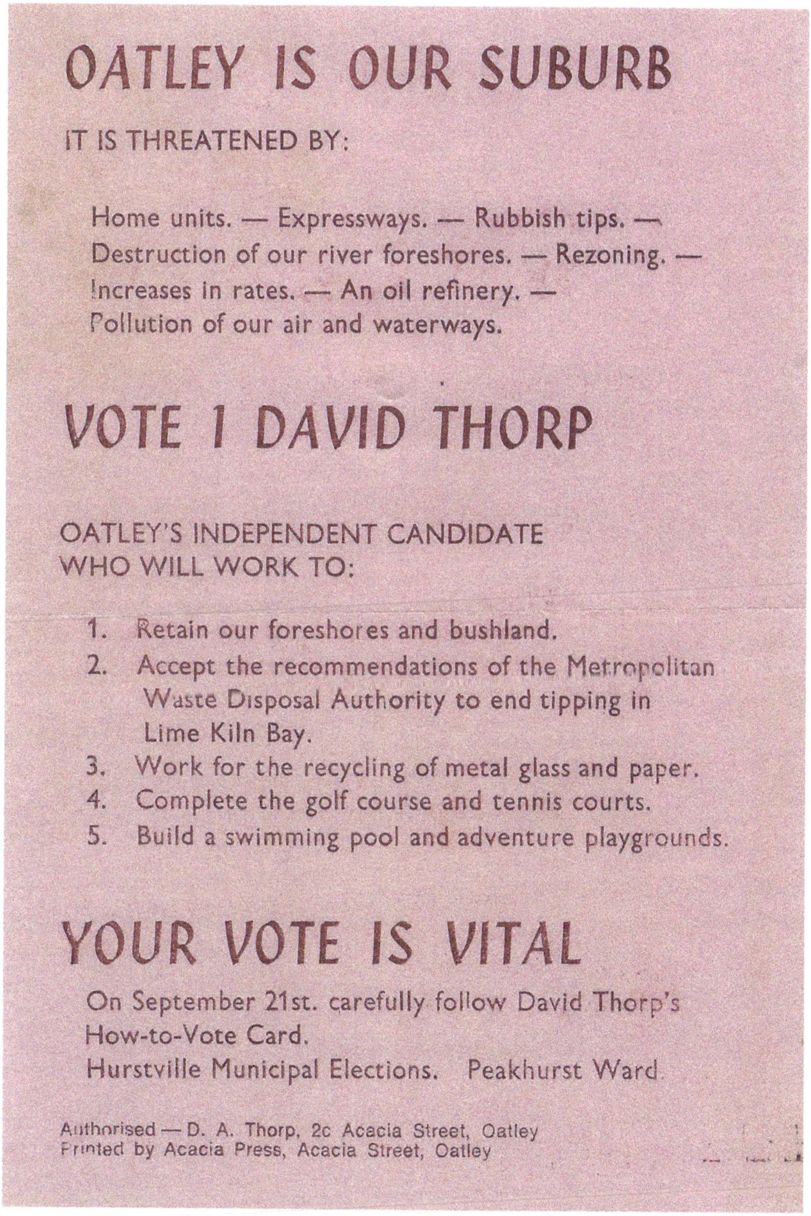

OATLEY IS OUR SUBURB

IT IS THREATENED BY:

Home units. — Expressways. — Rubbish tips. —
Destruction of our river foreshores. — Rezoning. —
Increases in rates. — An oil refinery. —
Pollution of our air and waterways.

VOTE 1 DAVID THORP

OATLEY'S INDEPENDENT CANDIDATE
WHO WILL WORK TO:

1. Retain our foreshores and bushland.
2. Accept the recommendations of the Metropolitan
   Waste Disposal Authority to end tipping in
   Lime Kiln Bay.
3. Work for the recycling of metal glass and paper.
4. Complete the golf course and tennis courts.
5. Build a swimming pool and adventure playgrounds.

YOUR VOTE IS VITAL

On September 21st. carefully follow David Thorp's
How-to-Vote Card.
Hurstville Municipal Elections.   Peakhurst Ward.

Authorised — D. A. Thorp, 2c Acacia Street, Oatley
Printed by Acacia Press, Acacia Street, Oatley

Figure 11.4: 'Oatley is Our Suburb', David Thorp election flyer, September 1974.

Courtesy of Dave Koffel, LKBPC Archive.

The group appealed to community members to see Lime Kiln Bay as their own, hoping they would want to defend it together, as a collective commitment. They were even able to obtain a page in the local Anglican Church newsletter, *Span*, in which they invited residents to 'take a walk and see for yourself'. They offered a map and an informative walking tour guide to build attachment and protectiveness. Rather than telling people what to think or how to vote, their approach was to encourage independent thinking, asking readers to have a look and make their own decision: 'Should it be destroyed or saved?'[41]

This energetic campaign was successful in wards close to the river in bringing more sympathetic councillors, like David Thorp and Julian Sheen, into the councils of both Hurstville and the adjoining Kogarah. They could not, however, mobilise enough votes in the wards away from the river to remove all the councillors who were committed to reclamations. After this election, the negotiations with the council were easier, but it was still not certain that the eastern arm of Lime Kiln Bay could be kept safe.

The campaigners had taken an active role in reaching out widely across the community throughout the year, so their work for the September election had extended this outreach even further. Yet, they had little knowledge of earlier movements. Just as Kevin Howard, the Bankstown health inspector had not known at all about the 1950s Picnic Point campaigners who had won the national park, despite sitting on the trust himself, so the Lime Kiln Bay committee knew nothing about the activists in their own area even in 1968 and 1969, let alone those who might have come before. It was only later in the campaigning in which Dave Koffel was involved that the petition written in 1968 came to light.[42]

While the LKBPC had not been aware of earlier movements, they had learnt more about the council's plans to 'reclaim' all the bays under its control. The committee had heard informally that council had applied for permission as early as 1971 to carry out the work. This application had demonstrated that council's goal was to fill in not just Lime Kiln Bay but Jewfish and Gungah bays too. But Hurstville Council had refused to release these plans.

---

41   *Span*, St Peter's Anglican News, Mortdale, August 1974, vol. 19, no. 6, 4, LKBPC Archive.
42   Koffel, interview.

In numerous community venues from January 1974, LKBPC activists explained that the council intended to fill all the bays. But the community simply did not believe them. Most local residents saw themselves as relatively economically well-off and correspondingly politically powerful. As Dave recalled:

> Well, people just said – 'Oh they're not going to fill in Edith Bay, this is Lugarno!' Or 'They're not going to fill in Jewfish Bay. We live on Landsdowne Parade, you know!' The class system actually cut in, you know? And 'We're silvertails, no one's going to put rubbish in our bays'. This is what they would say to you![43]

In 1976 the ALP came to power in New South Wales under Neville Wran and the supportive local member Frank Walker became minister for lands. He ordered Hurstville Council to release its plans for the bays, which it finally did in May 1976. These plans revealed that, indeed, the council did plan to fill in all the bays along the northern shore. There was immediate community uproar and an avalanche of support for the campaigners trying to stop the reclamations. In August 1976, a public meeting formed the Preserve Oatley West Resident Action Group (POW) to which the LKBPC was happy to affiliate. Together they collected 4,300 signatures on a petition to state parliament. Hurstville Council continued to raise the possibility of allowing the bays to be 'naturally reclaimed' with siltation – after which the council would then build playing fields! The Wran government assured POW and the LKBPC that no government approval would ever be issued, taking the plans effectively off the table permanently. Dave Koffel's summary of the campaign in 2005 for Alan Fairley's book ended cautiously with: 'It would appear that finally we had won!'[44]

---

43   Ibid.
44   Dave Koffel, notes and summary for Alan Fairley, March 2005, LKBPC Archive.

12

Mud, 'Mangrovites' and Oatley Bay

The protest at Oatley Bay was against both reclamation and dredging. There were two major tributaries into Oatley Bay and, by the 1960s, the western one, Renown Creek, had been largely destroyed by dumping, while the eastern one, Poulton Creek, and the surrounding Poulton Park, were both threatened with 'reclamation' by council dumping. While some of the material to be dumped was from rubbish, much of it was to be dredged up from Oatley Bay itself, through which the council aimed to deepen the bay and make it more accessible for watercraft. The active campaign in the 1960s and 1970s was focused on saving the eastern tributary, Poulton Creek, and its park, but the dredging of the whole bay was always just as crucial to this campaign as was the dumping on both the creeks.

This overall protest campaign was distinctive because of the rising strategic importance of education – both formal and informal – as the argument for conservation. There were activist teachers in the simultaneous campaign at Lime Kiln Bay, but they were focusing on mobilising political support at community and government level. Around Oatley Bay, while formal protests were written to politicians, the argument for an end to dumping, dredging and 'reclamation' was based fundamentally on the need to learn from the natural environment. This campaign argued that the mangrove and swampland and the natural bush and its wildlife provided a crucial educational resource for the community and within formal schooling, with teachers and students more prominently represented among the campaigners than in the upstream disputes.

These protests were distinctive too in that they demonstrated the complexity of the local community, showing alliances among residents but also revealing the tensions between them. Those trying to protect Poulton Creek and its bushland included oyster farming families as well as those employed on land. But, at the same time, churchgoing conservationists were accosted by religious ministers who sided with the council. Finally, the conflicts were distinctive because, even more obviously than in the Lime Kiln Bay conflicts with Hurstville Council, these disputes with Kogarah Council showed an intense focus on mangroves by all sides.

Some members of the longer-established Oatley Flora and Fauna Society (OFF) were attracted by the persistent advocacy undertaken in the Lime Kiln Bay conflicts. Others within OFF, however, were troubled by what they saw as 'activism', by which they meant putting public pressure on local and state government through petitions, media and running candidates in local elections. The more conservative members wished only to stick to their self-education approaches, as was clear in the *OFF News* Editorial in January 1969, which reported that, in the committee:

> The opinion has been expressed that the greater activity in conservation matters during the year may be against the wishes and inclinations of some members who would prefer just to hold our monthly evening meetings with their entertaining and instructive lectures and our enjoyable field days. This view has been strongly opposed, but the Committee feel that this is a matter for discussion at the AGM so that the incoming Committee will have a clear understanding of the wishes of members.[1]

By the late 1960s, such polite activity was losing favour, and indeed visiting experts like Allen Strom often argued for strong 'citizen-based conservation' advocacy. Nevertheless, this self-education activity had built up general and widespread community knowledge about the presence and values of native bushland. In the AGM the following month, members supported the view that OFF should take a more activist position. Subsequently the order of aims in its constitution was reworded so that 'the furtherance of conservation' was placed ahead of 'encouraging the growth of native plants'.[2] Yet the threats to bushland were coming ever closer to home as the momentum built up to further dredge the bay to fill in Poulton Creek.

---

1   *OFF News*, January 1969, 1–2.
2   'Annual General Meeting', *OFF News*, February 1969, 3.

Kogarah was further downstream than Hurstville, along the northern shore of the Georges River, stretching around to the shores of Botany Bay, making it even further away than Hurstville from the factories and the Housing Commission hostels and settlements of Milperra and Herne Bay. The river waters, however, were not isolated from the waste flowing from the old industrial areas like Mortdale, which was in the Hurstville local government area but encompassed Renown Creek, which flowed into the western arm of Oatley Bay, in the Kogarah area. The massive Judd brick pits and other smaller industries all lay around Mortdale until the 1930s or later, draining waste into Renown Creek. The contents of such dumped and leached toxic materials had not ever been recorded but had persisted in the soils of the creek bed as well as the floor of Oatley Bay itself.[3]

On the land close to the Georges River there were far more boat owners living in the Kogarah area than there were in the upstream areas controlled by Hurstville. There were also fewer industrial unionists although there were many with only moderate levels of education and income. Kogarah Council had a significant proportion of professional residents, with some who were economically comfortable, but others, like teachers, who were not only less affluent but had a history of unionised activism in the New South Wales Teachers Federation. Nature study had been given attention in the New South Wales education curriculum since 1905; however, with the first manned space flights in the 1960s – Yuri Gagarin in 1961 and the moon landing in 1969 – the profile of science education was rising. So too was concern about the impacts of new technologies. Consequently, teachers were being asked to teach more about the environment in their secondary schools.[4]

Like Bankstown and Hurstville, the upstream councils on the northern side of the Georges River, Kogarah had been dredging and reclaiming small patches of low-lying land over many years. The northern end of Kogarah Bay, for example, had long before been turned into Beverley Park and a golf course. The Kogarah area boat owners had not been satisfied with the access gained to Kogarah Bay and continued to apply pressure for more dredging. Renown Creek, with its load of toxic waste from Mortdale, had already largely disappeared under silt dredged up

---

3   Kogarah Council, 'Moore Reserve Plan of Management', 3.
4   Mitchell, *Teachers, Education, and Politics*; Kass, *Educational Reform*; Goodall, Randerson and Ghosh, *Teacher for Justice*.

from Oatley Bay in the days after World War II (WWII) to become 'Moore Reserve'. 'Reclamation' continued until eventually Renown Creek was destroyed altogether and replaced with concrete pipes.

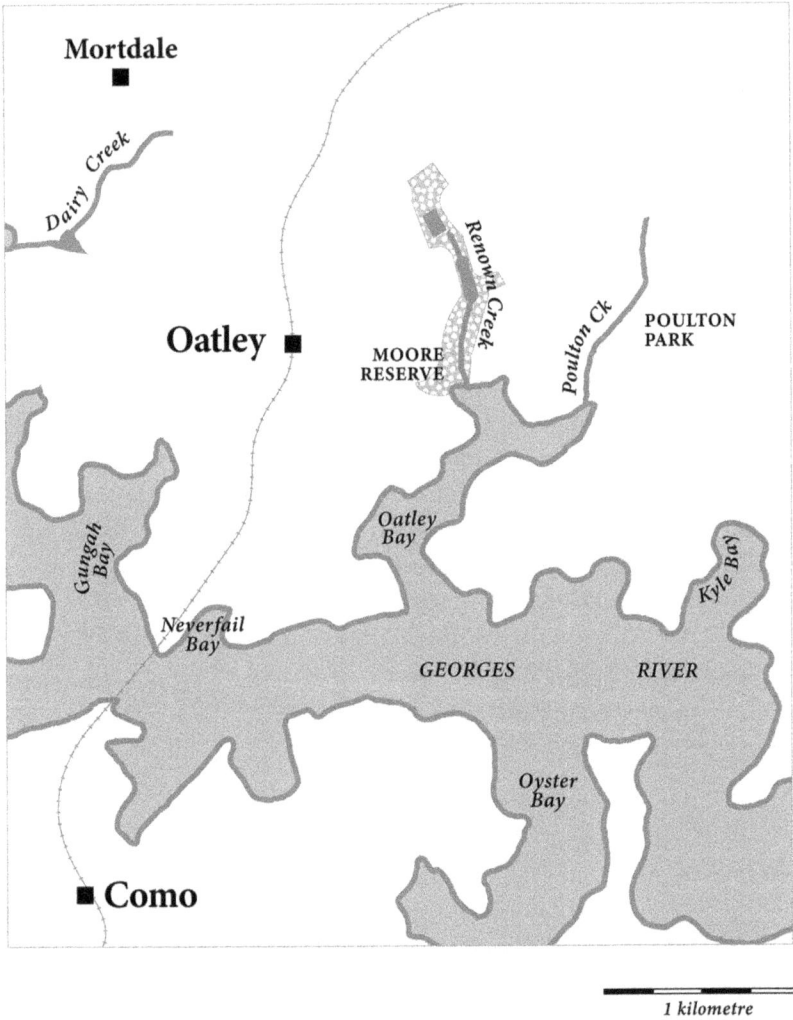

Map 12.1: Oatley Bay, Renown and Poulton creeks.
Cartography: Sharon Harrup.

As early as 1936 Kogarah had applied for permission to dredge still more of the bay in order to reclaim not only the more easterly Poulton Creek but also the deeper, eastern arm where this creek joined Oatley Bay, which would lead to the formation of Poulton Park. Although the Depression and

WWII had slowed this work, the rising tide of household and industrial waste after the war ensured that this 'reclamation' plan re-emerged. Today men who were young boys at Mortdale Public School in the 1940s have fond memories of sneaking out of school to hide in the caves and play in the swamps.[5] A small section of land along Poulton Creek had been filled by the late 1960s, but there was still a large area of saltmarsh and mangroves on the lower edges of the creek near its entrance to the bay.

The continued presence of these swamplands did not weigh on the conscience of Kogarah councillors, who talked of 'filthy mangroves'.[6] The council proposed building a causeway across the eastern arm that would cut off the creek and upper waters of the eastern arm from the river, starving the mangroves and saltmarsh of the saline, tidal water they needed to survive.

But the reclamation of the western arm for Moore Reserve had not been going to plan. In 1971, the Kogarah Council engineer, John Lindsay, reported to the 5 July council meeting that the dredged mud from the riverbed that had been dumped onto the Moore Reserve surface had not solidified.[7] Instead, it had remained slimy and mobile and was, in fact, slowly sliding back down into the bay. He reported that the dredged mud was causing substantial problems:

> After four years it is still moving. It has never dried out. All the mud in the tip is moving under the garbage and I don't know how we can control this.[8]

The problem was so pronounced that what had been suggested as a children's soccer field could not be opened. Instead, it lay idle, behind a cyclone wire fence with a sign forbidding entry because of the danger of quicksand. Even the hopes for its use had faltered. In 1977 Kogarah Council called a meeting to canvass local residents about their preferred use for the reclaimed area: did they want passive or active recreation? Residents attending the meeting voted overwhelmingly for passive

---

5 Robert Haworth, pers. comm. 29 April 2020.
6 Fairley, *Being Green*.
7 At the council meeting on 5 July 1971. John Lindsay (1920–2010) was Kogarah Council engineer and town planner (1956–72). He was outspoken and 'trod on toes' at Kogarah, which he accused in the mid-1960s, in an article in the *St George and Sutherland Shire Leader* (hereafter *Leader*), of treating him with 'dog in the manger antics'. Andrew Tink, Obituary, 1 September 2010, *Sydney Morning Herald*.
8 Cited in Fairley, *Being Green*, 52.

recreation – like the picnics and family gatherings that Ruth Staples had wanted to be able to retain at Lime Kiln Bay. It was not, however, what the council wanted.

Even more problematically for all concerned was the realisation that the waste and silt that had been dumped included high levels of zinc, lead, chromium and mercury, discovered because the unstable dredged layers were leaching liquids from the waste into the bay.[9] There had been no accurate accounting of the composition of the dumped waste, making it impossible to assess the degree of toxicity.[10] The Wran Labor government came to power at state level in 1976 and when local member Frank Walker became acting environment minister in the following year he was able to impose a halt to further work on the site. All dumping ceased at Moore Reserve from July 1977.[11]

Meanwhile, the faltering reclamation of Poulton Park had been under debate since the late 1960s. At the same 1971 meeting at which engineer John Lindsay had reported on the unstable silt at Moore Reserve, he used the evidence from that western arm to warn against further dredging and dumping onto the eastern Poulton Park. He argued that the dredged silt would exhibit the same unstable behaviour there. Regardless, Kogarah councillors voted at that meeting to go ahead with the dredging and to dump the silt onto Poulton Park. OFF members wrote in protest against the decision to kill the mangroves, demanding first that the council at least consider installing large pipes underneath the causeway to allow tidal water to flow to the mangroves and marshes and, second, that the whole area be made a flora and fauna conservation area. At the same time, attempting to counter the simplistic binaries that council was asserting of 'conservationists vs the community', OFF insisted that it did not oppose the dredging, believing that additional tidal flow would, in fact, benefit the mangroves.[12]

---

9   Ibid., 53.
10   At the Senate Select Committee Hunt explained that no records had been kept prior to 1969 of the composition of garbage dumped or of toxic waste released into river. The Bill before the New South Wales Parliament when he gave evidence (5 August 1969) set the maximum allowable discharge of any chemical, but he argued that this was not workable, as ascertaining the composition of a mixed discharge of chemicals would be impossible and/or unworkably time-consuming. In the later Poulton Park case, the New South Wales State Pollution Control Commission, the body arising from the 1969 Bill, had simply refused to act, telling the campaigners that all future correspondence must be directed to the municipal council.
11   Cited in Fairley, *Being Green*, 53.
12   Ibid., 43.

There continued to be those in OFF who wanted to take a stronger position, so the Save Poulton Park Campaign Committee was set up. Initiated by Ray and Evol Knight, together with some other OFF members, it drew in many concerned residents who had wider networks. Although neither Ray nor Evol had had the benefit of much formal education, they were both lifelong learners, and had become tireless advocates for the environment at Oatley. Ray, an immigrant from the south of England in 1957, had left school at the age of 11 to go to work and, by 1971, was general manager of a printing business in Ultimo. He had been active in promoting native plants and a bushland environment ever since his arrival, becoming vice-president of OFF.

Evol was just as active, although, as was common along the river, she was not ever the public face of conservation advocacy. Her involvement became particularly important in this campaign: she was a member of the Derwent family, so she belonged to the large network of oyster growing families. Consequently, Evol was able to form a sustained link between the oyster farmers and the conservationists. Her father, Charles John Derwent, her brothers and her cousins all farmed oysters and Evol had grown up among them in Wyong Street, which led down to Neverfail Bay where the industry was based and where Evol kept her own small rowboat. After Evol and Ray married, they stayed close by, settling directly behind Wyong Street, on a bush block on Letitia Street where they could retain all the native trees and shrubs. From there, they took a strong interest in both water quality and land-based environments in the area.

Evol had been frustrated in her own education, having fulfilled family wishes to leave school at 15 to train as a secretary. She grew up to be tireless in her environmental advocacy, writing endless letters to politicians and creating educational opportunities, particularly in schools. With Ray, she established a native plant garden at Oatley Public School, which survived as long as there was a sympathetic principal. They continued their work by setting up a creative leisure centre, which fostered environmental interest as well as other leisure activities. In what spare time she had, Evol would gather native plants like banksia from the bush around Oatley and take the cuttings into a school at Redfern to teach students there about the native plants they could no longer see in their heavily built-up inner-city area.

Figure 12.1: Save Poulton Park Campaign Committee stickers.

These stickers were printed by Ray Knight, chairman of the Save Poulton Park Campaign Committee. Alexandra Knight handed them out at school and gave them away as she gathered signatures for the petition opposing Kogarah Council's 'reclamation'. Note especially the 'Keep bushland in our suburbs' and 'Protect our wetlands' stickers. This is the only use of the term 'wetlands' in any of these campaigns along the river. Courtesy of Dr Alexandra Knight, Save Poulton Park Campaign Archive, private collection.

Kogarah Council continued to insist on 'reclaiming' the eastern arm by dumping garbage and silt, so the Save Poulton Park Campaign Committee geared up the attempt to save it. A petition was mounted and Alexandra Knight remembers going from door to door as a child across the suburb to gather signatures. As a printer, Ray understood the impact of graphic statements to remind people of what they stood to lose if the creek and banks were smothered in silt. He printed a set of stickers that Alex took with her to hand out to petitioners and around her school. Each sticker carried the name of an important species of bird, animal or plant that could be found, and the whole message of the campaign was summed up by one sticker, which could have been the slogan for all the anti-reclamation campaigns along the river: 'Keep bushland in our suburbs' (see Figure 12.1). It may be significant in this sense that this was the only one of the estuary campaigns that used the term 'wetlands': all others used terms like 'bush', 'mangrove swamp' or just 'mangroves' as the metonym for all the vegetation in low-lying swampy areas.

These were not campaigns to defend a historic built environment or even to defend working-class housing. Nor were they to defend distant and supposedly 'pristine' environments. Instead, this campaign and all the others on the river were attempting to defend a damaged and polluted river and the scarred remnants of its endemic bushland. They were driven by a commitment to saving what they could in order to create a future for the river lands.

The committee was now in touch with the wider emerging environmental activist movement. Unlike the Lime Kiln Bay activists, they do not seem to have attempted to contact unions as potential allies, perhaps having learnt from the refusal of the Municipal and Shire Council Employees' Union to support the Lime Kiln Bay campaign! Nor did this campaign focus its attention on mobilising political allies. Instead, its primary strategy was to focus on education.

Poulton Creek activists were able to build links to teachers interested in education as a means to defend the environment. Through teachers, the committee was able to draw in Alan Reid, who became a part of the Oatley Bay story. Reid had already been a conservationist and teacher in Melbourne when he began studying science part-time at Monash University in 1969 to better understand the environment he was teaching about. He became involved with both the Gould League and the Australian Conservation Foundation (ACF) where he took up a position as education liaison officer, making nationwide and international connections for the ACF among teacher environmentalists and developing strategy for the Curriculum Development Centre, sponsored by the federal Ministry for Conservation and Environment. During 1970, the ACF asked Reid to work on setting up state-based associations for environmental studies with the goal of building a national organisation on the model of the Field Studies Council in the UK.[13] In December 1970, Reid recalled that

---

13   Alan Reid, pers. comm., 2 May 2020, citing diary records from the period. The centre was eventually set up in 1975. The Environmental Studies Associations in each state became a national body in 1980. The UK Field Studies Council continues to exist. Field Studies Council, 'Outdoor Learning and School Trips', accessed 21 January 2021, www.field-studies-council.org/.

the broad environmental movement was shaken up by William Stapp from the University of Michigan who spoke at a Canberra conference and challenged teachers and environmentalists to work together to build curriculum for all age groups that would inform them about ecological science, empower them to investigate their local urban environments and build their skills to communicate their findings and concerns.[14] Strom had also been impressed by Bill Stapp's talk, drawing on it to support his own advocacy of 'citizen-based environmental activism'.[15]

Another source of organising energy for local activists was the Society for Social Responsibility in Science (SSRS), which included university students studying in the field of science and medicine. SSRS had generated an adult education program and Peter Ellyard, then a policy researcher, organised high school science students in Canberra on similar principles in 1970 – what would today be called today 'inquiry-based' or 'problem-based' education – to learn about biology by investigating their local environments. This drew on the approaches that had been developed by the earlier progressive education movement and can be seen as the seeds of today's 'citizen science'.[16] This program was called INSPECT – an acronym for 'INquiry into the State of Pollution and Environmental Conservation by Thoughtful People'. Ellyard and Roger Gifford reported in 1971 on the school students' program in their *Bad Luck, Dead Duck,* which circulated rapidly among environmental educators (see Figure 12.2).[17] As Ellyard explained it, the INSPECT approach began with talks to the students by visiting speakers, staff and fellow students, then students would select problems and, guided by scientists, teachers and planners who had some idea of the problem chosen, would develop a research plan. They could administer surveys, do literature searches and/ or undertake laboratory studies. They would then gather the data together in a form that would be useful for agencies responsible for the correction of the problem. INSPECT groups developed in many schools, drawing on similar approaches to develop their own strategies depending on local conditions and problems.

---

14   Reid, interview. Stapp was keynote speaker at an Australian Academy of Science conference. Stapp, 'A Strategy for Curriculum Development'.

15   Allen Strom's comments on Bill Stapp can be found in Fox, *Chief Guardian*, Ch. 11.

16   Progressive education in Australia had been associated with the New Education Fellowship (active in the UK, Europe, India and South Africa) and with John Dewey's work in the US. For its political impacts, see Goodall, Randerson and Ghosh, *Teacher for Justice*. For an introduction to 'citizen science' see Simpson, 'What is Citizen Science?'

17   Gifford and Ellyard, *Bad Luck, Dead Duck*. The following year they published *What a Mess! Let's Confess: The Report of INSPECT 1971*.

BAD LUCK, DEAD DUCK

the Report of

INSPECT 1970

Figure 12.2: Cover, *Bad Luck, Dead Duck: The Report of INSPECT 1970*, by Roger Gifford and Peter Ellyard.

The title was taken from a moving poem published on the inside cover, written by 13-year-old high school student, Nicholas Davey, which began: 'Lying there amongst the muck / Bad luck, dead duck; / Oil pollutes your river bed, / How sad, too bad … / As you lie between the weeds, / No-one cares; no-one sees; / You'll lie there for years and years; / Bad luck, dead duck'. Image courtesy of National Library of Australia.

Ray and Evol Knight were regularly holding the meetings of the Save Poulton Park Campaign Committee in their home. They invited SSRS to send a member and so met Philip Sutton, a veterinary science student at the University of Sydney, who had become the Sydney convenor of INSPECT.[18] Evol, with her relationship with Oatley Public School, worked with Sutton to develop an INSPECT program to investigate the conflict over the dredging and reclamation of Poulton Park. Together, they drew a number of local secondary schools into the INSPECT study program on the intended council-backed dredging and dumping plan as a focus for inquiry-based learning. Philip Sutton lived close to Oatley Bay for a month to work with the committee to develop its strategy, inviting Alan Reid, in his ACF role, as well as Dexter Dunphy, a sociologist who was then a professor in the Business Faculty at the University of New South Wales. Dunphy was the younger son of Myles Dunphy and so brought with him a substantial background in environmental politics.[19] As well, the campaign drew on high-profile scientists like the well-known head of the Fisheries Branch, Don Francois, and the ever-supportive local member, Frank Walker. The Save Poulton Park Committee was able to move quickly, organising for Philip Sutton and Dexter Dunphy to speak before Kogarah Council to argue the value of the swamps, pointing out the educational as well as environmental roles of the mangroves and saltmarsh. Letters were written to the press and publicity achieved in radio and television. By 11 July the petition for which Alexandra Knight had been working had been presented to council, carrying 3,000 signatures calling for an end to the plan to dredge, build the causeway and dump the sludge on the blocked wetlands. Eric Willis, still chief secretary, intervened again as he had done in the Great Moon Bay conflict, writing to Kogarah Council and the committee that the earlier 1936 permission to dredge and dump was to be withdrawn on the basis that 'the conservation principles were not then understood'.[20]

---

18 This approach appears to have been coordinated through the Sydney branch of the Social Responsibility in Science group. Correspondence with Vince Serventy, held in Papers of Vincent Serventy, MSS 4605, Class 8, consignment received 11 July 1994, File 18, Box 307, National Library of Australia.
19 Meredith, *Myles and Milo*; Orlovich, 'Dunphy, Milo Kanangra (1929–1996)'.
20 Cited in Fairley, *Being Green*, 43.

Tensions ran very high within the community during this period. One family of active campaigners were shocked to find that they were confronted by their local minister of religion at the end of a Sunday service. He accused family members of sabotage by destruction of the machinery of the dredges operating in the bay, an act that none of them had – or would have – contemplated, despite their strong commitment to the cause. The minister's unfounded accusations so dismayed them that they stopped going to church altogether.[21]

Despite the significant forces that the Save Poulton Park Campaign Committee had mobilised against the reclamation, the council refused to give up the idea, persisting in pushing forwards over the next three years. In 1973, the council reapplied to the state government, still in conservative hands. Its approach was to ask the recently created State Pollution Control Commission (SPCC) to review its earlier objection. As a result, the SPCC approved a modified Environmental Impact Statement (EIS) on the potential impact of the reclamation project and the dredging. Jack Beale, the minister for the environment, then approved this revised proposal to dredge on the grounds that it had been modified to conserve the mangrove area by the insertion, as OFF had suggested, of three large pipes underneath the causeway to allow tidal water to flow easily to the mangroves and saltmarsh areas.[22] The Save Poulton Park Campaign Committee was shocked and angered that the SPCC had backed down on its earlier objection. In January 1974 the campaigners wrote to Tom Lewis, the minister for lands, protesting that the SPCC had accepted a biased EIS:

> Consideration given to benefits accruing to water-based activities and organised sports is more extensive than that given to educational, social and aesthetic losses likely to be generated. This bias makes the EIS quite unsatisfactory as a basis for making an objective decision.[23]

21 Pers. comm.

22 'Dredging in Oatley Bay', letter to the editor, *Leader*, 5 November 1973, 2. Beale was minister for the environment (1971–73) in the Askin Liberal government. He championed water resources and set up the State Pollution Control Board. Eric Willis was no longer in a position to object, having moved from being chief secretary in 1972 to being minister for education.

23 Save Poulton Park Campaign Committee to Minister for Lands and Tourism Tom Lewis, 19 January 1974, Dr Alexandra Knight, Save Poulton Park Campaign Archive, private collection.

As will have been clear in earlier chapters – and evident in the press and the records held by the resident action campaigners – there had never been regular or sympathetic communication between these local anti-reclamation groups and the oyster farmers of the Georges River estuary. Even though oyster beds remained in the open waters off Lime Kiln Bay and the industry was well known downstream, the many oyster farming families had felt they had been on their own in their campaign for cleaner water even when they had protested against the leaching of dumped garbage into the water around their oyster racks as they had done in 1969. Nor had the oyster farmers been drawn on to support the campaigns against 'reclamation' by dredging or garbage dumping, even though their concerns were so similar. In this Poulton Creek campaign, however, Evol Knight played a crucial role in bring the two groups together. She organised for her brother, John Derwent, to take the members of the Save Poulton Park Campaign Committee along the river to see for themselves the damage being done in other areas as well as to learn more about the oyster farmers' concerns (see Figure 12.3).

Figure 12.3: Boat trip, organised by Evol Knight, allowing oyster farmers and Poulton Creek campaigners to view river problems together.

Looking back from the front of the boat, this photo shows in first row: John Derwent, front right and Evol Knight, left (without hat). Second row: Ida Carder in hat. Back row: a scientific member of OFF on left, John Derwent Jnr on right steering boat. Courtesy of Dr Alexandra Knight, Save Poulton Park Campaign Archive, private collection.

Strengthened by this alliance, the campaign continued to oppose both the dredging and reclamation. The importance of the Poulton Creek wetlands as a teaching resource was a prominent element in the group's opposition to the council, with INSPECT taking a key role in organising student and teacher visits to the area to affirm the value of observing ecological networks in process. Mangroves were particularly well suited to this educational role: while the immature fish and other species were hard to see and the saltmarsh was often unremarkable, the large mangrove trees and the protruding pneumatophores were easy to identify and to recognise as essential parts in the wider ecological network.

Kogarah Council was at pains to marginalise the role of education, as it demonstrated in February 1974. The Save Poulton Park Campaign had worked with Philip Sutton through INSPECT to organise a teaching field day at Poulton Park where Alan Reid led invited secondary students and teachers from various schools in the area, including nuns from a local Catholic school, in discussion about questions around reclamations of mangrove and saltmarsh areas. Reid, who was visiting Sydney for the ACF, had been interested in mangroves and saltmarsh since teaching nature craft at children's school camps at Westernport Bay (1959–66) where he had studied bird populations with fellow researcher Bill Davis.[24] A group of Kogarah Council aldermen and boat-owning residents interrupted the event. The *St George and Sutherland Shire Leader* reported the intervention sympathetically, transforming the teachers into 'protesters'. Headlined 'Angry Residents Rout Protesters', the article continued: '200 angry residents drove about 40 conservationists from Poulton Park last week and took control of a meeting the conservationists had organised'.[25] Arguing that council was simply following majority resident requests, one of the attending aldermen said:

> The people of Oatley are sick and tired of having a stinking, mosquito-infested swamp in their backyards. They are also weary of the conservationists hindering council clearing up the area and turning it into something useful for the kids … That's why the people who elected us to council mainly on this issue and gave us a clear mandate to reclaim the park, came out to stop the meeting.[26]

24 Alan Reid, pers. comm., 2 May 2020, citing diary records from the period. See also 'Teachers' Park Probe', *St George Pictorial*, 28 February 1974, 8.
25 'Angry Residents Rout Protesters', *Leader*, 27 February 1974, 3; 'Editorial: The Silent Have a Say', *Leader* 27 February 1974, 2.
26 'Angry Residents Rout Protesters', *Leader*, 27 February 1974, 3.

The following night, council once again endorsed the reclamation plan, with Alderman R. MacKenzie arguing that:

> 'It was not right to call the groups "conservationists"'. He said he had made up a new name for them – 'mangrovites'. 'Why should they want to conserve a dirty, stinking mass at Poulton Park which is not an asset to the community?' Alderman A. H. Hardiman agreed: 'Perhaps we can see if we can save a patch of the mud at Poulton Park for the "mangrovites" to wallow in.'[27]

Philip Sutton wrote a broad analysis of the threat to bays in general for the *St George Pictorial*, using Poulton Park as the example. His article was headlined 'Poulton Park: Waste or Wonderland?' and the *Pictorial* by-lined him as 'a common-sense expert'. Sutton pointed to recent Victorian Government support for the Environmental Studies Association and urged New South Wales to recognise the educational value of all estuarine swamps:

> One of the most utilitarian values of bushland in general and Poulton Park in particular is that it is an exceptionally useful tool for educational purposes. Environmental education and the associated field studies are becoming ever more important in the school curriculum … If we allow Poulton Park to be submerged under tons of silt we will be severely disadvantaging the children in the St George area.[28]

Sutton pointed out that only those lucky enough to live close to such resources, or who had the money to travel to them, would benefit from such richness of education, and he warned that 'it is the less well-off who will suffer most'.[29]

***

Although Minister Beale had not assisted the Save Poulton Park Campaign, the conservative state government, of which Beale and Willis were both members, began to move to address the problem of massive solid waste

---

27 'Teachers' Park Probe', *St George Pictorial*, 28 February 1974, 8; 'Angry Residents Rout Protesters', *Leader*, 27 February 1974, 3; 'Committee Fights Council Move to Reclaim Park', *Sydney Morning Herald*, 29 January 1974, 16; 'Garbage Plans for Oatley', *Sydney Morning Herald*, 8 February 1974, 9; 'Conservationists at Poulton Park', *Leader*, 6 March 1974. All cited in Fairley, *Being Green*, 49.

28 'Poulton Park: Waste or Wonderland?', *St George Pictorial*, 27 March 1974, 16. In its early planning, the Environmental Studies Association was identified, in Reid's diary notes, as the Association for Environmental Education.

29 Ibid.

accumulation. Harold Hunt had argued in his report to Bankstown Council and before the Senate Select Committee on Water Pollution that state and federal governments had to recognise their responsibilities to address the problem of waste, whether liquid, gaseous or solid, so that there were overarching standards rather than individual councils setting their own rules. In August 1974, the Metropolitan Waste Disposal Authority announced that there would be 10 regional garbage depots across Sydney with a number of councils entitled to take their waste there rather than operating their own tip within municipal boundaries. The waste depot for the Georges River councils was to be at Menai so Hurstville and Kogarah councils were directed to take their collected rubbish to that tip and to cease their own garbage disposal.

Both Hurstville and Kogarah councils were outraged and refused to stop their use of garbage for reclaiming land. Hurstville Council said that continuing to dump at Lime Kiln Bay and other areas was simply 'cheaper than other methods and will result in much-needed sporting areas'.[30]

Kogarah Council asked for an extension of time on its garbage dumping programs, particularly those at Oatley Bay, wanting permission to dump rubbish for 'several more years'. Councillors' attitudes to land and vegetation were made very clear by former mayor, Alderman Ernest A. Duggan (1965–68), who argued: 'All we want is the right to dump in our own municipality, so we can establish more playing and recreation areas out of wasteland'.[31]

---

30 'Tipping Cheapest!', *Leader*, 31 July 1974, 7.
31 Fairley, *Being Green*, citing *Leader*, 28 August 1974.

13

Atoms and Airports:
Towra Point

Bernie Clarke had grown up on the Georges River. Born in 1921, he lived most of his life at Oyster Bay, on the southern shore of the river, just opposite the mouth of Oatley Bay. He had followed the family profession and become a commercial fisherman after serving in Papua New Guinea in World War II. So he knew about mangroves, tropical and temperate. Bernie had begun his activist career in 1952 when he was arrested for setting up a roadblock to try to stop the oil refinery being built at Kurnell in Botany Bay. A Sutherland man, he was the archetype of all the older Georges River activists. He would have been comfortable in the Picnic Point Regatta Association (PPRA) – and perhaps he was. Like the early campaigners for the national park, Bernie was the activist in his family. His wife, Belle, was a strong supporter of all his campaigns but, in 1996, was said to be 'operating quietly behind the scenes' in the same way that Min Jacobsen and Eileen Stills had done.[1] Bernie was a fisherman who fished for pleasure as well as a job, a working-class man who knew the beaches, tides and fish up and down the river and into the bay.

Yet Bernie Clarke – like all the local residents in Sutherland – was faced with two of the most difficult problems of modernity. Compared to the councils along the northern shores, Sutherland had far fewer conflicts about reclamations because it had attempted far fewer of them; it had fewer people to generate garbage, fewer expensive yachts and powerboats

---

1   Borschmann, 'Guardian of Botany Bay', 10; Goodall and Cadzow, *Rivers and Resilience*.

to dredge for moorings and fewer bays to reclaim. And, where volumes of garbage did become a problem, Sutherland had the new Menai tip within its own borders.

Precisely because of its low population, however, Sutherland had been made the site of Australia's first nuclear reactor, an extreme expression of the military uses of land that had characterised the government's acquisition of Holsworthy. The High Flux Australian Reactor, perched on an escarpment at Lucas Heights, on the watershed between the Woronora River and Mill Creek, and operating from 1958, was a Cold War military experiment in nuclear fuel creation rather than an experiment in the production of electricity. In the end, its only acknowledged role was in the production of radioactive material for medical purposes and, at times, for environmental research. Through the early 1950s, British atomic testing in Western and South Australia had gone largely unnoticed by Australians, but the severe problems arising from the US Bravo test in the South Pacific at the Marshall Islands in March 1954 had alerted many people to the unpredictable and uncontrolled effects of radioactivity.[2] So the Lucas Heights reactor was given an uneasy welcome, and fears circulated about what toxic waste it might be releasing into the Woronora River, Mill Creek and downstream.[3] The original waste pipeline went into the Woronora River, but was later rerouted to go up, over the river and into waste storage on the eastern ridge of the Woronora. Mill Creek rises in the nearby toxic waste depot, and also receives some surface storm water from the reactor grounds. Tests done in later years (after 1980) showed that the natural pooling structure of Mill Creek had kept any more dangerous material at its source.[4]

This nuclear anxiety was compounded by plans discussed from the early 1960s to build a second airport on Towra Point, the sandy promontory that sheltered the mouth of the Georges River as it entered Botany Bay. Aircraft noise and pollution from Kingsford Smith Airport, opened in 1933, had been causing great trouble to the area's residents. Fishermen like Bernie Clarke were acutely aware of how the wave patterns were altered by the runway protruding into Botany Bay and he was later to make dredging a major target.

---

2   Niedenthal, 'A Short History'.

3   'Pollution from Atomic Plants', *Canberra Times*, 5 August 1969, 8. Reporting Denis Winston's evidence at the Senate Select Committee, under questioning from Senator Mulvihill as well as that by H. C. Hunt, Bankstown's chief health inspector, about both the reactor and the toxic industrial waste depot located close to it. See Senate Select Committee on Water Pollution, *Minutes of Evidence*, vol. 20, 4637.

4   Robert Haworth, a member of that water quality research team, pers. comm., June 2020.

Figure 13.1: Bernie Clarke in 1975 demonstrating how dredging was damaging the foreshore of the 'important estuaries of south Botany Bay'.
Obituary, *St George and Sutherland Shire Leader*, 17 January 2019. Courtesy of Nine Publishing.

Moreover, as discussed in earlier chapters, there were people on the Sutherland Shire Council who were sympathetic to the new ecology. So, when reclamations had been attempted, there were councillors who spoke out against them. Notably, in 1965 and 1966, when the Georges River National Park Trust and Sutherland Shire planned to reclaim two large low-lying swamps at Mickey's Point and Alfords Point on the southern bank of the river, the plan was opposed by the chair of the Parks and Playgrounds Committee, ALP Alderman Kevin Skinner, who commented ruefully that:

> The Council's policy is that the flat areas of the river foreshores should be used for playgrounds and this may or may not be bad. We would not like to see the National Park turned into one big oval or a Coney Island. I oppose the whole of the Georges River

being treated as a reclamation area. I hope the river will be allowed to stay in its natural state for the use of future generations. It will be a sin if this is not done.[5]

This second airport was to be a particular Sutherland anxiety, despite holding some implications for the northern shores of the river. The proposed flight path – and all its attendant noise – was not only planned to go to the south-west, thus crossing all of Sutherland, but also planes would be travelling low right over the only place on that southern side of the river that had begun to rise in value: the canal suburb of Sylvania Waters. The airport plan brought the dispersed population together like nothing else. The major strategy of Sutherland Shire in supporting – and indeed fanning – this local opposition to the airport was to demonstrate what this flight path noise would mean.[6] A meeting of over 1,400 people was held in the car park at Miranda Fair in 1968 while a recording of jet engines under full throttle was played through loudspeakers. A council station wagon was then fitted with loudspeakers and driven round the shire streets. Arthur Gietzelt described the process:

> Council's ganger and former councillor, Jimmy Stansell, in ear-muffs, drove the system over 700 miles around the shire, broadcasting the noise at about 40 times the level of ordinary public address broadcasting. The effect was dramatic. When the vehicle parked in shopping centres and let off a blast, the shopkeepers promptly appeared and signalled the driver on with rude gestures – if only we could get rid of jet noise that easily! When it parked outside blocks of home units, the reaction was similarly spontaneous – windows and doors slammed shut. The minute-and-a-half broadcast of jet noise was followed immediately by an apology from Council and an explanation of the fact that unless a protest was made, the noise could well become a daily occurrence in the life of the shire's residents.[7]

---

5   'Survey Planned for Waterways', *St George and Sutherland Shire Leader* (hereafter *Leader*), 14 December 1966, 11. Later, Skinner was mayor for six terms, 1973–74 and 1982–86.
6   Cullis, 'Holsworthy'; 'Homes to be Under Jet Alley', *Leader* 19 July 1967, 1; 'Editorial: What Is Going on at Towra?', *Leader*, 19 July 1967, 2.
7   Gietzelt, *Sticks and Stones*.

Map 13.1: Towra Point and Botany Bay.
Cartography: Sharon Harrup.

Yet, despite the very local concerns, this dispute had implications for all urban residents in relation to noise and environmental justice. With more success than the Lime Kiln Bay campaigners had in their appeal to the Municipal Employees' Union, the Sutherland campaigners against the Towra Point airport called on the support of the Amalgamated Metal Workers Union who saw themselves as representing the residents of Kogarah, Rockdale and Hurstville as well as those in the Sutherland area. The union was particularly concerned to support the residents in opposing the second airport – or indeed any airport extension – because they wanted to stop the spread of high-rise or even medium-density development from eroding residents' amenities.[8]

---

8   'Extension of Sydney Airport Suggested: Union Represents Residents', *Canberra Times*, 14 December 1973, 12.

There was also a widely endorsed environmental concern about the vulnerability of Towra Point. This sandy promontory had been cleared in the 1850s for Thomas Holt's grazing stock and the bays reshaped for his oyster leases, which had been managed by William Rowley, the Aboriginal man who later moved upriver into the Salt Pan Creek Aboriginal community, contributing to their demands for civil rights in the 1920s.[9] Holt's attempts at commercial uses had eventually failed, however, and Towra Point had been little used, with its wetlands no longer disturbed and its vegetation left to regrow unharvested. By the 1960s, it looked like wilderness and certainly offered shelter for birds and aquatic species. But it was being threatened by expanding commercial activities in Botany Bay, such as dredging to enable the passage of large tankers to the new oil refineries, potential oil spills and the continual wash of the ships as they moved.

Bernie Clarke was a tireless advocate for the conservation values of the promontory, arguing strongly against further dredging and in support of the now wildly beautiful place. He knew little, however, about the wildlife or vegetation there. Characteristic of many of the Georges River campaigners, Clarke as a fisherman could tell you about the riverbed and the sea creatures there but not about the land creatures or their habitat. During this campaign against the second airport, however, he was approached by Arnold McGill, an amateur ornithologist, who had been surveying birdlife on Botany Bay. McGill introduced Clarke to the long journey of the migratory waders – birds that flew over 20,000 kilometres to get to Botany Bay from their northern hemisphere breeding grounds in Siberia, Alaska, Asia and the Arctic Circle.[10] Clarke appreciated the importance of the birds of the area, taking up McGill's concern and adding the protection of birdlife to the campaign to save Towra Point. Yet he admitted to conservationist Gregg Borschmann that his battles to save the river and bay up to then had been based on his lifelong love of the river as a fisherman:

> I didn't know the difference between a pigeon and a wading bird, or an angophora and a blackbutt tree. Back then, a bird was a bird and a tree was a tree.[11]

---

9   Goodall and Cadzow, *Rivers and Resilience*; Irish, *Hidden in Plain View*, 130.
10   Borschmann, 'Guardian of Botany Bay'.
11   Bernie Clarke, quoted in Borschmann, 'Guardian of Botany Bay', 12.

Figure 13.2: Bernie Clarke with migratory wading birds at Towra Point in 1990.

Photographer: Robert Pearce, Fairfax. Obituary, *St George and Sutherland Shire Leader*, 17 January 2019. Courtesy of Nine Publishing.

Clarke was joined by others across the shire and on the northern shores as well, including the Cooks River Valley Association.[12] The pressure mounted by the conservation argument (and, perhaps, local reaction to the aircraft noise demonstration) led Liberal Prime Minister John Gorton to retreat in 1969 from the plan to put the second airport on Towra Point, fearing the loss of votes in the coming elections.[13] Whitlam's Labor Party won government in 1972, which saw Gietzelt in federal parliament as a senator for New South Wales, and an enthusiastic environment minister, Moss Cass. With continuing lobbying from the Sutherland Shire Council and residents, the Whitlam government set about trying to protect Towra Point.[14] The airport plan was discarded permanently and the federal government tried to convince the state government (as state governments hold all power over land under the Australian Constitution) to purchase the promontory from its three private owners. The conservative state government refused to do so. In May 1973 Whitlam announced the dramatic decision that the federal government would compulsorily acquire the land through its Department of Services and Property under the *Land Acquisition Act* and would set the land aside as a national park.

---

12 Tyrrell, *River Dreams*, 152; Muir, *A History of Cooks River*, 8, 172.
13 Borschmann, 'Guardian of Botany Bay'.
14 Wildlife Park Plans', *Canberra Times,* 8 May 1974, 3; '"Threat" to Historic Site', *Canberra Times*, 27 July 1974, 7.

The UNESCO Ramsar Convention was repeatedly raised by Whitlam and Cass, but this international treaty carried no actual power for the Australian Government. It would be a decade before the High Court would decide (in the Franklin Dam case) that the federal government did indeed have foreign affairs power to conserve internationally valued heritage land, so this decision to acquire Towra Point was a groundbreaking precursor to later environmental activism. As Moss Cass explained: 'This will be the first time that any Australian Government has owned and managed land for nature conservation purposes within a State.'[15] Moreover, Towra Point was a complex area, with many different types of valuable environmental sites including sand dunes, wetland and revegetated clearing. All these types of habitat were mentioned in initial announcements of the attempts to have the area protected.

Yet the press focused on the key environmental element that had become dominant in the many concurrent environmental conflicts along the river: mangroves. This was reported very directly in the local press as an issue about mangroves and it was picked up in the national press, with *The Canberra Times* headlining its story about the acquisition 'Mangrove Area to be Reserve'.[16] While the detailed statements of the federal minister and activists like Bernie Clarke explained the complexity of the site, by 1975 the mangroves there had become iconic in all estuarine disputes – they were a metonym, standing in for the whole issue no matter how much more complex it might be.

For Bernie Clarke, too, the mangroves were the key element of the landscape. He may not have known many botanical details about them before the mid-1960s, but he knew about their role in nurturing the fish that he caught. He devoted the rest of his life not only to protecting the mangroves but also to educating people about them and replanting them. He was involved in many campaigns in later years, but what was always closest to his heart was protecting the mangroves. He led school trips along newly constructed boardwalks through the mangroves and he encouraged children to plant mangrove seedlings.

---

15   'Mangrove Area to be Reserve', *Canberra Times,* 21 March 1975, 3.
16   Ibid.

Figure 13.3: Bernie Clarke showing Towra Point mangroves to local primary school students, 1989.

Obituary, *St George and Sutherland Shire Leader*, 17 January 2019. Courtesy of Nine Publishing.

From the early 1990s, Bernie Clarke – and the many school children and fellow conservationists who helped him – planted more than 7,500 mangrove plants on Towra promontory. When Borschmann asked Clarke how he wanted to be remembered, he replied: 'If someone comes along and says, "Bernie Clarke planted those mangroves," that's all the satisfaction I want'.[17]

17   Borschmann, 'Guardian of Botany Bay', 13.

.

Part V: Conclusions

14

Reflections, 1945–80

This book has asked two questions. First, what can we learn about 'suburban resident environmentalism' from the seven environmental conflicts along the Georges River from 1945 to 1980, which have been invisible in the histories of conservation in Australia?

The second question has been to ask about the relationship between these human histories and the histories of the non-human species that were the focus of their conflicts.

The first question is the more familiar one for historians: any activism is shaped by its time and place. This study shows that characterisation of this unquestionably 'suburban' life as if it were focused only within the private blocks of individually owned land is inadequate. Instead, environmental activism on the Georges River in the mid-twentieth century is comparable to the areas Sellers discusses, in that the broader environment was as important for residents as their individual block and house.[1] It will have become clear in these pages that suburbs aren't monolithic or uniform, and that within areas often dismissed as 'suburban' there are wide differences. This book has considered seven 'suburban' environmental campaigns: one in the 1950s, another in the early 1960s, and the other five occurring close together along the river and often interacting from the mid-1960s to the mid-1970s and beyond. Each of these campaigns was distinctive, as earlier chapters have shown, but just as important, there were many common themes. This chapter, while recognising the diversities, will consider what those common themes were.

---

1   Sellers, *Crabgrass Crucible*.

The residents were there for different reasons, but for all of them, the river was a part of their vision of the place. This was not an area where people saw their lives confined by the fences around their blocks. Some of the residents in the area in the postwar years were there by choice, and proximity to the river and open space were a strong factor in such choices. Others had not chosen to be there – the international refugees, the assisted migrants or the 'slum cleared' inner-city people – but some of them had used the river and its parklands to make new homes for themselves, or at least to make their stay there more meaningful. So for all of them, the river was a central part of their lives.

The suburban environmental campaigns, as suggested in earlier chapters and discussed below, were largely monocultural and rarely if ever recognised that Aboriginal people had a continuing presence along the river.[2] Yet, despite little consideration of colonialism and its continuing impacts, there was an awareness – expressed most clearly among the East Hills campaigners – that Aboriginal societies prior to British invasion and settlement had valuable practices in environmental management. In keeping with Aboriginal principles, a recurrent theme among upper estuary working-class residents like the Jacobsen family, who fished and hunted game for food, was that wildlife was not to be hunted for sport, nor wasted, but was instead to be utilised fully.[3] Maria Nugent has pointed out that settlers often accorded a limited role to Aboriginal people in their own histories as a source of authenticity about places and practices.[4] The theme was common among bushwalkers and early conservationists too that settlers who cared for environments and wildlife were under an obligation – as heirs to the idealised Aboriginal people assumed to be former owners – to honour such principles.[5] This romanticised vision of being heirs to vanished but noble environmentalists empowered conservationists although it also sustained the continued marginalisation of the many Aboriginal families who still lived in the area.

The early campaign in the 1950s to achieve the first Georges River National Park was fuelled by both the hopes and fears generated by the impacts of World War II. Federal decisions to increase industrialisation and population had very specific impacts on the Georges River, where

---

2   For evidence to the contrary see Goodall and Cadzow, *Rivers and Resilience*.
3   Kevin, Colin and Carol Jacobsen, interview, 12 July 2006.
4   Nugent, 'Historical Encounters'.
5   Harper, 'The Battle for the Bush'; White and Ford, *Playing in the Bush*; Nugent, *Botany Bay*; Nugent, 'Historical Encounters'; Banivanua Mar, *Decolonisation and the Pacific*.

state government goals to reduce inner-city overcrowding combined with rising manufacturing and immigration to increase the population in the Bankstown area at a faster rate than anywhere else in the city. The County of Cumberland Plan (CCP) brought hope but also fear. It proposed a 'green zone' stretching from the Royal National Park in Sutherland all the way to the Georges River, stimulating the hope that the bushland along the river would be valued as 'national' and belong to local people. Yet the CCP also argued for increased density in township 'residential' areas, worsening the fear that 'a rash of soulless blocks of two-storey flats' would 'run riot' across the area.[6]

In class terms, the resident action groups were mixed. Gentrifying residents (in areas newly subdivided like Padstow Heights overlooking Little Salt Pan Creek on the north side and downstream in Bonnet Bay and Sylvania Waters on the southern side) contributed both to the Georges River Oyster Lease Protest Association (GROLPA), which opposed the oyster farms, and to the Little Salt Pan Creek campaign against reclamation and garbage dumps. Yet many of those activists who could be considered professional, like the teachers in Lime Kiln Bay and those in Oatley Bay, had a history of Australian Labor Party and union activism. They saw themselves as being in opposition to the more affluent residents. Residents of the Oatley area contacted by Dave Koffel saw themselves as 'silvertails', but in the end discovered they held very little power.

Another complicated group were the oyster farmers. The work they did was hard manual labour, often in difficult and unpleasant conditions, whether handling trays on the water or shucking and bottling oysters in the sheds. At the same time, they were an aspirational group who saw their enterprises as small businesses, and insisted they be called 'farmers'. Yet they were dismissed by both councils and new gentrifying residents as unsightly and outdated, cluttering up the river views no matter how luxurious their products. It was only to be newly built alliances between such unlikely groups as the teachers and the oyster farmers that gave the campaigners the numbers they needed to put pressure on local government. Such alliances were often – eventually – successful in staving off the loss of the riverfront bushland environments.

---

6   Editorial, *Bankstown Torch*, 27 December 1972, 2.

Each of the campaigns hoped to gain attention to achieve their goals, but their varied situations gave them differing supporters. The gentrifying residents with expensive land 'with a view' – like those at Little Salt Pan Creek and GROLPA at Sylvania Waters – received editorial sympathy from local press and even, at times, from local government, perhaps because of the rates they paid. The fishing people at the Moon bays had little support from either the press or councils, but were strongly supported by ecologists and the activist state Fisheries Branch, and, surprisingly by Eric Lewis, chief secretary in a conservative state government but nevertheless a geographer with an interest in environment. This question of river water quality activated also at least some of the professionals in local government, like Hunt and Howard from Bankstown, whose evidence to the Senate Select Committee claimed the spotlight at a national level.

Those who faced the most bitter local government opponents, almost simultaneously, were at Lime Kiln Bay, facing off against Hurstville Council, and those at Oatley Bay, confronting Kogarah Council. These campaigns chose different strategies, with Lime Kiln Bay campaigners proving highly effective in drawing in the state Opposition politicians from the Australian Labor Party, forcing the deteriorating conditions of the river into the metropolitan press and onto the state political agenda. Those around Oatley Bay – in the Save Poulton Park Campaign and in the Oatley Flora and Fauna Society – focused on education, mobilising networks of large conservation organisations as well as student and academic networks like the Society for Social Responsibility in Science. Yet, each of these campaigns also aimed to build alliances. The Lime Kiln Bay Committee practised energetic outreach to local people across all types of organisations as well as political figures, while the Poulton Park and OFF campaigners joined forces with the oyster farmers as well as the educators.

None of these campaigns achieved all the goals they wanted and some of the activists were left with a deep sense of failure. Yet, together – with different strategies and alliances – they changed the public conversation across these suburbs as well as in state and national politics.

Across most of the conflicts, from the early campaign to achieve the Georges River National Park, to the later downstream ones opposing dredging, dumping and reclamation, there was at least one common theme. Few of the uses to which residents put the river and parklands – even the powerboat races and water skiing that GROLPA wanted –

were solitary. There may have been some who fished or walked alone, exploring and observing, but most people were seeking social interactions: picnics among family or friends, or those organised by church groups, unions or progress associations; fishing with mates or talking with nearby fishers about baits and catches. Even the quieter areas associated with assignations – illicit or unconventional sexual contacts, beats or secret meetings – were expressions of social networks, however marginalised or repressed. Sociality was, therefore, a sustained element in the uses of the open spaces of this suburban area, and of the places that were defended in these environmental movements of the 1960s and 1970s.

The changes on the river were directly related to the changing postwar economy. There was a massive increase in population and industrial activity along the river, which brought significant diversification in class. Land prices rose more rapidly where river views were accessible, so, by the early decades of the twenty-first century, more affluent residents lived closer to the river while lower-income residents lived further away from the river. Yet it was lower-income residents who were the most common users of the parks.[7] There had been little progress in acquiring new open public space away from the river after the 1970s.[8] It had been the rugged, sandy or boggy areas close to the river that continued to offer the majority of open spaces for parks or remaining bushland in all the local government areas through which the Georges River ran.[9] Oyster farmers too needed the continued mangrove and saltmarsh swamps not only as a cleansing habitat but also to break the force of the tides and the wakes from the increasing numbers of speedboats on the estuary.

The socialities of the lower Georges River environmental campaigns had not been cross-cultural. During the mid-twentieth century, there were gatherings of Italian and Greek immigrants as well as of the continuing Aboriginal populations in the area, but these communities were not included in the more public gatherings of the majority Anglo-Irish populations along the river in the years from 1945 to the mid-1970s. Nor were members of the non-Anglo communities invited into, or included in, the suburban environmental campaigns considered in this paper. The state government pushed both residents and local government

---

7   Byrne, Goodall and Cadzow, *Place-Making in National Parks*; Cadzow, Byrne and Goodall, *Waterborne*; Goodall, Byrne and Cadzow, *Waters of Belonging*.

8   News South Wales Department of Environment and Planning, 'Open Space in the Sydney Region'.

9   Cunneen, 'Hands Off the Parks!'.

out of parklands management in the 1980s on the grounds of lack of diversity, but the government was concerned about formal qualifications and gender imbalances, not about cultural imbalances, and it took no action to redress such isolations.

Nevertheless, despite being relatively monocultural, it was sociality rather than solitary interactions with nature that was the more likely characteristic of all the Georges River campaigns from 1945 to 1980. A sense of working together motivated the activists in each of these campaigns and, as Dave Koffel and others have explained, involved extensive time and emotional commitments, with long hours after work and stressful meetings with local government councillors and officials. So the shared work and the shared anxieties all strengthened commitments.

Gender was a factor in these resident action environment campaigns. Families shared in all this campaigning, as memories and documents of each of these campaigns show – husbands and wives, sons and daughters, all took part in the letterboxing, fundraising and, often, in the planning. Most important, as was demonstrated by Evol Knight in the Poulton Creek dispute, was the role women could play in building person-to-person relationships across previously separated groups. There had been little interaction across decades between the oyster farming families and those of their neighbours who worked in land-based jobs, yet their interests had often been very similar. It was the personal and 'behind the scenes' roles that women could play as neighbours, friends and spouses that could draw people together in order to see how closely their goals coincided.

Further, in each campaign, from East Hills to Oatley Bay, women took active roles in initiating activities and in resourcing – through cooking and managing – the social events and working parties that kept these campaigns going. It seems too that it was women particularly whose interests in informal sociality were a theme in all the campaigns. The playing fields for competitive sport for which local government councils were so often calling for garbage dumping and reclamation were still often in use for sporting codes that, at their most elite levels, were predominantly for male players. At the level of local sports, girls were increasingly likely to be visible, taking part in long-established netball and hockey competitions and also, occasionally, in newly formed girls' soccer and AFL teams. Nevertheless, the campaigns against escalating reclamation of swampland to create sporting fields were often fuelled by undercurrents of resentment against the loss of wild places for the informal and non-competitive sociality that was shown in each campaign to be valued highly by women along the river.

Yet, in most groups, whether oyster farmers or land-based residents, it was men who were recognised as the spokespeople of the campaigns. It reflects the gender order of these areas that it was accepted both within the families and by formal bodies like local government councils that it would be men who took roles of public responsibility. Unmarried men or women, however silent they may be about sexual orientation and identification, were less visible; these suburban environments were undoubtedly difficult for men and women who were homosexual or in any way divergent from the nuclear family models.

Another thread that runs through all these campaigns is the fear of loss of spaciousness, a rising population and the erosion of open spaces. Yet these campaigns were each quite clear that what they wanted was not simply 'green space' – the generic term in use today in which 'green' can refer to grass or manicured parks and playing fields. These campaigns all wanted to keep native, uncultivated and wild bushland – exactly as the Poulton Creek campaign had printed on its sticker: 'Keep bushland in our suburbs.' They were each campaigning to protect *bush* – vegetation that was understood to be endemic and that was not manicured or tailored into a 'garden' but instead reflected some sort of original condition. Mangroves were the key representative of all the rest of the 'bush' that these campaigns were trying to protect; if they could save the mangroves, they could save the adjacent, more complex, habitats, both on land and underwater, and so protect the animal, fish and birdlife that might need that habitat.

During interviews, few people remembered faecal contamination of the river as one of their motivating factors, even though it had resulted from the population increase of which they were so anxiously aware. Instead, campaigners focused on a horror of being suffocatingly crowded. One of the qualities about suburban life in the Georges River area was the sense of an uncrowded world in which ready access to the river was central. The river was a core of the imagined landscape within which local people lived. This had been central to the campaign to gain the Georges River National Park in the 1950s and to defend it in the 1960s.

As the population increased more rapidly in the Bankstown local government area (LGA) than in most other areas, the anxiety about losing this sense of spaciousness rose rapidly through the decades. The example of neighbouring LGAs was often raised, where medium-density housing had mushroomed with walk-up blocks of four-storey flats.[10] But whereas the campaigners in the 1950s were anxious about losing access to daily living and recreational space, the campaigners of the later 1960s and 1970s, with greater awareness of ecology and the relationships between species – human and non-human – were fearful not only of crowding among people but also of the irretrievable loss of habitats and environmental networks in the more-than-human world. All these elements had been present in the Little Salt Pan Creek campaign: the anxieties of long-term residents about losing spaciousness and the fears of newer, more affluent, residents about losing their views of native bushland.

These environmental campaigns were attempts to conserve riverine environments, above and below the water. So, while most were focused on the low-lying waterlogged places called swamps, few of these campaigns demonstrated the interests that appear most commonly in the conservation campaigns to defend what are today called 'wetlands', which often focus on birdlife. This was despite the fact that, in earlier years, there had been evidence of many species of birds on the Georges River and its large swamplands like Kelso. Population increase, subdivisions and small-scale 'reclamations' for golf courses from the 1920s had reduced these habitats and undermined the bird population.

Instead, the most tenacious defence of the Georges River swamps from 1945 to 1980 came from fishing people. In working within the river's waters, fishers shared many interests with oyster farmers, but fishing people had an even greater commitment to the uncultivated and 'wild' dimensions of the river's ecology. This interest was present in the campaign for the original Georges River National Park but became particularly prominent in the campaigns around Great Moon Bay and Towra Point, where the threat to fish from dredging was most urgent. Yet, in all the campaigns, the swamps that were to be destroyed by 'reclamation' were valued as nurturing environments for aquatic species, including immature fish and crustaceans. This concern highlighted the role of mangroves in linking with networks of living species, demanding a refusal to privilege

---

10   As noted in Editorial, *Bankstown Torch*, 27 December 1972, about neighbouring suburbs where blocks of flats had 'run riot'.

an orientation to land only but rather to recognise the ecology of the whole river, above and below the waterline. This was compounded in the postwar years by well-founded anxieties about toxic discharge from the rapidly increasing number of factories along the river as well as from the experimental Lucas Heights nuclear reactor.

There was virtually no regulation nor accounting of the contents of factory discharges into the river and very little about volumes, as the Senate Select Committee found in sittings from 1969.[11] Yet the State Pollution Control Commission, established by the New South Wales Government to respond to the same popular concerns as the federal Senate Committee, proved itself in the Oatley Bay dispute to have little real power over the Kogarah Council, which was committed to garbage dumping and reclamation for sports grounds. The experience of fishing people extended from the killing associated with hunting through to insight into the psychology of aquatic species, as well as awareness of preferred habitats and concerns over sustainability. It has been the case in Africa and South Asia that hunters have become some of the most effective conservation advocates as they have shifted their knowledge from predator to protector. On the Georges River, the tireless conservationist Bernie Clarke, as a former commercial fisher, is one example, as is Kevin Howard, the Bankstown health inspector who drew on his recreational fishing experience to inform his approaches to the problems of garbage disposal and river conservation. It is notable that Clarke learned about birdlife and migratory species only while he was campaigning to save Towra Point, although he rapidly incorporated this into his advocacy.

The determination of the Georges River campaigners to focus on the environment they lived with, however polluted it was, is one of the reasons these campaigns do not appear in the histories of Australian conservation. Unlike mainstream conservation organisations, which tended to be more interested in wilderness, the suburban environmentalists wanted to intervene in, and improve, environmental quality where they lived – even if it was damaged. This was a particularly distinctive element in the Oatley Bay campaign for Poulton Creek and its banks, which came to focus on the educational value of these polluted and compromised estuarine ecologies for inquiry-based learning for schools and for the public. This had been raised in other campaigns, like that at Lime Kiln Bay, but it was most

---

11   Birch, Evenden and Teutsch, 'Dominance of Point Source', demonstrated the validity of the concerns, although there was little confirmation at the time.

developed downstream around Poulton Creek and Oatley Bay. And across all these campaigns, both the working-class campaigners of the 1950s and the aspirational teachers and oyster farmers of the lower Georges River in the 1970s were focused on their own surroundings. They chose not to spend their energy on distant 'wilderness' areas. Instead, the Georges River suburban environmentalists, even as the area gentrified, campaigned in the present to protect the polluted, damaged river at their doors – however much they might hope to heal that damaged environment in the future.

Perhaps the other reason these campaigns have not attracted analysis as conservation campaigns is that, despite their attempts, they did not gain support from the progressive union movement. The New South Wales Builders Labourers' Federation (BLF) had, by this time, initiated their widely publicised 'green bans' strategy (see Chapter 8), but there was very little involvement of the BLF in the Georges River area. The Lime Kiln Bay campaigners appealed to the Municipal and Shire Council Employees' Union for support, as it covered the workers who dug up the mangroves and bushland at the councils' instructions and then dumped the silt and garbage on the razed mangroves and swamplands. The leadership of this union was aligned with the conservative wing of the Trades and Labor Council and demonstrated emphatically, in its rejection of residents' calls for support, that it was not interested in challenging the councils on this issue or developing a policy on environmental matters.

Despite their green bans, even the rank and file leadership of the BLF recognised that union members were divided on questions of support for heritage conservation and urban planning to foster social justice and environmental conservation. Only after many meetings and internal debates did a significant proportion – although still not all – of the membership decide to support the green bans policy.[12] This process and policy attracted articulate and politically active groups in university and conservation circles, drawing attention to a whole series of inner-city disputes in which unionists were prepared to confront big, multinational development corporations in order to defend low-income and socially disadvantaged residents' interests.[13]

---

12 Burgmann and Burgmann, *Green Bans, Red Union*.
13 Bacon, 'They Huffed and They Puffed'; Jakubowicz, 'The Green Ban Movement'.

The resulting alliances, including the development of the Total Environment Centre (TEC) in 1972, forced shifts in the environment movement, directing attention to urban questions, social justice conflicts and the role of major development companies in environmental questions. The TEC, founded by two Georges River residents, Milo Dunphy and Bob Walshe (then still teaching but increasingly involved with environmental politics), reflected the motivating force of the environmental problems at their backs – on the Georges River. Yet the TEC focused attention throughout most of the 1970s on confrontations with big multinational corporations, like the oil companies with refineries in Botany Bay, rather than on less dramatic and small-scale confrontations with local government councils over the intractable problems of waste disposal. The 1976 TEC report on the Cooks River was important but was not to be repeated in other suburban rivers. The enemies of the Georges River resident environmental advocates did not pose such dramatic David and Goliath confrontations – they were not global transnational corporations. It was harder to mobilise strong support for campaigns about confrontations with local councillors (however ridiculous those confrontations might be) concerning unpleasant but common problems like human waste and fly-blown garbage.

The second question of this study – about how the human and non-human histories of the river were related – remains unresolved, but it is possible to sketch out some conclusions.

As always, non-human species were changing – often rapidly – and, in urban conditions, this was occurring at unprecedented rates by the mid-twentieth century. While many species were undergoing changes, the most apparent were those occurring in the large aquatic plants (or macrophytes) along the river. Mangroves drew most of the attention, both from the environmental campaigners and their opponents, even though they were not the only species undergoing changes in distribution or behaviour. But they were the largest and the most visible. And they had also accumulated a large amount of cultural baggage in European culture and medicine, being historically viewed as sources of miasmas and diseases at the most mundane level, and of malignant spiritual forces at the more immaterial level. This cultural baggage from Europe had been intensified among white Australians as they had experienced colonial control and then warfare in the tropical areas of South-East Asia and Papua New Guinea. The long-established European fears of 'fens' and 'bogs' had been exacerbated by persistent post-traumatic stress disorders after the horrors of tropical mangrove swamp battlefields in South-East Asia in WWII for many of the Australians who had, like Brewer, taken on public service as municipal engineers or in similar roles.[14] Mangroves, both in myths and in recent wartime experiences, were the species that inhabited *both* land and water, meaning they were seen as unnatural as well as malevolent.

For opponents of environmental campaigns, mangroves were a continuation of this negative past of disease and evil. Mangroves were a pest species that indicated a damaged environment that needed to be 'reclaimed' and healed to become dry land. Such hostility was often directed at the activists campaigning to save them. As Dave Koffel remembers, the Hurstville aldermen told him and the other Lime Kiln Bay campaigners that they were 'all communists defending a mosquito-ridden swamp'.[15] Such vitriol (and such politicised hostility) was seldom made public, although there were some councillors from Hurstville and Kogarah who allowed themselves to be quoted along these lines, including Albert Brewer, Hurstville's municipal engineer who called mangroves 'a foul and noxious weed and a cancerous growth' in 1969, and the Kogarah councillors who called mangroves 'a stinking, mosquito-infested swamp' and a 'dirty, stinking mass' in February 1974.[16]

The more common public stance was that of the 1974 Hurstville Engineer's Report, written by a different municipal engineer, E. Anderson. His report was just as negative as Brewer's 1969 statement, but Anderson was able to give even more evidence that mangroves were expanding in that area. He drew on recent quantification of mangrove distribution since 1930 to argue that what the council proposed was really going to be for the best (it would mean more playing fields, about which the councils were under so much lobbying pressure) and would make very little difference to the existing mangrove cover.

The environmental campaigners opposed 'reclamation' altogether, arguing that it would lead to the removal of all estuarine species and the creation of flat playing fields, picnic areas and golf courses. So they argued against

---

14 'Editorial: Why Keep an Eyesore?', *Leader*, 7 August 1974, 2. See also the editor's response about 'witnessing first-hand what damage mangroves can do in Papua New Guinea and Queensland', in letter to the editor, 'Mangroves Do Give Support for Wildlife', *Leader*, 21 August 1974, 21; Gullett, *Not as a Duty Only*, 9.

15 Koffel, interview.

16 Hurstville Shire Engineer A. H. Brewer, quoted in Dunstan, 'Some Early Environmental Problems and Guidelines in NSW Estuaries', 3; 'Angry Residents Rout Protesters', *St George and Sutherland Shire Leader*, 27 February 1974.

the uprooting not only of mangroves but also of saltmarsh overall, and all the associated salt-tolerant species like casuarinas and ti-trees. At first the expansion of mangroves along the sheltered banks of the lower estuary was little noticed. It was only in the 1950s that the groups considered here began to identify the changing accessibility of the river's banks. While there was open conflict among the Picnic Point Regatta Association and Georges River National Park campaigners, some people drew a general distinction between mangroves and other endemic species, which allowed Alf Stills, for example, to condone mangrove removal, although George Jacobsen held out for total protection.

By the later 1960s, the mangroves were impossible to ignore; however, the rapidity of their expansion was hard to admit in a campaign that was arguing that nature was fragile and needed protection. To do so would risk undermining their case. Nor were the causes of mangrove expansion understood. No campaign documents link local causes like sewage contamination of river water with mangrove expansion and there was no recognition at all of global human-induced climate change in that period, so sea level or temperature rise was simply not considered.

During this time too, knowledge of ecological relationships was just beginning to be disseminated, demonstrating the importance of mangroves for the health of the river itself. This drew both fishing people and commercial users like oyster farmers into the earlier coalitions of land-based riverbank users who had protested the 'reclamations'. By no means could it be said that mangroves became anyone's much-loved 'charismatic species', but attitudes were shifting. Many dimensions of mangrove biology were becoming better known and some were useful for campaigning, such as the mangroves' capacity to filter and clean river water.

Most notably, the elements of mangrove biology that were invariably drawn on for campaigning emphasised their nurturing capacity; that is, their capacity to protect and feed the immature life stages of fish and other aquatic species. This anthropomorphic, nurturing and *maternal* role for mangroves was consistently used in campaign literature and appeals, no doubt because it was the most likely to evoke empathy among audiences and counter existing prejudices against the species.

While such arguments formed the expressed campaign language of press releases and correspondence, the very size and visibility of the expanding mangroves made them valuable to the campaigners – it allowed them a clear body of vegetation to defend. The 'bush' that campaigners wanted to retain was complex and had many species, so it was easy to refer to in general, but harder to specify. Saltmarsh was nondescript and unobtrusive in Sydney, which was towards the northerly upper limit of its range, so it was much less noticed, even by botanists at that stage, who did not begin to research temperate saltmarsh until around 1990.[17] Saltmarsh too, therefore, made a less useful 'environment' to defend. Instead, it was the broader complex, called 'mangrove swamp', that could use the better known and more visible mangrove plant as a symbol of the wider landscape – both saltmarsh and 'bush' – that needed to be conserved.[18]

On the Georges River estuary, the human histories came to be shaped by mangroves, whether the opposing groups responded with disgust, like the advocates of 'reclamation', or with protective defence, like the resident environmental campaigners, the 'mangrovites'. Had the mangroves not been invading both saltmarsh and open water, the municipal 'reclaimers' would have had fewer strategies to solve their exploding garbage problem. Had there been no expanding, smelly, confronting mangroves, pushing into everyone's attention, the activists would have had little readily identifiable 'bush' to defend in order to save the social relationships they valued. While the mangroves themselves were not pleasant, furry or cuddly, their representation as maternal nurturers of baby fish allowed them to play a role as charismatic species to save the wider swamps and bushlands.

---

17   Peter Fairweather, pers. comm., 2019; Fairweather, 'Ecological Changes Due to Our Use of the Coast'; Saintilan, *Australian Saltmarsh Ecology*. There is only one early article on mangroves and saltmarsh, but it's not Georges River–focused and is concerned with zoning and distribution. See Clarke and Hannon, 'The Mangrove Swamp'.
18   LKBPC, Press Release 1, December 1973, LKBPC Archive; *OFF Newsletter*, August 1974.

15

Afterword: Disasters, Regenerations and Ambiguities

Disasters

The battle between the Georges River oyster farmers and the cashed-up waterfront block owners at Sylvania continued across the 1970s. The waterfront landowners were represented by the Georges River Oyster Lease Protest Association, enthusiastically supported by the *St George and Sutherland Shire Leader*. Then disaster struck, in July 1978, with 2,000 people across Australia developing acute gastroenteritis after eating Georges River oysters.[1] Contributing to the resulting panic, and without any proof, the *Leader* suggested that the poisoning was caused through contamination of oysters by parvovirus, a virus rarely found in humans (and in whom it has very different symptoms than those of gastroenteritis) but with a canine variant with which many readers would have been familiar.[2]

---

1 'Oyster Ban "Disaster for Farmers"', *St George and Sutherland Shire Leader* (hereafter *Leader*), 19 July 1978, 5; 'Oyster Famers to Meet Over Freeze on Sales', *Leader*, 2 August 1978, 11; 'Oyster Farmers Start Afresh', *Leader*, 23 August 1978, 9; 'Safeguards for Oysters', *Leader*, 6 September 1978, 2.
2 '"Ghost" Ban on Oysters: "No Evidence"', *Leader*, 4 October 1978, 1; 'Oyster Firm Shells Out to Prove Point', *Leader*, 11 October 1978, 15.

It took 16 months, to October 1979, until the results of research into the contamination were published in the *Medical Journal of Australia*. The authors, Murphy, Grohmann and Christopher, with others, found that the harmful contaminant in the oysters had indeed been a virus, not bacteria, but that it had not been parvovirus. Their bacteriological tests showed that, while 'some batches of oysters were contaminated by sewage', it was not any bacterial contaminant in the oysters that had been passed on to the people who became ill after eating the oysters. Instead, what had affected them had been Norwalk virus, 'a known cause of acute non-bacterial gastroenteritis' that 'has not been identified previously outside the United States of America and has not been linked to food-borne gastroenteritis before'.[3]

This result was a surprise for people who had assumed it was the sewage contamination that had caused the problems, although it did little to dispel the general disquiet. In response, Georges River oyster farmers withdrew their oysters from sale and the Minister for Fisheries introduced 'fishing closure' restrictions under the *Fisheries and Oyster Farms Act 1935* to prohibit the taking of oysters from the estuary. Sites were chosen further into Botany Bay at, for example, Weeney Bay and Quibray Bay on the eastern side of Towra Point, where oysters could be held before marketing to allow cleansing from contaminants by natural elimination. In addition, many oyster farmers began the installation of expensive purification equipment.[4]

But the damage had been done. After two decades of troubling headlines about sewage pollution, and despite strenuous efforts by oyster farmers to repair the image of their product, consumers responded by turning away from oysters grown in the river. There were faltering restarts but the industry was then afflicted by further troubles: first by poisonings of the oysters by TBT (an ingredient in anti-fouling paint put onto watercraft prohibited in many countries and eventually in New South Wales); second, by the aggressive impacts of the introduced Pacific oyster; and, finally, in 1994, by QX disease, a parasite that killed up to 90 per cent of all the rock oysters in the Georges River.[5] By 2000, oyster farming

---

3   Murphy et al., 'An Australia-Wide Outbreak', 329.
4   'Safeguards for Oysters', *Leader*, 6 September 1978, 2; 'Oysters Get Clean-Up', *Leader*, 8 November 1978, 2; 'Breakthrough Claim in Clean Oyster Study', *Leader*, 15 November 1978, 9; 'Oyster Growers "Saved": Mammoth Job Ahead after Lifting of Four-Month State Ban', *Leader*, 22 November 1978, 2; Derwent, interview.
5   Nell, 'The History of Oyster Farming', 20.

closed down on the Georges River almost entirely, continuing only in one isolated leasehold, with Sydney rock oyster production now continuing in coastal locations to the north and south of Sydney.[6]

The impact on members of the extended oyster farming families among Georges River residents has continued to be distressing. Some oyster farmers, like Laurie Derwent, had left the industry before the problems from 1978 emerged. He retrained in environmental studies and worked in conservation, administration and legal roles in state government agencies.[7] Others retired,[8] but some were simply shattered, forced onto the dole for the first time in their lives and left with few possibilities for productive work.[9]

Regenerations

The campaigns of the 1970s built on the work of the 1950s campaigners and carried the new wave of the river lands' regeneration. For all their limitations, their monoculturalism and their localisms, these campaigns halted the rush of local and state governments to solve both sewage and garbage problems by dumping waste into the river or onto the surrounding wetlands. By saving the riverbed, water quality and at least some of the foreshores, these campaigns allowed a breathing space. Some of the new wave of regeneration was led by ideas introduced very directly by these campaigners.

One idea was about recycling as a way to address the unmanageable explosion of garbage. The very first press release of the Lime Kiln Bay Preservation Committee directed Hurstville Council to take up the separation and sorting of solid waste into different types of materials and to seek out ways to use these products fruitfully: 'We just cannot go on forever tipping into our rivers and estuaries. No mangrove area is safe anymore.' Recycling was not being used by any local government in

6   Drake, interview. The only remaining oyster lease on the Georges River, originally developed by Bob Drake, president of the Oyster Farmers Association from 1978, was covered in ABC TV *Landline*, Sunday 22 June 2020.
7   Derwent, interview.
8   Drake, interview.
9   Knight, interview.

Australia at that time, but the sustained pressure from campaigners like the Lime Kiln Bay group has led to the situation now where recycling is widespread.[10]

Another of the ideas raised from the beginning of the Lime Kiln Bay campaign was to work with engineers and biologists to better manage household run-off so that water coming into the river was made cleaner. Continued pressure from the Lime Kiln Bay campaigners on Hurstville Council led to the successful development of an artificial wetlands scheme there, which has in turn drawn back the abundance of bird and native animal life as well as expanding the spaces for sociality and picnics along with walking places for local residents and their dogs.

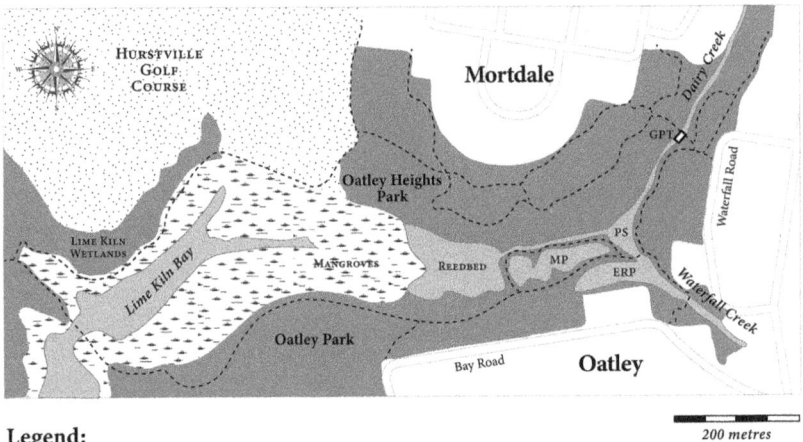

Legend:

GPT Gross Pollutant Trap
MP Macrophyte Pond
PS Primary Sediment Pond
ERP Eastern Ridge Pond
---- Walking Track

200 metres

Map 15.1: Saving Lime Kiln Bay.

The Lime Kiln Bay Preservation Committee argued for a filtration system to protect the bay from polluting run-off from surrounding suburbs. The result is shown here in the present-day Dairy Creek pollution trap and pond filtration system, eventually built by the state government, to protect Lime Kiln Bay from storm water run-off. Map redrawn for this volume with permission from Mo (2015). Cartography: Sharon Harrup.

---

10   LKBPC Press Release 1, [December 1973], reported in 'Hands off Lime Kiln Bay, Petition Urges', *Leader*, 9 January 1974, 11 and 'Study Need Before Bay Reclaimed', *Leader*, 23 January 1974, [supplement, 10]; 'It's Getting Worse: Mangrove Dumping Protest', *St George Pictorial*, 9 January 1974, 1.

Figure 15.1: Ruth Staples, bank regenerator, 2009.

Ruth Staples continued to be active in bush regeneration along the Georges River until she became unwell in the last year of her life. She is shown here exploring the saltmarsh area on lower Mill Creek (Guragurang). Photographer: Heather Goodall.

Yet another Lime Kiln Bay proposal was that the vegetation on creek and riverbanks should be restored to a healthy state, both aiding in the improvement of water quality and the environment of living creatures in the water and on the foreshores. The method the Lime Kiln Bay campaigners suggested was the Bradley method for bush regeneration, another early strategy that was to prove effective and was widely adopted.

Although labour intensive, it has demonstrated its value in removing invasive species and fostering regrowth among locally endemic species. Further, because it demands such intensive labour, it has been organised through groups of volunteers, thus offering a new way to practice and expand the sociality that had been so important in earlier uses of the river lands. When funding has been available, councils have managed such regeneration work, but the local volunteer groups have continued whether or not there were paid coordinators available. This has remained a local resident-driven environmental process.[11]

As the local campaigns in the 1970s demonstrated, children were involved along with their parents in the campaign work, dropping off leaflets and stickers, collecting signatures for petitions and spreading the word among school friends. At least some of these younger members of the campaigning families went on to careers in environmentally related professions.[12] The Georges River blues have, of course, continued, with a recent conflict in 2018 when Hurstville Council and then the Georges River Council sought to sell off the former Oatley Bowling Club site (being part of Myles Dunphy Reserve) for housing development. There was strong local resident protest, including younger members of families who had been involved in earlier protests against reclamation. Only after this local protest did the Department of Planning step in, refusing permission for the sale as there was too little public open space left in the area.[13]

The local municipal and shire councils to which the campaigners became increasingly opposed were themselves divided. At times such divisions aligned with party affiliation, but it was not always so simple. Some left-wing representatives and officers were focused on playing fields, like the Australian Labor Party Hurstville councillor, Alderman Lawrance. There were others, however, considered to be conservatives, at local government and state government level, like Eric Willis, who were very responsive

---

11 Staples, interview, 27 October 2005; Koffel, interview; David Koffel, notes of a meeting with Hurstville Municipal Council, 28 February 1975, LKBPC Archive; Australian Association of Bush Regenerators, 'The Bradley Method', accessed 21 January 2021, www.aabr.org.au/learn/what-i-bush-regeneration/general-principles/the-bradley-method/. Now part of Georges Riverkeeper program, when funding is available, see Salt et al., 'Georges Riverkeeper'. See also Benson and Howell, *Taken for Granted*.

12 Robert Haworth, from Lime Kiln Bay (Ruth Staples's younger brother); Laurie Derwent and Alexandra Knight (from the Derwent oyster farming families who became active in the Oatley Bay campaign) are examples. Even with less direct involvement in the environmental campaigns, the experience of growing up on a threatened river was motivation for studies in ecology. Saintilan, interview.

13 Laurie Derwent, pers. comm., describing his daughter's participation to protest the sale.

to emerging environmental ideas and rising pressure from residents. Always there were competing demands – in gentrifying suburbs with very different class and real estate values, and between waterfront landowners and oyster farmers – as well as the persistence of myths and wartime experiences, so it was only to be expected that the councils were unreliable allies. Yet, some officers, like Hunt and Howard in Bankstown, as well as councillors like Gietzelt and Skinner in Sutherland, and Julian Sheen in Hurstville, were able to offer support as the emerging campaigns took shape. Eventually, the Georges River Council's Riverkeeper program was initiated in the 1990s, bringing together many councils in improving the health of the river.[14] Alongside the campaigners and local government officials and representatives, those who most brought about change were unquestionably the Fisheries Branch biologists Don Francois, W. B. Malcolm and others who gave up their time to engage in what is often called 'outreach' to teach and learn with local people about how best to intervene in damaged, suburban riverine environments. It was this patient interchange over many years that ensured that groups like the Lime Kiln Bay Preservation Committee and the Save Poulton Park Campaign had the information and language needed to power their campaign.

Ambiguities

The campaigns had consequences that were often different from those that activists had imagined. The river and its foreshore parklands had been more or less saved through their activism, which drew together diverse interest groups from fishers and oyster farmers through to picnickers and birdwatchers through to health professionals and aquatic ecologists. Their campaigns enabled the continuation of the mixed open space of the river and foreshores, with a combination of picnic spaces, playing fields and bushland. The spaces still allowed for socialities, but they were not necessarily the ones expected by the campaigners. The continuing expansion of the population meant that all the quiet market gardens and backwater creeks where non-Anglo groups had gathered for their shared meals, games and ceremonies in earlier years had all been subdivided and sold. Increasingly, as the population aged, the young people for whom the campaigners had wanted to save the bushland or build the playing fields had grown up and moved away.

---

14   Salt et al., 'Georges Riverkeeper'; Cavanaugh, 'The Aboriginal Riverkeeper Team'.

Figure 15.2: Australia Day, Burrawang Reach, Georges River National Park, 2005.

Picnickers at the Georges River National Park include many immigrant families, who come from many different places, including Vietnam and the Middle East. Georges River Arabic-speakers include Christians, Mandaeans and Muslims, such as these women in hijab sitting beside the river. Photographer: Heather Goodall.

Now, in the twenty-first century, there are new immigrants and refugees coming to work in the factories or live in the hostels along the river. Since the 1990s, the people who have come to the parklands and the river to picnic or play sport have not come from old Anglo and Irish families. Instead they have been Vietnamese, Arabic-speaking, Pacific Islander or African families, bringing their old people to remember the homes they had left behind and their children to hear those stories of lost homes or to explore and play games to learn more about their new homes.[15] In many ways, these new gatherings looked different from the old Sunday school picnics or factory Christmas parties or the earlier shared meals around fires that had created the middens. They might involve prayer times and naming ceremonies as well as football games across the picnic ground.

---

15   Byrne, Goodall, Cadzow, *Place-Making in National Parks*; Cadzow, Byrne and Goodall, *Waterborne*; Goodall, Byrne and Cadzow, *Waters of Belonging*; Byrne and Goodall 'Placemaking and Trans-Nationalism'; Goodall, 'Memory, Mobility & the More-Than-Human World'; Goodall, 'Remaking the Places of Belonging'.

Such gatherings are not often welcomed by older Anglo-Irish residents who have lived on the Georges River. For some, these new picnickers reflect something very different from their 'own' community and many remain troubled by difference. However, others, like Elliot Goodacre, are excited by these innovations and welcome the variety of new foods and customs introduced to the picnic grounds!

Regardless, it is sociality that continues to bring people to the river foreshores, the picnic grounds, the bush or the playing fields as well as onto the river itself, swimming, fishing or just remembering. In a very real way, this represents a continuity with the Anglo-Irish river land crowds at East Hills in the 1950s and at Lime Kiln Bay or Poulton Creek with its bushland in the 1970s. It is, in fact, the victory of those earlier campaigns, which saved the inlets from 'reclamation', that enable these culturally diverse socialities – the unfamiliar picnics, prayer mats and foods – to be experienced now so widely across the riverbanks. This might seem to have been an ambiguous victory to the old campaigners, but it has been a victory nonetheless.

The areas that were 'reclaimed' and turned into playing fields are – similarly – ambiguous for those people who might have seen themselves as victors in the battles to bring sport to the area. The open, levelled and ordered playing fields, often neatly ringed with seating and shade trees, become empty for all the time when no sports are being played. For some local people, and particularly for women, these empty spaces are unwelcoming after dark, places of foreboding and threat. The vast emptiness of the sports ground – even with lighting, is no comfort. For others, as Matthew Gandy and Denis Byrne have argued, the reclaimed spaces, along with their ring of bushes and trees, become safe and secluded spaces once again as beats for exploratory sexual assignations, whether heterosexual or homosexual.[16]

And the mangroves? Has their elevation to the status of (almost) 'charismatic species' been sustained? Are they still seen as the endearingly maternal and nurturing species portrayed in the 1970s campaigns?

The river land environment has continued to change, sometimes noticed by humans and sometimes not. While mangroves are threatened by encroaching development in many parts of the world, those on the

---

16 Gandy, 'Queer Ecology'; Byrne, 'Time on the Waterline'.

Georges River have continued to expand at the expense of the saltmarsh, making the water–land boundary harder to decipher as well as more challenging and – for some – more malevolent. At Towra Point, 62 per cent of saltmarsh has been lost, largely due to mangrove encroachment.[17]

How humans have responded – or even whether they have recognised such changes – remains varied and unresolved. In some parts of the estuary, mangroves have also encroached on former seagrass beds as siltation has raised the riverbed above the range of seagrasses, particularly *Zostera capricorni*. Perhaps even more significant has been the smothering of mangroves, seagrasses and saltmarsh by drifting sand from Towra Point to Pelican Point. These changes have been widely attributed to the dredging of Botany Bay from the mid-1970s for the construction of airport runways into the bay and Port Botany. Such dredging is claimed to direct significantly more storm wave energy entering from the Tasman Sea to the vulnerable south side of the bay than it had faced prior to the dredging.[18] How such changes might have expanded or reduced the possibilities for sociality are a question for a later study.

There has been a new recognition of the interests of Aboriginal people over the marine protected area at Towra Point. The promontory includes Pelican Point, William Rowley's birthplace and the home of other Aboriginal families throughout the nineteenth century who lived and fished in the area. Rowley was one who, before he moved to Salt Pan Creek, had been employed by Thomas Holt when he first attempted to set up oyster leases in the shallow waters around Weeney Bay on the eastern side of the Towra promontory.

In the early years of the twenty-first century an unprecedented collaboration between the New South Wales National Parks and Wildlife Service (NPWS) and the Aboriginal communities of the area led to the establishment of the 'Towra Team'. This was a group of 10 young Aboriginal conservation trainees from the La Perouse community, the youngest being 15 with most in their 20s, supported by two older Aboriginal mentors. The whole group was led by Dean Kelly, born in 1967 into the La Perouse community and later employed by NPWS as a community liaison officer. Aiming to distribute opportunities evenly

---

17 Kelleway et al., 'Seventy Years of Continuous Encroachment'; DECCW, *Towra Point Nature Reserve*, 81.
18 DECCW, *Towra Point Nature Reserve*, 57; Laurie Derwent, pers. comm.

across the Aboriginal community, Kelly selected participants from all the families in the La Perouse area. Each of these young people was chosen because of their interest in learning and the responsibilities for country that the job offered. Kelly pointed out that they had become separated from an active involvement with the land:

> These kids are very urban, their environment is [made of] concrete. A lot of them had lost that connection to country and bushland, even though it was so close. They were pretty much disconnected from it and distracted by the bright lights that the city hosts.

Their roles as trainees, however, had allowed them not only to learn more about their country and its history, but also to bring home the remains of their people that had been held in museums for decades. Kelly continued:

> The other thing is, within the same area, and only a couple of hundred meters or so from where the birds' nest, we've returned in the last five years approximately 70 Aboriginal remains that came back from the Museums, as part of the Sydney Metropolitan repatriation program … So there you are, there's another special area there that's very deeply [important] to the Aboriginal community.[19]

More recently still, a team of young Aboriginal people joined the Riverkeeper program in the Georges River Council, incorporating the old Hurstville and Kogarah councils. The program drew the ecological knowledge of the river together with the cultural interests of its diverse riverside communities.[20] Many of the actors in the Georges River campaigns – from George Jacobsen to the activists trying to save Lime Kiln Bay, Poulton Creek and Towra Point – referred to their goal of honouring the approaches of Indigenous people on the river: hunting, fishing and harvesting only for food, not sport; taking only what they needed to survive, not to accumulate or for competitive show. Yet, until recently, none of those campaigners have taken the step of contacting the many Aboriginal people who survived along the river or who lived at La Perouse. An imagined vision of what was understood to be tradition was always present, but it was not one that led to real alliances.

---

19 These quotations all arise from Dean Kelly's paper and later discussion on the Towra initiative, recorded at the *Cities Nature Justice* symposium at University of Technology Sydney, 10 December 2008.
20 Cavanaugh, 'The Aboriginal Riverkeeper Team'. This program functioned from 2014 to 2017 with government funding. The Indigenous team are now part of the NPWS management of Towra Point.

Figure 15.3: The Towra team in 2005.
These young Aboriginal trainees looked after the Towra Point Marine Conservation area while they were in training as rangers with what was then called the Department of Environment and Conservation. Source: Goodall and Cadzow, *Rivers and Resilience*.

For the campaigners in the period on which this book has focused (1945–80), and for the council officers and representatives, the lines of communication and the memories across time to earlier campaigns were very weak. While some political parties allowed memories of early conflicts to be transmitted, there were a disturbing number of situations in which almost no memories or documents had survived from earlier campaigners, even from those who had been active only a few years before. This remains true today; there are few who remember this period of intense activity along the Georges River when so many people tried to save its waters and bays from reclamation.

This makes activist Dave Koffel's extraordinary personal archive about Lime Kiln Bay, Esme Clisby's visual archive of East Hills Park, Alexandra Knight's collection of the papers and slides of the Save Poulton Park Campaign and Andrew Molloy's tireless local history work about Padstow, East Hills and Milperra all the more important. The stories of these local suburban campaigns to save damaged river lands – the campaigners' compromised, polluted but *lived* environments – have become lost amid the more glamorous and higher profile campaigns for supposedly 'pristine' and remote 'wilderness'. These suburban environmental campaigns need to have their stories recognised and celebrated.

The River I Learned about …

This book has been about the river that I came to know as I listened to the people who had taken part in these campaigns. Its pages record many of the conversations I have had as I learned. This was my river, but it was a river I had failed to notice when I had the chance, a river I had missed because I left too soon.

I still have conflicted feelings about mangroves, but I understand better where my concerns came from, and my responses are far more nuanced now. I see more than those strategic campaign images of maternal and nurturing mangroves. I have learned from the many people I have talked with who have shared their warm and affectionate memories of the river and its mangroves.

There will be other ways to look at each of the campaigns I have considered on the estuary and, indeed, there will have been other campaigns that I did not consider at all.

But it has not just been me who has failed to notice this river. In fact, this whole stretch of the estuary, from Milperra to Towra Point, from 1945 to 1980 has been invisible in histories of the environmental movement, of urban heritage campaigns and of social activism. It has been too polluted, too damaged, too compromised, too 'suburban' to be noticed.

So, despite its limits and omissions, this book might open some doors into the dynamism and tenacity of the living beings – human, plant and animal – who all belong to this changing river.

Figure 15.4: Mangrove sunrise, Cabbage Tree Bay.

Taken at Port Hacking, just south of Botany Bay. The moon is visible in this dawn photo. Courtesy of the photographer and ecologist William Gladstone, more of whose photographs can be found on Instagram @williamgladstonephotography.

Bibliography

Interviews

Byron, Ed and Noeline. Interview by Allison Cadzow. 31 May 2006.

Campbell, Jacko. Interview by Heather Goodall. 14 July 1982.

Campbell, Jacko and Ted Thomas. Interview by Heather Goodall. 24 September 1980.

Chester, Judy. Interview by Heather Goodall, 25 March and 4 September 2005.

Chester, Judy and Janny Ely. Interview by Heather Goodall, 12 October 2006.

Chester, Judy, Janny Ely and Robyn Williams. Interview by Heather Goodall, 13 March 1992, 8 August 1999 and 24 February 2002.

Connell, Kel and Frances Seitch. Interview by Heather Goodall. 5 May 2006.

Cullis, Fred and Sharyn. Interview by Allison Cadzow. 13 June 2007.

Cullis, Sharyn. Interview by Allison Cadzow. Notes. 10 May 2007.

Derwent, Laurie. Interview by Heather Goodall. 19 June 2020.

Drake, Robert. Interview by Heather Goodall. 21 June 2020.

Goodacre, Elliott and Val. Interview by Heather Goodall. 23 May 2002.

Goodacre, Glenn. Interview by Heather Goodall. 13 September 2019.

Goodall, Craig and Mark. Interview by Heather Goodall. 2 August 2006.

Groves, Jason. Interview by Allison Cadzow. 29 August 2006.

Haworth, Robert. Interview by Heather Goodall. 17 November 2005.

Hekmat, Khali Bibi. Interview by Heather Goodall. Interpreter Latifa Hekmat. 16 December 2015.

Howard, Kevin. Interview by Heather Goodall and Allison Cadzow. 13 February 2006.

Jacobsen, Carol. Interview by Heather Goodall. 22 November 2005 (with Alf and Eileen Stills); 22 March 2006 (with various former members of the Picnic Point Regatta Association); and 12 July 2006 (with her brothers, Colin and Kevin Jacobsen).

Jacobsen, Colin (aka Col Joye), Kevin and Carol. Interview by Heather Goodall. 12 July 2006.

Kelleway, Jeff. Interview by Heather Goodall. Notes. 26 March 2019.

Knight, Alexandra. Interview by Heather Goodall. 20 July 2020.

Koffel, David. Interview by Heather Goodall. 16 October 2019.

Lennis, John. Interview by Allison Cadzow. 12 September 2006.

PPRA (gathering of former members of the Picnic Point Regatta Association). Interview by Carol Jacobsen, assisted by Heather Goodall and Allison Cadzow. 22 March 2006.

Reid, Alan. Interview by Gregg Borschmann. 3–5 December 1996. Environmental Awareness in Australia Oral History Project. National Library of Australia.

Saintilan, Neil. Interview by Heather Goodall. Notes. 26 March 2019.

Staples, Ruth. Interview by Heather Goodall. 27 May 2005 and 27 October 2005.

Stills, Alf, Eileen Stills and Carol Jacobsen. Interview by Heather Goodall. 22 November 2005.

Willis, Elizabeth. Interview by Heather Goodall. 26 October 2019.

Zaim, Wafa. Interview by Heather Goodall. 26 May 2015.

Government Reports

Australian Government, Department of Agriculture, Water and the Environment. 'Royal National Park and Garawarra State Conservation Area'. Accessed 4 May 2020. www.environment.gov.au/cgi-bin/ahdb/search.pl?mode=place_detail; place_id=105893.

Commonwealth of Australia, Senate Select Committee on Water Pollution. *Minutes of Evidence*. Vols. 8, 19 and 20. Canberra: Government Printer, 1970.

Commonwealth of Australia, Senate Select Committee on Water Pollution. *Report*. Canberra: Government Printer, 1970.

Hunt, H. C. *Garbage Disposal in the Sydney Metropolitan Area*. Bankstown: Bankstown Municipal Council, 1968.

New South Wales. *The Fisheries and Oyster Farms Act 1935*. Sydney: Government Printer, 1988.

New South Wales Coastal Conference. *Estuary Management Manual*. New South Wales Coastal Conference: 1992.

New South Wales Department of Environment and Planning. 'Open Space in the Sydney Region: Research Study 5'. In *1982 Open Space Survey*. Sydney, Department of Environment and Planning, 1985.

New South Wales Department of Primary Industries. *Seagrasses: Prime Facts*, no. 692. September 2007.

New South Wales Legislative Council. *Votes and Proceedings*, vol. 54, 1964.

Theses and Unpublished Material

Beder, Sharon. 'From Pipe Dreams to Tunnel Vision: Engineering Decision-Making and Sydney's Sewerage System'. PhD thesis, University of New South Wales, 1989.

Cadzow, Allison. 'Waltzing Matildas: A Study of Select Australian Women Explorers'. PhD thesis, University of Technology Sydney, 2002.

Cullis, Sharyn. 'Holsworthy: The Nature, Impact and Legacy of a Community Campaign against an Airport'. MA thesis, University of New South Wales, 2004.

Howard, Kevin. 'An Essay on Contemporary Change and Prospects of the Georges River'. Report submitted for the Diploma of Environmental Studies, Macquarie University, 1973. Copy held in Kevin Howard's personal archive.

Kelleway, Jeff. 'Ecological Impacts of Recreational Vehicle Use on the Saltmarshes of the Georges River, Sydney'. Hons thesis, University of New South Wales, 2004.

Books, Articles, Conference Papers

Adam, Paul. 'Australian Saltmarshes in Global Context'. In *Australian Saltmarsh Ecology*, edited by N. Saintilan. Collingwood, Vic.: CSIRO, 2009.

Adam, Paul. 'Mangroves and Saltmarsh Communities'. In *Plants in Action. Adaptation in Nature, Performance in Cultivation*, edited by B. J. Atwell, P. E. Kriedemann and C. G. N. Turnbull, 563–564. Melbourne: Macmillan, 1998.

Aird, W. V. *The Water Supply, Sewerage and Drainage of Sydney*. Sydney: Metropolitan Water Sewerage and Drainage Board, Government of NSW, 1961.

Allison, Glenys. 'Bankstown Soldier Settlement Milperra'. *Dictionary of Sydney*. 2010. Accessed 4 May 2020. dictionaryofsydney.org/entry/bankstown_soldier_settlement_milperra.

Allport, Carolyn. 'Castles of Security: The New South Wales Housing Commission and Home Ownership 1941–1961'. In *Sydney: City of Suburbs*, edited by Max Kelly, 95–124. Kensington, NSW: UNSW Press in association with the Sydney History Group, 1987.

Allport, Carolyn. 'The Unrealized Promise: Plans for Sydney Housing in the Forties'. In *Twentieth Century Sydney*, edited by Jill Roe, 48–68. Marrickville, NSW: Hale & Iremonger in association with the Sydney History Group, 1980.

Alongi, Daniel M. 'Impact of Global Change on Nutrient Dynamics in Mangrove Forests'. Review article. *Forests* 9, no. 10 (2018): 569. doi.org/10.3390/f9100596.

Ashton, Paul and Robert Freestone. *Town Planning*. Sydney: University of Technology, 2008. doi.org/10.5130/sj.v1i2.590.

Bacon, Wendy. 'They Huffed and They Puffed and They Blew the Doors Down'. *The Living Daylights*, 8–14 January 1974, 3–6.

Baker, Robert G. V., Robert Haworth and Peter G. Flood. 'Inter-Tidal Fixed Indicators of Former Holocene Sea Levels in Australia: A Summary of Sites and a Review of Methods and Models'. *Quaternary International* 83–85 (2014): 257–273. doi.org/10.1016/S1040-6182(01)00044-1.

Baker, Robert G. V., Robert Haworth and Peter G. Flood. 'An Oscillating Holocene Sea-Level? Revisiting Rottnest Island, Western Australia, and the Fairbridge Eustatic Hypothesis'. *Journal of Coastal Research* 42 (2005): 3–14.

Banivanua Mar, Tracey. *Decolonisation and the Pacific: Indigenous Globalisation and the Ends of Empire*. Cambridge: Cambridge University Press, 2019.

Benson, Doug and Georgina Eldershaw. 'Backdrop to Encounter: The 1770 Landscape of Botany Bay, the Plants Collected by Banks and Solander and the Rehabilitation of Natural Vegetation at Kurnell.' *Cunninghamia* 10, no. 1 (2007): 113–37.

Benson, Doug and Jocelyn Howell. *Taken for Granted: The Bushland of Sydney and Its Suburbs.* Sydney: Kangaroo Press in association with the Royal Botanic Gardens Sydney, 1996.

Bino, G., K. Jenkins and R. T. Kingsford. 'Adaptive Management of Ramsar Wetlands'. Report. National Climate Change Adaptation Research Facility, 2013.

Birch, G. F., D. Evenden and M. E. Teutsch. 'Dominance of Point Source in Heavy Metal Distributions in Sediments of a Major Sydney Estuary (Australia)'. *Environmental Geology* 28, (1996): 169–74. doi.org/10.1007/s002540050090.

Bird, Juliet. 'The Nineteenth-Century Soap Industry and its Exploitation of Intertidal Vegetation in Eastern Australia'. *Australian Geographer* 14, no. 1 (1978): 38–41. doi.org/10.1080/00049187808702731.

Blewett, Graham. *Ferries and Farms: A History of Lugarno.* Accessed 20 January 2021. sites.google.com/site/lugarnohistory/.

Boon, Paul. *The Hawkesbury River: A Social and Natural History.* Melbourne: CSIRO Publishing, 2017. doi.org/10.1071/9780643107601.

Borschmann, Gregg. 'Guardian of Botany Bay: Bernie Clarke'. *Wetlands Australia Newsletter* 7 (1997): 10–13.

Boyd, Robin. *The Great Australian Ugliness.* Ringwood, Vic.: Penguin, 1960.

Brooks, Barbara and Colleen Burke, eds. *The Heart of a Place: Stories from the Moorebank Women's Oral History Project Covering the Suburbs of Moorebank, Chipping Norton, Hammondville and Holsworthy in the Liverpool City Council Area.* Liverpool: Liverpool City Council, 1992.

Burgmann, Meredith and Verity Burgmann. *Green Bans, Red Union: Environmental Activism and the New South Wales Builders Labourers' Federation,* Sydney: UNSW Press, 1998.

Butlin, N. G., ed. *Sydney's Environmental Amenity, 1970–1975.* Canberra: Australian National University Press, 1976.

Byrne, Denis. 'Time on the Waterline: Coastal Reclamations and Sea Walls in Sydney and Japan'. *Journal of Contemporary Archaeology* 5, no. 1 (2018): 53–65. doi.org/10.1558/jca.33282.

Byrne, Denis and Heather Goodall. 'Placemaking and Transnationalism: Recent Migrants and a National Park in Sydney, Australia', *Parks* 19.1 (March 2013): 63–72. doi.org/10.2305/IUCN.CH.2013.PARKS-19-1.DB.en.

Byrne, Denis, Heather Goodall and Allison Cadzow. *Place-Making in National Parks: Ways that Australians of Arabic and Vietnamese Background Perceive and Use the Parklands along the Georges River, NSW.* Sydney: Office of Environment and Heritage, 2013. Accessed 5 February 2021. www.environment.nsw.gov. au/research-and-publications/publications-search/place-making-in-national-parks-ways-that-australians-of-arabic-and-vietnamese-background.

Cadzow, Allison, Denis Byrne and Heather Goodall. *Waterborne – Vietnamese Australians on Sydney's Georges River Parks and Green Spaces.* UTS ePress, 2011. doi.org/10.5130/978-0-9924518-1-3.

Cadzow, Allison, Heather Goodall and Denis Byrne. 'Waterborne: Vietnamese Australians and River Environments'. *Cities Nature Justice, Transforming Cultures eJournal* 5, no. 1 (2010): 112–42. doi.org/10.5130/tfc.v5i1.1558.

Cahill, Rowan. 'An Activist for All Seasons'. Obituary for Bob Walshe, Radical Sydney/Radical History. 2018. radicalsydney.blogspot.com.au/p/an-activist-for-all-seasons.html (site discontinued).

Cavanaugh, Vanessa. 'The Aboriginal Riverkeeper Team Project – Building Indigenous Knowledge and Skills to Improve Urban Waterways in Sydney's Georges River Catchment'. Paper delivered at the 8th Australian Stream Management Conference, Leura, 2018.

Clark, Herbert H. 'Social Actions, Social Commitments'. In *Roots of Human Sociality: Culture, Cognition and Interaction*, edited by N. J. Enfield and Stephen C. Levinson, 126–52. Oxford: Routledge, 2006.

Clarke, Lesley D. and Nola J. Hannon. 'The Mangrove Swamp and Salt Marsh Communities of the Sydney District: I. Vegetation, Soils and Climate'. *Journal of Ecology* 55, no. 3 (November 1967): 753–71. doi.org/10.2307/2258423.

Clune, David. 'Mulvihill, James Anthony (1917–2000)'. Biographical Dictionary of the Australian Senate. Accessed 14 January 2021. biography.senate.gov.au/mulvihill-james-anthony/.

Cook, Margaret. *A River with a City Problem: A History of Brisbane Floods.* St Lucia, Qld: University of Queensland Press, 2019.

Coward, Dan Huon. *Out of Sight: Sydney's Environmental History 1851–1981*. Canberra, ACT: Department of Economic History, Australian National University, 1988.

Cox, Frances E. G. 'History of the Discovery of Malaria Parasites and their Vectors'. *Parasites and Vectors* 3, no. 5 (2010). doi.org/10.1186/1756-3305-3-5.

Cross, John. *Jungle Warfare: Experiences and Encounters*. Barnsley, South Yorkshire: Pen and Sword Books, 2008.

Cunneen, Chris. '"Hands Off the Parks!" The Provision of Parks and Playgrounds'. In *Twentieth Century Sydney*, edited by Jill Roe, 105–19. Marrickville, NSW: Hale & Iremonger in association with the Sydney History Group, 1980.

Davies, Jaqueline, Dorothy Mulholland and Nora Pipe. *West of the River Road*. Picnic Point: Towrang Publications, 1979.

Davison, Aidan. 'Australian Suburban Imaginaries of Nature: Towards a Prospective Theory'. *Australian Humanities Review*, 37 (December 2005).

Davison, Aidan. 'Stuck in a Cul-De-Sac? Suburban History and Urban Sustainability in Australia'. *Urban Policy and Research* 24, no. 2 (2006): 201–16. doi.org/10.1080/08111140600704137.

Davison, Aidan. 'The Trouble with Nature: Ambivalence in the Lives of Urban Australian Environmentalists'. *Geoforum* 39 (2008): 1284–95. doi.org/10.1016/j.geoforum.2007.06.011.

DECCW. *Towra Point Nature Reserve Ramsar Site: Ecological Character Description*. Sydney: NSW Department Environment, Climate Change and Water and Sydney Metropolitan Catchment Authority, 2010.

Deery, Phillip. 'Community Carnival or Cold War Strategy? The 1952 Youth Carnival for Peace and Friendship'. *Labour and Community: Historical Essays*, edited Ray Markey, 313–45. Wollongong: University of Wollongong Press, 2001.

Derwent, Laurie. 'Oysters: The Canaries of Our Estuary'. Lecture to Oatley Flora and Fauna Conservation Society, 24 October 2016. Accessed 21 July 2020. off.oatleypark.com/2016/10/25/oysters-canaries-of-our-estuary/.

Drake, Maxine. *Georges River Tales*. Melbourne: Maxine Drake, 2019.

Dunstan, D. J. 'Some Early Environmental Problems and Guidelines in New South Wales Estuaries'. *Wetlands Australia* 9, no. 1 (2009): 1–6. doi.org/10.31646/wa.140.

Earnshaw, Beverley. *The Land Between Two Rivers: The St George District in Federation Times*. Kogarah: Kogarah Historical Society, 2001.

Enfield, Nicholas J. and Stephen C. Levinson, eds. *The Roots of Human Sociality: Culture, Cognition and Interaction*. London: Routledge, 2006.

Fairley, Alan. *Being Green: Oatley Flora and Fauna Conservation Society: The First 50 Years, 1955–2005*. Oatley: Oatley Flora and Fauna Conservation Society Inc., 2005. Accessed April 2020. off.oatleypark.com/wordpress/wp-content/uploads/2010/03/Being-Green-first-50-yrs-OFF.pdf.

Fairweather, P. G. 'Ecological Changes Due to Our Use of the Coast: Research Needs Versus Effort'. *Proceedings of the Ecological Society of Australia* 16 (1990): 71–77.

Flick, Isabel and Heather Goodall. *Isabel Flick: Many Lives*. St Leonards: Allen and Unwin, 2008.

Foley, Denis. *Repossession of Our Spirit: Traditional Owners of Northern Sydney*. Canberra: Aboriginal History Inc., 2001.

Foley, Denis and Peter Read. *What the Colonists Never Knew*. Canberra: National Museum of Australia Press, 2020.

Ford, Caroline. *Sydney Beaches: A History*. Coogee, NSW: NewSouth Publishing, 2014.

Fox, Allan. *Chief Guardian: The Life and Times of Allen Strom*. [Sydney]: Australian Association for Environmental Education, 2016.

Gandy, Matthew. 'Queer Ecology: Nature, Sexuality, and Heterotopic Alliances'. *Environment and Planning D: Society and Space* 30 (2012): 727–47. doi.org/10.1068/d10511.

Gapps, Stephen. *Cabrogal to Fairfield City: A History of a Multicultural Community*. Fairfield: Fairfield City Council, 2010.

Gaynor, Andrea. 'Grappling with "Nature" in Australian Home Gardens 1890–1960'. *Environment and History* 24 (2018): 23–38. doi.org/10.3197/096734018X15137949591828.

Gaynor, Andrea. *Harvest of the Suburbs: An Environmental History of Growing Food in Australian Cities*, Perth: UWA Press, 2006.

Gietzelt, Arthur. *Sticks and Stones*. Sutherland: A. T. & D. Gietzelt & Family, 2014.

Gifford, Roger M. and Peter Ellyard. *Bad Luck, Dead Duck: The Report of INSPECT, 1970*. Canberra: Dalton Publishing Company, 1971.

Gifford, Roger M. and Peter Ellyard. *What a Mess! Let's Confess: The Report of INSPECT 1971*. Canberra: Dalton Publishing Company, 1972.

Gilbert, Alan. 'The Roots of Anti-Suburbanism in Australia'. In *Australian Cultural History*, edited by S. L. Goldberg and F. B. Smith, 33–49. Cambridge: Cambridge University Press, 1988.

Goodall, Heather. '"Assimilation Begins in the Home": The State and Aboriginal Women's Work as Mothers in New South Wales: 1900s to 1960s'. In *Aboriginal Workers*, edited by Ann McGrath and Kay Saunders with Jackie Huggins. Special issue of *Labour History* 69 (1995): 75–101. doi.org/10.2307/27516392.

Goodall, Heather. 'Frankenstein, Triffids and Mangroves: Anxiety and Changing Urban Ecologies'. *Australian Folklore* 21 (2006): 82–98.

Goodall, Heather. 'Memory, Mobility & the More-Than-Human World: Oral History and Environmental History'. In *Telling Environmental Histories: Intersections of Memory, Narrative and Environment,* edited by Katie Holmes and Heather Goodall, 31–50. Basingstoke: Palgrave Macmillan, 2017.

Goodall, Heather. 'Remaking the Places of Belonging: Arabic Immigrants and the Urban Environment Along Sydney's Georges River'. *Miradas en Movimiento* 5 (2011), www.espaciodeestudiosmigratorlos.org/es/miradas-en-movimiento-mem (site discontinued).

Goodall, Heather and Allison Cadzow. 'The People's National Park: Working Class Environmental Campaigns on Sydney's Urban Georges River, 1950 to 1967'. In *Red, Green and In-Between*. Special issue of *Labour History* 98 (2010): 17–35. doi.org/10.5263/labourhistory.99.1.0017.

Goodall, Heather and Allison Cadzow. *Rivers and Resilience: Aboriginal People on Sydney's Georges River*. Sydney: UNSW Press, 2009.

Goodall, Heather, Allison Cadzow and Denis Byrne. 'Mangroves, Garbage and Fishing: Everyday Ecology on an Industrial City River'. *Cities Nature Justice, Transforming Cultures eJournal* 5, no. 1 (2010): 52–83. doi.org/10.5130/tfc.v5i1.1555.

Goodall, Heather, Denis Byrne and Allison Cadzow. *Waters of Belonging: Al-miyahu Tajma'unah: Arabic Australians and the Georges River Parklands*. UTS ePress, 2012. doi.org/10.5130/978-0-9872369-3-7.

Goodall, Heather, Helen Randerson and Devleena Ghosh. *Teacher for Justice: Lucy Woodcock's Transnational Life*. Canberra: ANU Press, 2019. doi.org/10.22459/TJ.2019.

Goodger, Betty. 'History Notes'. *Bankstown Historical Society Newsletter*, October 1992, 12.

Gowers, Richard. 'Dunphy, Myles Joseph (1891–1985)'. *Australian Dictionary of Biography*. National Centre of Biography, Australian National University. Published first in hardcopy 2007. Accessed 21 January 2021. adb.anu.edu.au/biography/dunphy-myles-joseph-12446/text22381.

Griffiths, Tom. 'Environmental History, Australian Style'. *Australian Historical Studies* 46, no. 2 (2015): 157–73. doi.org/10.1080/1031461X.2015.1035289.

Gullett, H. S. *Not as a Duty Only: An Infantryman's War*. Carlton, Vic.: Melbourne University Press, 1976.

Gwyther, Gabrielle. 'Western Sydney: From Cowpastures to Pigs' Heads'. *Dictionary of Sydney.* 2008. Accessed 13 January 2019. dictionaryofsydney. org/entry/western_sydney.

Halliday, Stephen. 'Death and Miasma in Victorian London: An Obstinate Belief'. *British Medical Journal* 323 (2001): 1469–71. doi.org/10.1136/bmj. 323.7327.1469.

Harper, Melissa. 'The Battle for the Bush: Bushwalking vs Hiking between the Wars'. *Journal of Australian Studies* 19, no. 45 (1995): 41–52. doi.org/10.1080/14443059509387226.

Harper, Melissa. *The Ways of the Bushwalker: On Foot in Australia*. Sydney, NSW: NewSouth Publishing, 2007.

Harper, Melissa and Richard White. 'How National Were the First National Parks? Comparative Perspectives from the British Settler Societies'. In *Civilizing Nature: National Parks in Global Historical Perspective*, edited by Bernhard Gissibl, Sabine Höhler and Patrick Kupper, 50–67. Munich: Berghahn Books, 2012.

Haworth, R. J. 'Bush Tracks and Bush Blocks: The Aerial Photographic Record from Southwest Sydney, 1930–1950'. *People and Physical Environment Research* 49 (1995): 32–42.

Haworth, R. J. 'Changes in Mangrove/Salt Marsh Distribution in the Georges River Estuary, Southern Sydney, 1930–1970'. *Wetlands* (Australia) 20, no. 2 (2003): 80–103. doi.org/10.31646/wa.237.

Haworth R. J., Robert G. V. Baker and Peter G. Flood. 'A 6000-Year-Old Fossil Dugong from Botany Bay: Inferences about Changes in Sydney's Climate, Sea Levels and Waterways'. *Australian Geographical Studies* 42, no. 1 (2004): 46–59. doi.org/10.1111/j.1467-8470.2004.00242.x.

Haworth R. J., Robert G. V. Baker and Peter G. Flood. 'Predicted and Observed Holocene Sea-Levels on the Australian Coast: What Do They Indicate about Hydro-Isostatic Models in Far-Field Sites?' *Journal of Quaternary Science* 17, no. 5–6 (2002): 581–91. doi.org/10.1002/jqs.718.

Head, Lesley and Pat Muir. *Backyard: Nature and Culture in Suburban Australia.* Wollongong: University of Wollongong, 2007.

Hogan, Michael. *Almost Like Home: Living in Bradfield Park.* Gordon: Ku-ring-gai Historical Association, 2012.

Hogan, Michael. 'Postwar Emergency Housing in Sydney – the Camps that Never Were'. *Journal of the Royal Australian Historical Society* 97, no. 1 (2011): 7–24.

Hogan, Trevor. '"Nature Strip": Australian Suburbia and the Enculturation of Nature'. *Thesis Eleven* 74 (2003): 54–75. doi.org/10.1177/0725513603074 1005.

Houston, Toni. 'Former Bird Calling Champions of Gould League of Bird Lovers Reunite in Merimbula'. *Magnet News*, 28 November 2016. Accessed 14 January 2021. www.edenmagnet.com.au/story/4320318/reunion-for-champion-birds-of-a-feather-video/.

Hunter, John. *An Historical Journal of the Transactions at Port Jackson and Norfolk Island: With the Discoveries Which Have Been Made in New South Wales and in the Southern Ocean Since the Publication of Phillip's Voyage, Compiled from the Official Papers.* London: John Stockdale, 1793.

Hutton, Drew and Libby Connors. *A History of the Australian Environment Movement.* Melbourne: Cambridge University Press, 1999.

Huxley, John. 'Down Binoculars as Bird League Calls it a Day after 100 Years'. *Sydney Morning Herald*, 2 April 2011. Accessed 14 January 2021. www.smh.com.au/environment/conservation/down-binoculars-as-bird-league-calls-it-a-day-after-100-years-20110401-1crk2.html.

Innes, David J. *The Story of Golf in New South Wales, 1851–1987.* Darlinghurst: New South Wales Golf Association, 1988.

Irish, Paul. *Hidden in Plain View: The Aboriginal People of Coastal Sydney.* Sydney: UNSW Press, 2017.

Jackson, Greg and Pam Forbes. 'Oysters on the Georges River'. *Sutherland Shire Historical Society Inc. Bulletin* 210 (February 2019): 31. Accessed 21 January 2021. www.shirehistory.org/uploads/1/0/9/1/109164607/210_2019_february.pdf.

Jakubowicz, Andrew. 'The Green Ban Movement: Urban Struggle and Class Politics'. In *Australian Urban Politics: Readings in Sociology*, edited by John Halligan and Chris Paris. Melbourne: Longman Cheshire, 1984.

James, Peggy. *Cosmopolitan Conservationists: Greening Modern Sydney*. Melbourne: Australian Scholarly Press, 2013.

Karskens, Grace. *People of the River: Lost Worlds of Early Australia*. St Leonards: Allen and Unwin, 2020.

Kass, Dorothy. *Educational Reform and Environmental Concern: A History of School Nature Study in Australia*. London: Routledge, 2018. doi.org/10.4324/9781315625256.

Kass, Terry. 'Cheaper than Rent: Aspects of the Growth of Owner-Occupation in Sydney, 1911–61'. In *Sydney: City of Suburbs,* edited by Max Kelly, 77–94. Kensington, NSW: UNSW Press in association with the Sydney History Group, 1987.

Kelleway, J. J., N. Saintilan, P. I. Macreadie, C. G. Skilbeck, A. Zawadzki, P. J. Ralph. 'Seventy Years of Continuous Encroachment Substantially Increases "Blue Carbon" Capacity as Mangroves Replace Intertidal Salt Marshes'. *Global Change Biology* 22 (2016): 1097–109. doi.org/10.1111/gcb.13158.

King, Peter, ed. *Australia's Vietnam: Australia in the Second Indo-China War*. St Leonards: Allen and Unwin, 1983.

Kingsford, R. 'Conservation Management of Rivers and Wetlands under Climate Change – a Synthesis'. *Marine and Freshwater Research* 62 (2011): 217–22. doi.org/10.1071/MF11029.

Kingsford, R. 'Ecological Impacts of Dams, Water Diversions and River Management on Floodplain Wetlands in Australia'. *Austral Ecology* 25 (2000): 109–27. doi.org/10.1046/j.1442-9993.2000.01036.x.

Kogarah Council. 'Moore Reserve Plan of Management'. 23 August 1999. Accessed 8 February 2021. kogarahresidents.files.wordpress.com/2020/07/moore-reserve-hurstville-grove-plan-of-management-pom-adopted-1999.pdf.

Lake, Meredith. 'Hammondville'. *Dictionary of Sydney*. 2012. Accessed 29 July 2020. dictionaryofsydney.org/place/hammondville.

Larkum, A. W. D., G. A. Kendrick and P. J. Ralph, eds. *Seagrasses of Australia: Structure, Ecology and Conservation*. Cham, Switzerland: Springer 2018. doi.org/10.1007/978-3-319-71354-0.

Logan, M. I. 'Suburban Manufacturing: A Case Study'. *Australian Geographer* 9, no. 4 (1964): 223–34. doi.org/10.1080/00049186408702425.

Macintyre, Stuart. *Australia's Boldest Experiment: War and Reconstruction in the 1940s.* Kensington: NewSouth Publishing, 2015.

McKenzie, Peter and Ann Stephen. 'La Perouse: An Urban Aboriginal Community'. In *Sydney: City of Suburbs*, edited by Max Kelly, 172–91. Kensington: UNSW Press in association with the Sydney History Group, 1987.

McKillop, Bob. 'The Royal National Park Line'. *Dictionary of Sydney.* 2017. Accessed 4 May 2020. dictionaryofsydney.org/entry/the_royal_national_park_line.

McLeod, Anne. *The Summit of Her Ambition: The Spirited Life of Marie Byles.* Sydney: Anne McLeod, 2016.

McLoughlin, Lynne. 'Estuarine Wetlands Distribution along the Parramatta River, Sydney, 1788–1940: Implications for Planning and Conservation'. *Cunninghamia: A Journal of Plant Ecology for Eastern Australia* 6, no. 3 (2000): pp 579–610.

McLoughlin, Lynne. 'Mangroves and Grass Swamps: Changes in Shoreline Vegetation, Lane Cove River, Sydney'. *Wetlands* 7, no. 1 (1987): 13–24. doi.org/10.31646/wa.113.

McLoughlin, Lynne. *The Middle Lane Cove River: A History and a Future.* Sydney: Centre for Environmental and Urban Studies Macquarie University, 1985.

McLoughlin, Lynne. *The Natural Environment of Bankstown.* Bankstown: Bankstown City Council, 1994.

McManus, Phil. 'Mangrove Battlelines: Culture/Nature and Ecological Restoration'. *Australian Geographer* 37, no. 1 (2006): 57–71. doi.org/10.1080/00049180500511970.

Madden, Brian. *Hernia Bay: Sydney's Wartime Hospitals at Riverwood.* Campsie, NSW: Canterbury and District Historical Society, 2001.

Mansell, Ken. '"Taking to the Streets against the Vietnam War": A Timeline History of Australian Protest 1962–1972'. *Labour History Melbourne*, 8 May 2020. Accessed 1 November 2020. labourhistorymelbourne.org/taking-to-the-streets-against-the-vietnam-war-a-timeline-history-of-australian-protest-1962-1972-introduction/.

Mason, K. J. *Experience of Nationhood: Modern Australia since 1901.* 4th edn. New York: McGraw-Hill Education, 2001.

Melosi, Martin V. *Garbage in the Cities: Refuse Reform and the Environment* (revised edition). Pittsburgh: University of Pittsburgh Press, 2004.

Meredith, Peter. *Myles and Milo: The Story of Myles and Milo Dunphy.* St Leonards: Allen and Unwin, 1999.

Mitchell, Bruce. *Teachers, Education, and Politics: A History of Organisations of Public School Teachers in New South Wales.* St Lucia: University of Queensland Press, 1975.

Mo, Matthew. 'Herpetofaunal Community of the Constructed Lime Kiln Bay Wetland, South Sydney, New South Wales'. *Victorian Naturalist* 132, no. 3 (2015): 64–72.

Molloy, Andrew. *The History of Milperra.* Padstow Heights: Australian Media P/L, 2006.

Molloy, Andrew. *A History of Padstow.* Sydney: Australian Media P/L, 2004.

Molloy, Andrew. *The History of Panania, Picnic Point and East Hills.* Sydney: University Publishers, University of Sydney, 2006.

Moore, Keith. 'Bodgies, Widgies and Moral Panic in Australia, 1955–1959'. Paper presented to Social Change in the 21st Century conference, Centre for Social Changed Research, Queensland University of Technology, 24 October 2004. QUT ePrints.

Muir, Lesley. *A History of Cooks River.* Belmore: L. Muir, 1978.

Mulligan, Martin and Stuart Hill. *Ecological Pioneers: A Social History of Australian Ecological Thought and Action.* Cambridge: Cambridge University Press, 2001.

Murphy, A. M., G. S. Grohmann, P. J. Christopher, W. A. Lopez, G. R Davey and R. H. Milsom. 'An Australia-Wide Outbreak of Gastroenteritis from Oysters Caused by Norwalk Virus'. *Medical Journal of Australia* 2 (1979): 329–33. doi.org/10.5694/j.1326-5377.1979.tb104133.x.

Murphy, John. *Harvest of Fear: A History of Australia's Vietnam War.* St Leonards: Allen and Unwin, 1973.

Nash, Linda. *Inescapable Ecologies: A History of Environment, Disease and Knowledge.* Los Angeles: University of California Press, 2006. doi.org/10.1525/9780520939998.

Nell, John A. 'The History of Oyster Farming in Australia'. *Marine Fisheries Review* 63, no. 3 (2001): 14–25. Accessed 21 July 2020. aquaticcommons.org/9751/.

Nicholls, Jeff. *Cooks River Environmental Survey and Landscape Design.* Sydney: Total Environment Centre, 1976. Copy in Milo Dunphy Papers, State Library of New South Wales.

Niedenthal, Jack. 'A Short History of the People of Bikini Atoll'. Accessed 21 January 2021. marshall.csu.edu.au/Marshalls/html/History_Varia/Bikini_History/Bikini_History.html.

Nugent, Maria. *Botany Bay: Where Histories Meet.* Sydney: Allen and Unwin, 2005.

Nugent, Maria. 'Historical Encounters: Aboriginal Testimony and Colonial Forms of Commemoration'. *Aboriginal History* 30 (2006): 33–47. doi.org/10.22459/AH.30.2011.04.

O'Gorman, Emily. *Wetlands in a Dry Land: More-Than-Human Histories of Australia's Murray-Darling Basin.* Washington: University of Washington Press, 2021.

O'Gorman, Emily and Andrea Gaynor. 'More-than-Human Histories'. *Environmental History* 25, no. 4 (2020): 711–35. doi.org/10.1093/envhis/emaa027.

Orlovich, Peter. 'Dunphy, Milo Kanangra (1929–1996)'. *Australian Dictionary of Biography.* National Centre of Biography, Australian National University. Published online 2020. Accessed 15 January 2021. adb.anu.edu.au/biography/dunphy-milo-kanangra-25367/text33767.

Otto, Kristin. *Yarra: The History of Melbourne's Murky River.* Melbourne: The Text Publishing Company, 2011.

Pidgeon, I. 'The Ecology of the Central Coastal Area of NSW, III: Types of Primary Succession'. *Proceedings of the Linnean Society of NSW* 65 (1940): 221–49.

Pollon, Frances and Gerald Healy. *The Book of Sydney Suburbs.* North Ryde: Angus & Robertson, 1990.

Powell, D. *Out West: Perceptions of Sydney's Western Suburbs.* St Leonards, NSW: Allen and Unwin, 1993.

Powis, Jon. 'Ecology Action by the Text Book: How to Save Little Salt Pan Creek'. *Nation Review*, 29 January 1973, 8–9.

Poynting, Scott. 'The Youth Carnival for Peace and Friendship, March 1952'. *Labour History* 56 (May 1989): 60–68. doi.org/10.2307/27508927.

Purdy, J. S. 'Metropolitan Health Officer's Report for 1920', Sydney Municipal Council Archives, City of Sydney.

Purdy, J. S. 'Metropolitan Health Officer's Report, 1924', Sydney Municipal Council Archives, City of Sydney Archives.

Reef, Ruth, Ilya C. Feller and Catherine E. Lovelock. 'Nutrition of Mangroves'. *Tree Physiology* 30 (2010): 1148–60. doi.org/10.1093/treephys/tpq048.

Roberts, P. and D. Tribe. *The Gould League of New South Wales: from Bird Lovers to Environmentalists.* Sydney: Gould League of NSW, 2011.

Robin, Libby. *The Flight of the Emu: One Hundred Years of Australian Ornithology, 1901–2001.* Melbourne: Melbourne University Press, 2001.

Roddewig, Richard J. *Green Bans: The Birth of Australian Environmental Politics.* Washington: The Conservation Foundation, 1978.

Rogers, Kerrylee, Neil Saintilan, Peter Davies, Jeff Kelleway and Laura Mogensen. *Mangrove and Saltmarsh Threat Analysis in the Sydney Coastal Councils Region.* Sydney Coastal Councils Group, 2017.

Rosen, Sue. *Bankstown: A Sense of Identity.* Sydney: Hale & Iremonger, 1996.

Rosen, Sue. *Losing Ground: An Environmental History of the Hawkesbury-Nepean Catchment.* Sydney: Hale and Iremonger, 1995.

Saintilan, Neil, ed. *Australian Saltmarsh Ecology.* Collingwood, Vic.: CSIRO, 2009. doi.org/10.1071/9780643096844.

Saintilan, Neil. 'Relationships between Height and Girth of Mangroves and Soil-Water Conditions in the Mary and Hawkesbury River Estuaries, Eastern Australia'. *Austral Ecology* 23, no. 4 (1998): 322–28.

Saintilan, Neil, N. S. Khan, E. Ashe, J. J. Kelleway, K. Rogers, C. D. Woodroffe and B. P. Horton. 'Thresholds of Mangrove Survival under Rapid Sea Level Rise'. *Science* 368, no. 6495 (June 2020): 1118–21. doi.org/10.1126/science.aba2656.

Saintilan, Neil and Kerrylee Rogers. 'Woody Plant Encroachment of Grasslands: A Comparison of Terrestrial and Wetland Settings'. *New Phytologist* 205 (2015): 1062–70. doi.org/10.1111/nph.13147.

Saintilan, Neil, Kerrylee Rogers and Alice Howe. 'Geomorphology and Habitat Dynamics'. In *Australian Saltmarsh Ecology*, edited by Neil Saintilan. Collingwood, Vic.: CSIRO, 2009. doi.org/10.1071/9780643096844.

Saintilan, Neil, Kerrylee Rogers and Karen L. McKee. 'The Shifting Saltmarsh-Mangrove Ecotone in Australasia and the Americas'. In *Coastal Wetlands: An Integrated Ecosystem Approach*, 2nd ed., edited by G. M. E. Perillo, E. Wolanski, D. R. Cahoon and C. S. Hopkinson, 915–45. Amsterdam: Elsevier, 2019. doi.org/10.1016/B978-0-444-63893-9.00026-5.

Saintilan, Neil, Kerrylee Rogers, Jeff Kelleway, Emilie-Jane Ens and D. R. Sloane. 'Climate Change Impacts on the Coastal Wetlands of Australia'. *Wetlands and Climate Cha*nge 39 (2019): 1145–54. doi.org/10.1007/s13157-018-1016-7.

Saintilan, Neil and R. J. Williams. 'The Decline of Saltmarsh in Southeast Australia: Results of Recent Surveys'. *Wetlands* (Australia) 18 (2000): 49–54. doi.org/10.31646/wa.228.

Saintilan, Neil and R. J. Williams. 'Mangrove Transgression into Saltmarsh Environments in South-East Australia'. *Global Ecology and Biogeography* 8 (1999): 117–24.

Salt, E. B., D. Weir, A. C. Wales and S. M. Smith. 'Georges Riverkeeper: The Establishment and Evolution of a Catchment Management Organisation'. Paper delivered at the 9th Australian Stream Management Conference, Hobart, Tasmania, 2018. Accessed April 2020. georgesriver.org.au/sites/default/files/resources/2019-10/salt_reid_wales_smith_-_georges_riverkeeper_40_years_in_the_making_-_9asm_full_paper_final.pdf.

Sellers, Christopher C. *Crabgrass Crucible: Suburban Nature and the Rise of Environmentalism in Twentieth-Century America*. Chapel Hill: University of North Carolina Press, 2012.

Simpson, Greg and David Newsome. 'Environmental History of an Urban Wetland: From Degraded Colonial Resource to Nature Conservation Area'. *Geo: Geography and Environment* 4, no. 1 (2017). doi.org/10.1002/geo2.30.

Simpson, Robert. 'What is Citizen Science?'. *Conversation*, 15 August 2013. Accessed 21 January 2021. theconversation.com/explainer-what-is-citizen-science-16487.

Spearritt, Peter. *Sydney's Century: A History*. Sydney: UNSW Press, 2000.

Spearritt, Peter. *Sydney since the Twenties*, Sydney: Hale and Iremonger, 1978.

Staples, Arthur (Mick). *Paddo*. Sydney: Ure Smith, 1964.

Stapp, William B. 'A Strategy for Curriculum Development and Implementation in Environmental Education at the Elementary and Secondary Levels'. In *Education and the Environmental Crisis,* edited by Jeremy Evans and Stephen Boyden, 23–37. Canberra: Australian Academy of Science, 1970.

Strang, Veronica. 'Substantial Connections: Water and Identity in an English Cultural Landscape'. *Worldviews* 10, no. 2 (2006): 155–77. doi.org/10.1163/156853506777965820.

Sykes, Roberta B. and Sandy Edwards. *Murawina: Australian Women of High Achievement.* Sydney: Doubleday, 1993.

Taksa, Lucy. 'James Anthony Mulvihill'. Australian Society for the Study of Labour History. Accessed 21 January 2021. www.labourhistory.org.au/hummer/vol-3-no-6/james-anthony-mulvihill.

Tyrrell, Ian. *River Dreams: The People and Landscape of the Cooks River.* Sydney: NewSouth Publishing, 2018.

Waterhouse, David. 'Lime Kiln Bay – Then And Now'. *OFF News*, September-October 2002.

West, R. J. *Seagrasses.* Sydney: NSW Agriculture and Fisheries, 1989.

West, R. J., C. A. Thorogood, T. Walford and R. J. Williams. *An Estuarine Inventory for NSW, Australia.* Fisheries Bulletin no. 2. Sydney: Division of Fisheries, NSW Department of Agriculture, 1985.

Wheatley, Nadia. 'Meeting Them at the Door: Radicalism, Militancy and the Sydney Anti-Eviction Campaign Of 1931'. In *Twentieth Century Sydney*, edited by Jill Roe, 208–30. Marrickville, NSW: Hale & Iremonger in association with the Sydney History Group, 1980.

White, Richard and Caroline Ford, eds. *Playing in the Bush: Recreation and National Parks in New South Wales.* Sydney: University of Sydney Press, 2012.

Williams, Robyn. *The River in Sydney's Backyard: A Guide to Catchment Management.* Sydney: The Video Unit in association with Water Board, Environment Protection Authority, Georges River Catchment Management Committee, 1994.

Winston, Denis. *Sydney's Great Experiment: The Progress of the Cumberland County Plan.* Sydney: Angus and Robertson, 1957.

Woodroffe, Colin D., Kerrylee Rogers, Karen McKee, Catherine Lovelock, I. A. Mendelssohn and Neil Saintilan. 'Mangrove Sedimentation and Response to Relative Sea-Level Rise'. *Annual Review of Marine Science Journal* 8 (2016): 243–66. doi.org/10.1146/annurev-marine-122414-034025.

Archival

Alexandra Knight (private)

Save Poulton Park Campaign Archive.

Alf Stills Collection (private)

Picnic Point Regatta Association Archive.

David Koffel Collection (private)

Lime Kiln Bay Preservation Committee (LKBPC) Archive.

Hurstville Library, Georges River Council Libraries

Local Studies Archive
Hurstville Council Minutes.

National Parks and Wildlife Service – Georges River National Park Trust (NPWS Archive)*
Correspondence Enquiries, Ministerial Representations – Georges River National Park, A/1732.

Trust Appointments – Georges River SRA 1992/SR/109/32.

1982 Trustees Conference – Georges River SRA, 1992/SR/201/290.

* Note: these records may have been moved to the State Archives and Records Authority of New South Wales.

National Library of Australia

Papers of Vincent Serventy. MS 4655, MS Acc05.013, MS Acc06.156 (specifically, MSS 4605, Class 8, consignment received 11 July 1994, File 18, Box 307).

State Library of New South Wales

PXA 773/Box 1, Series 03 Box 1: Australian Indigenous Ministries pictorial material: pre 1960 photographs.

Newspapers

Australian Fisheries Newsletter
Bankstown Observer
Bankstown Torch
Biz (Fairfield)
Canberra Times
Courier Mail (Brisbane)
Cumberland Argus
Daily Mirror (Sydney)
Daily Telegraph (Sydney)
Leader (see *St George and Sutherland Shire Leader)*
Mail (Adelaide)
National Times
OFF News (Oatley Flora and Fauna Society)
Propeller (Sutherland)
St George and Sutherland Shire Leader
St George Call
St George Pictorial
Sun (Sydney)
Sydney Morning Herald
Tharunka (Kensington, NSW)
Tribune (Sydney)
Truth (Sydney)

Index

Page numbers in bold type indicate images. Page numbers containing 'n.' indicate a reference appearing in a footnote on that page.

Como Pleasure Ground 39, 41
Connell, Kel 147
contamination 107, 108, 127, 130
　faecal 116, 119, 120, 123, 127,
　　131, 249
　from fertilisers 39, 40
　from golf course 39
　from industry 124, 125, 131,
　　155, 181
　heavy metal 68, 119n.2
　of oysters 110, 115–16, 117,
　　257–8
　sewage 107, 108, 115–16, 120,
　　155, 255, 258
　see also chemicals; human waste;
　　sewage
Cook, James 25, 53, 98
Cook, Margaret 13
Cooks River 9, 10, 25, 55, 121, 156,
　185
　and residential development 66,
　　171
　and Total Environment Centre
　　165, 253
　as warning about pollution 9, 10,
　　94, 156
　industrial pollution 68, 121, 135
　pollution testing 156
　sewage discharge into 107, 108,
　　135
　social activities along 17, 202
　studies of 10, 13
Cooks River Improvement League
　(CRIL) 17
Cooks River Valley Association
　(CRVA) 17, 156n.5, 202n.29,
　237
Cornwell, Joy **82**
County of Cumberland 61
County of Cumberland Plan (CCP)
　61, **62**, **63**, 64–6, 73, 81, 88, 97,
　139, 171, 245
crabs, *see* crustaceans—crabs
Crestani family **45**, 46

crustaceans 6, 24, 25, 133, 177, 178,
　250
　crabs 28, 84, 146, 203
　prawns 44, 53, 84, 87, 89, 92,
　　203
CSIRO (Commonwealth Scientific
　and Industrial Research
　Organisation) 143n.17, 156n.4,
　177
Cumberland, *see* County of
　Cumberland
Cumberland Plain 181
Cunneen, Chris 140, 141
Curlisa, E. J. 111
Curlisa, Mick 197n.14
Cuttings Pleasure Ground **42**

Dane, W. H. 148, 149
Davis, Bill 227
Dawson, P. 110
Defence Department, *see* Department
　of Defence
Department of Agriculture 113, 121,
　184
Department of the Chief Secretary
　113, 136, 185
Department of Child Welfare 139
Department of Defence 171, 178
Department of Education 195, 196
Department of Environment and
　Conservation **268**
Department of Environment and
　Planning 141
Department of Fisheries 188, 196, 197
　see also Fisheries Branch (NSW)
Department of Health 113, 197
Department of Housing, *see* Housing
　Commission (NSW)
Department of Lands 18, 91, 183
Department of Planning 262
Department of Public Health 110, 112
Department of Services and Property
　237
Derwent, Charles John 219

www.ingramcontent.com/pod-product-compliance
Lightning Source LLC
Chambersburg PA
CBHW051443270326
41932CB00038B/3400